FOREIGN DIRECT INVESTMENT

Theory, Evidence and Practice

Also by Imad A. Moosa

EXCHANGE RATE FORECASTING

INTERNATIONAL FINANCE: An Analytical Approach

INTERNATIONAL PARITY CONDITIONS: Theory, Econometric Testing and Empirical Evidence (*with R. H. Bhatti*)

MACROECONOMICS (*with J. B. Taylor*)

MICROECONOMICS (*with J. B. Taylor and B. Cowling*)

Foreign Direct Investment

Theory, Evidence and Practice

Imad A. Moosa

332.67314
M82f

First published 2002 by
PALGRAVE
Houndmills, Basingstoke, Hampshire RG21 6XS and
175 Fifth Avenue, New York, N.Y. 10010
Companies and representatives throughout the world

PALGRAVE is the new global academic imprint of
St. Martin's Press LLC Scholarly and Reference Division and
Palgrave Publishers Ltd (formerly Macmillan Press Ltd).

ISBN 0–333–94590–5

This book is printed on paper suitable for recycling and made from fully managed and sustained forest sources.

Cataloguing-in-Publication Data

A catalogue record for this book is available from the British Library.

A catalogue record for this book is available from the Library of Congress.

10   9   8   7   6   5   4   3   2   1
11   10   09   08   07   06   05   04   03   02

Typeset by Integra Software Services Pvt. Ltd., Pondicherry, India
www.integra-india.com

Printed in Great Britain by
Antony Rowe Ltd.
Chippenham, Wiltshire

To Nisreen and Danny

Contents

List of Tables

List of Figures

Preface

Writing a book on foreign direct investment (FDI) is not an easy task, as at least two problems are encountered in embarking on this endeavour. The first problem arises from the fact that the literature on the subject is massive. Given manuscript constraints, one has to make some difficult choices concerning the selection of relevant pieces of work. The second problem is that it would seem difficult to come up with a book that differs significantly from what is already available in the form of books or lengthy survey articles.

I believe that these two problems have been dealt with effectively in this book. To start with, this book presents a comprehensive and up-to-date survey of the theory of, and evidence about, FDI determination and effects. To accomplish the objective of being comprehensive and up-to-date while taking into account the constraints of manuscript length, extensive use is made of lengthy tables that summarize the findings of the most recent studies, some of which appeared in 2001. To produce something different, this book was written to address not only the economics of FDI, but also its financial, accounting and management aspects in a rather integrated manner. As far as the economics of FDI is concerned, the book deals with both the macro and micro aspects of the subject, including the behaviour of multinational corporations that generate FDI. Even the political and social aspects of FDI are touched upon briefly, particularly when the effects of this activity are examined. This book, therefore, should be a useful reference for those engaged in research on FDI, and it could be used for advanced undergraduate or postgraduate subjects related to FDI and International Business.

The book is entitled *Foreign Direct Investment: Theory, Evidence and Practice*. While it is obvious what the terms 'theory' and 'evidence' refer to, it may not be obvious to tell to what the term 'practice' refers. This term, as far as this book is concerned, refers to the description of some of the practices in which multinational corporations indulge. The book, for example, describes capital budgeting techniques, the techniques of setting transfer prices, and the management of political risk, all of which are functions that are performed by multinationals. Moreover, the book presents on several occasions a comparison between the theory of the behaviour of multinationals and what actually happens in practice, as inferred from surveys that have been conducted by various authors.

The book is in ten chapters. The first three chapters examine the characteristics, determination, and the effects of FDI as well as the related behaviour of multinationals. In essence, these chapters present an exposition of the economics of FDI. A comprehensive survey of the theory of, and empirical evidence about, the determination and effects of FDI are presented in Chapters 2 and 3, respectively. I have endeavoured to present diverse views on various issues, given that FDI is, or can be, a contentious and politically-sensitive topic. It is left up to the reader to decide which of the views are more appealing. Despite the diversity of the theories that have been put forward to explain FDI, it is undoubtedly true that the profitability (or the perceived profitability) of FDI projects is of prime importance for multinationals. This is why Chapter 4 examines capital budgeting, describing the criteria that are used to determine the financial feasibility of FDI projects. We shall discover that financial feasibility is influenced by country risk, taxes and the cost of capital: Chapters 5, 6 and 7, respectively, deal with these issues. Therefore, Chapters 4–7 are concerned predominantly with the financial aspects of FDI. Finally, Chapters 8 and 9 focus primarily on the accounting and management aspects of FDI: Chapter 8 examines the critical issue of transfer pricing, while the subject matter of Chapter 9 is control and performance evaluation in multinational corporations.

Writing this book would not have been possible if it was not for the help and encouragement I received from family, friends and colleagues. My utmost gratitude must go to my small family, who had to bear the opportunity cost of writing this book. My wife, Afaf, proved once again to be my best research assistant by producing the figures shown in the book. Friends and colleagues have been supportive, directly or indirectly, by providing the intellectual and social environment that is conducive, among other things, to writing a book. Hence, I would like to thank Lee Smith who, under a tight schedule, provided efficient research assistance and read the manuscript from end to end, coming up with various suggestions for changes, and picking up some errors that I might have overlooked. Robert Waschik and Ryle Perera checked the mathematical derivations, for which I am grateful. I would also like to thank my colleagues Buly Cardak, Iain Fraser, Lionel Frost, Michael Harris, Darren Henry, Sisira Jayasuriya, Paul Kim, Liam Lenten, Judy Lock, Neil Perry, David Prentice, Michael

Schneider and Xiangkang Yin. I benefited particularly from discussion with some colleagues in the stimulating atmosphere of the *Eagle*, and for this reason my thanks go to Damian Lyons, Penny Fyffe and Kerri Ridsale for providing such an atmosphere. I would also like to thank my good friends, Sam and Maha, for providing the weekend entertainment needed after hard working weeks.

My thanks go to friends and former colleagues who live far away but provided help via telecommunications, including Kevin Dowd, Bob Sedgwick, Sean Holly, Dave Chappell, Dan Hemmings (who taught me capital budgeting for the first time in 1974), Ian Baxter, Scott MacDonald, Razzaque Bhatti and Nabeel Al-Loughani. Last, but not least, I would like to thank Zelah Pengilley, Steven Kennedy and Stephen Rutt, of Palgrave, who not only encouraged me to write this book but also showed understanding when I failed to deliver the manuscript on time, for reasons beyond my control.

Naturally, I am the only one responsible for any errors and omissions in this book. It is dedicated to my beloved children, Nisreen and Danny, whose favourite multinational corporation is McDonald's, the producer of their favourite meal, the Big Mac.

IMAD A. MOOSA

List of Abbreviations

APV	adjusted present value
ARIMA	autoregressive integrated moving average
BERI	Business Environment Risk Information Index
CAPM	capital asset pricing model
CEECs	Central and East European countries
CEO	chief executive officer
CFC	controlled foreign corporation
CIA	Central Intelligence Agency
CIP	covered interest parity
DISC	domestic international sales corporation
ECGD	export credits guarantee department
FDI	foreign direct investment
FIFO	first in, first out
GAPM	global asset pricing model
GATT	General Agreement on Tariffs and Trade
GDP	gross domestic product
GM	General Motors
GNP	gross national product
GST	goods and services tax
IBM	International Business Machines
ICI	Imperial Chemical Industries
ICSID	International Centre for Settlement of Investment Disputes
IFC	International Finance Corporation
IMF	International Monetary Fund
IRR	internal rate of return
LIFO	last in, first out
M&As	mergers and acquisitions
MAI	multilateral agreement on investment
MCC	marginal cost of capital
MIGA	Multi Investment Guarantee Agency
MNC	multinational corporation
MPE	multinational producing enterprise
MRI	marginal return on investment
NATO	North Atlantic Treaty Organization

NPV	net present value
NRV	net receivable value
OECD	Organization for Economic Co-operation and Development
OPIC	Overseas Private Investment Corporation
P/E	price/earnings
PPP	purchasing power parity
PRI	political risk indicator
PRS	political risk services
PTA	preferential trade agreement
PV	present value
R&A	research and development
RC	replacement cost
SEC	Securities and Exchange Commission
TRIP	trade related investment performance
UIP	uncovered interest parity
UNCTAD	United Nations Conference on Trade and Development
VAT	Value Added Tax
WPRF	world political risk forecasts
WTO	World Trade Organization

1 Introduction and Overview

WHAT IS FOREIGN DIRECT INVESTMENT?

Foreign direct investment (FDI) is the process whereby residents of one country (the source country) acquire ownership of assets for the purpose of controlling the production, distribution and other activities of a firm in another country (the host country).[1] The International Monetary Fund's *Balance of Payments Manual* defines FDI as 'an investment that is made to acquire a lasting interest in an enterprise operating in an economy other than that of the investor, the investor's purpose being to have an effective voice in the management of the enterprise'. The United Nations 1999 *World Investment Report* (UNCTAD, 1999) defines FDI as 'an investment involving a long-term relationship and reflecting a lasting interest and control of a resident entity in one economy (foreign direct investor or parent enterprise) in an enterprise resident in an economy other than that of the foreign direct investor (FDI enterprise, affiliate enterprise or foreign affiliate)'.[2] The term 'long-term' is used in the last definition in order to distinguish FDI from portfolio investment, the latter characterized by being short-term in nature and involving a high turnover of securities.[3]

The common feature of these definitions lies in terms like 'control' and 'controlling interest', which represent the most important feature that distinguishes FDI from portfolio investment, since a portfolio investor does not seek control or lasting interest. There is no agreement, however, on what constitutes a controlling interest, but most commonly a minimum of 10 per cent shareholding is regarded as allowing the foreign firm to exert a significant influence (potentially or actually exercised) over the key policies of the underlying project. For example, the US Department of Commerce regards a foreign business enterprise as a US foreign 'affiliate' if a single US investor owns at least 10 per cent of the voting securities or the equivalent. Both equity and debt-financed capital transfers to foreign affiliates are included in the US government's estimates of FDI. Sometimes, another qualification is used to pinpoint FDI, which involves transferring capital from a source country to a host country. For this purpose,

1

investment activities abroad are considered to be FDI when (i) there is control through substantial equity shareholding; and (ii) there is a shift of part of the company's assets, production or sales to the host country. However, this may not be the case, as a project may be financed totally by borrowing in the host country.

Thus, the distinguishing feature of FDI, in comparison with other forms of international investment, is the element of control over management policy and decisions. Razin *et al.* (1999b) argue that the element of control gives direct investors an informational advantage over foreign portfolio investors and over domestic savers. Many firms are unwilling to carry out foreign investment unless they have one hundred per cent equity ownership and control. Others refuse to make such investments unless they have at least majority control (that is, a 51 per cent stake). In recent years, however, there has been a tendency for indulging in FDI co-operative arrangements, where several firms participate and no single party holds majority control (for example, joint ventures).

But what exactly does 'control' mean in the definition of FDI? The term 'control' implies that some degree of discretionary decision-making by the investor is present in management policies and strategy. For example, this control may occur through the ability of the investor to elect or select one or more members on the board of directors of the foreign company or foreign subsidiary. It is even possible to distinguish between the control market for shares and the non-control or portfolio share market as an analogy to the distinction between direct investment and portfolio investment. It may be possible to exercise control via contractual (non-equity) arrangements. The non-equity forms of FDI include, *inter alia*, subcontracting, management contracts, franchising, licensing and product sharing. Lall and Streeten (1977) argue that a majority shareholding is not a necessary condition for exercising control, as it may be achievable with a low equity share and even without an explicit management contract.

So, it is possible (in theory at least) to define and characterize FDI, but measuring FDI in practice is a totally different 'game'. There are inherent problems in measuring FDI, particularly when the investment takes the form of machinery or capitalized technological contributions. There are also gaps in the FDI statistics available from the source and host countries on FDI. Most countries do not publish comprehensive information on the foreign operations of their companies, for reasons of secrecy. Because of these problems, inconsistency between measures of FDI flows and stocks are the rule rather than the exception.[4] Furthermore, Cantwell and Bellack (1998) argue that the current practice of reporting FDI stocks on a historical cost basis (that is, book value) is unsatisfactory, because it does not take into account the age distribution of stocks, which makes international comparisons of FDI stocks almost impossible.

Interest in FDI, which has motivated attempts to come up with theories that explain its causes and effects, is attributed to the following reasons.[5] The first reason is the rapid growth in FDI and the change in its pattern, particularly since the 1980s. In the 1990s, FDI accounted for about a quarter of international capital outflows, having grown relative to other forms of international investment since the 1970s. The rapid growth of FDI has resulted from global competition as well as from the tendency to free up financial, goods and factor markets. It has been observed that FDI flows continue to expand even when world trade slows down. For example, when the growth of trade is retarded by trade barriers, FDI may increase as firms attempt to circumvent the barriers (see for example, Jeon, 1992; and Moore, 1993). It has also been observed that even when portfolio investment dried up in Asian countries as a result of the crisis of the 1990s, FDI flows were not affected significantly. Lipsey (1999) argues that FDI has been the least volatile source of international investment for host countries, with the notable exception of the USA. The latest available OECD figures show the following: FDI inflows to OECD countries increased from US$249 billion in 1996 to US$684 billion in 1999, whereas FDI outflows increased from US$341 to US$768 during the same period. This growth is rather dramatic (we shall examine the relevant statistics in more detail later).

The second reason for interest in FDI is the concern it raises about the causes and consequences of foreign ownership. The views on this issue are so diverse, falling between the extreme of regarding FDI as symbolizing new colonialism or imperialism, and the other extreme of viewing it as something without which the host country cannot survive. Most countries show an ambivalent attitude towards FDI. Inward FDI is said to have negative employment effects, retard home-grown technological progress, and worsen the trade balance. A substantial foreign ownership often gives rise to concern about the loss of sovereignty and compromise over national security. Outward FDI is sometimes blamed for the export of employment, and for giving foreigners access to domestic technology.

The third reason for studying FDI is that it offers the possibility for channelling resources to developing countries. According to this argument, FDI is becoming an important source of funds at a time when access to other means of financing is dwindling, particularly in the aftermath of the international debt crisis that emerged in the early 1980s. Lipsey (1999) argues that FDI has been the most dependable source of foreign investment for developing countries. Moreover, FDI is (or can be) important in this sense not only because it entails the movement of financial capital but also because it is normally associated with the provision of technology as well as managerial, technical and marketing skills. But it has to be emphasized here that FDI does not necessarily involve the movement of financial capital, as the investor may try to raise funds by borrowing from financial institutions in the host country. Moreover, the other benefits of FDI may not materialize, or they may materialize at a very high cost for the host country. All of these issues will be examined in the following chapters.

Finally, FDI is thought to play a potentially vital role in the transformation of the former Communist countries. This is because FDI complements domestic saving and contributes to total investment in the (host) economy. It is also because FDI brings with it advanced technology, management skills and access to export markets. Again, these positive effects may not arise, or they may arise simultaneously with some adverse effects.

TYPES OF FDI

FDI can be classified from the perspective of the investor (the source country) and from the perspective of the host country. From the perspective of the investor, Caves (1971) distinguishes between horizontal FDI, vertical FDI and conglomerate FDI. Horizontal FDI is undertaken for the purpose of horizontal expansion to produce the same or similar kinds of goods abroad (in the host country) as in the home country. Hence, product differentiation is the critical element of market structure for horizontal FDI. More generally, horizontal FDI is undertaken to exploit more fully certain monopolistic or oligopolistic advantages, such as patents or differentiated products, particularly if expansion at home were to violate anti-trust laws. Vertical FDI, on the other hand, is undertaken for the purpose of exploiting raw materials (backward vertical FDI) or to be nearer to the consumers through the acquisition of distribution outlets (forward vertical FDI).

For example, for a long time, US car makers found it difficult to market their products in Japan because most Japanese car dealers have close business relationships with Japanese car makers, thus making them reluctant to promote foreign cars. To overcome this problem, American car dealers embarked on a campaign to establish their own network of dealerships in Japan to market their products. The third type of FDI, conglomerate FDI, involves both horizontal and vertical FDI. In 1999 horizontal, vertical and conglomerate mergers and acquisitions (which is one of two forms of FDI, as we shall see later) accounted for 71.2 per cent, 1.8 per cent and 27 per cent, respectively, of the total value of mergers and acquisitions worldwide.

From the perspective of the host country, FDI can be classified into (i) import-substituting FDI; (ii) export-increasing FDI; and (iii) government-initiated FDI. Import-substituting FDI involves the production of goods previously imported by the host country, necessarily implying that imports by the host country and exports by the investing country will decline. This type of FDI is likely to be determined by the size of the host country's market, transportation costs and trade barriers. Export-increasing FDI, on the other hand, is motivated by the desire to seek new sources of input, such as raw materials and intermediate goods. This kind of FDI is export-increasing in the sense that the host country will increase its exports of raw materials and intermediate products to the investing country and other countries (where the subsidiaries of the multinational corporation are located). Government-initiated FDI may be triggered, for example, when a government offers incentives to foreign investors in an attempt to eliminate a balance of payments deficit. A similar, trade-related classification of FDI is adopted by Kojima (1973, 1975, 1985). According to Kojima's classification, FDI is either trade-orientated FDI (which generates an excess demand for imports and excess supply of exports at the original terms of trade) or anti-trade-orientated FDI, which has an adverse effect on trade.

Finally, FDI may be classified into expansionary and defensive types. Chen and Ku (2000) suggest that expansionary FDI seeks to exploit firm-specific advantages in the host country. This type of FDI has the additional benefit of contributing to sales growth of the investing firm at home and abroad. On the other hand, they suggest that defensive FDI seeks cheap labour in the host country with the objective of reducing the cost of production. Chen and Yang (1999) suggested that a multinomial logit model can be used to identify the determinants of the two types of FDI in the case of Taiwan. Their empirical results indicated that expansionary FDI is influenced mainly by firm-specific advantages such as scale, R&D intensity, profitability and motives for technology acquisition. Defensive FDI, on the other hand, is shown to be influenced by cost reduction motives and the nexus of production networks. Both types of FDI are affected by the characteristics of the underlying industry.

WHAT ARE MULTINATIONAL CORPORATIONS?

Most FDI is carried out by multinational corporations (MNCs) which have become household names. Examples (without any particular order in mind) are Toyota, IBM, Phillips, Nestlé, Sony, Royal Dutch Shell, IBM, GM, Coca-Cola, McDonald's, Daimler-Benz, and Bayer. It is, however, difficult to pinpoint what constitutes an MNC, and there is not even an agreement on what to call these firms. The literature shows various 'labels' for these firms, consisting of the words 'international', 'transnational', or 'global' followed by any of the words 'corporations', 'companies' and 'enterprises'. What is more important is that there is no single definition for an MNC. For example, the United Nations (1973) lists twenty-one definitions for MNCs, or whatever they may be called (the UNCTAD in fact calls them TNCs).

Sometimes, however, a distinction is made between the terms 'international', 'multinational' and 'transnational'. The term 'multinational firm' has evolved from changes in the nature of international business operations. The term 'international business firm' referred traditionally to the cross-border activity of importing and exporting, where goods are produced in the domestic market and then exported abroad, and vice versa. The financial implications of these transactions pertain to the payment process between buyers and sellers across national frontiers. As international operations expand, the international firm may feel that it is desirable, if possible, to expand in such a way as to be closer to foreign consumers. Production will then be carried out both at home and abroad. Thus, a multinational firm carries out some of its production activity abroad by establishing a presence in foreign countries via subsidiaries, affiliates and joint ventures (these terms will be defined later). The financial implications become more significant. The foreign 'arms' of a multinational firm normally have a different base or functional currency, which is the currency of the country where they are located. This setup results in a greater currency and financial risk in general. As cross-border activity expands even further, the distinction between 'home' and 'abroad' becomes blurred, and difficulties arise as to the identification of the 'home country'. What is created in this case is a 'transnational firm'. It remains the case that the relationship between multinationals and FDI is very simple: firms become multinational (or transnational) when they undertake FDI. Thus, FDI represents an internal organizational expansion by multinationals. In this book, we shall use the term 'multinational corporation' (MNC) generally to imply the firms that indulge in FDI.

The link between FDI and MNCs is so close that the motivation for FDI may be used to distinguish between MNCs and other firms. Lall and Streeten (1977) distinguish among economic, organizational and motivational definitions of FDI. The economic definition places emphasis on size, geographical spread and the extent of foreign involvement of the firm. This definition allows us to distinguish between an MNC and (i) a large domestic firm that has little investment abroad; (ii) a small domestic firm that invests abroad; (iii) a large firm that invests in one or two foreign countries only; and (iv) a large portfolio investor that does not seek control over the investment. Parker (1974) classified 613 of the largest manufacturing firms in the world into 'MPE2', 'MPE1' and 'not MPE' (MPE standing for 'multinational producing enterprise'). According to this classification, MPE2 represents firms with more than five foreign subsidiaries, or more than 15 per cent of total sales produced abroad; MPE1 represents firms that are less globally orientated and have 2–5 subsidiaries or 5–15 per cent of sales produced abroad; and not MPE represents the rest of the firms. The organizational definition takes the size and spread for granted and emphasizes factors that make some firms more multinational than others. These factors pertain to the organization of these firms, centralization of decision-making, global strategy and the ability to act as one cohesive unit under changing circumstances. Finally, the motivational definition places emphasis on corporate philosophy and motivations. For example, an MNC is characterized by a lack of nationalism, and by being concerned with the organization as a whole rather than with any constituent unit, country or operation.

The 1999 *World Investment Report* (UNCTAD, 1999) defines multinational corporations (which it calls transnational corporations) as 'incorporated or unincorporated enterprises comprising parent enterprises and their foreign affiliates'. A parent enterprise or firm is defined as 'an enterprise that controls assets of other entities in countries other than its home country, usually by owning a certain equity capital stake'. A foreign affiliate is defined as 'an incorporated or unincorporated enterprise in which an investor, who is resident in another economy, owns a stake that permits a lasting interest in the management of that enterprise'. Foreign affiliates may be subsidiaries, associates or branches.[6] UNCTAD (1999) distinguishes between them as follows:

- A subsidiary is an incorporated enterprise in the host country in which another entity directly owns more than a half of the shareholders' voting power and has the right to appoint or remove a majority of the members of the administrative, management or supervisory body.
- An associate is an incorporated enterprise in the host country in which an investor owns a total of at least 10 per cent, but not more than a half, of the shareholders' voting power.
- A branch is a wholly or jointly-owned unincorporated enterprise in the host country, which may take the form of a permanent office of the foreign investor or an unincorporated partnership or a joint venture. A branch may also refer to land, structures, immovable equipment and mobile equipment (such as oil drilling rigs and ships) operating in a country other than the investor's country.

Moreover, the UNCTAD (1999) lists the following facts and figures about multinationals:

1. Multinationals comprise over 500 000 foreign affiliates established by some 60 000 parent firms.[7]
2. The MNC universe comprises large firms mainly from developed countries, but also from developing countries and more recently from the countries in transition.
3. In 1997, the 100 largest non-financial MNCs held US$1.8 trillion in foreign assets, sold products worth US$2.1 trillion abroad and employed six million people in their foreign affiliates.
4. In 1997, the top fifty non-financial MNCs based in developing countries held US$105 billion in foreign assets. Most of these companies belong to Korea, Venezuela, China, Mexico and Brazil.
5. The twenty-five largest MNCs in Central Europe (excluding the Russian Federation) held US$2.3 billion in foreign assets and had foreign stakes worth US$3.7 billion.

6. The value of output under the common governance of MNCs amounts to about 25 per cent of global output, one third of which is produced in host countries. In 1998, foreign affiliate sales were about US$11 trillion.[8]

The question as to what MNCs are has been dealt with in the academic literature. Lall and Streeten (1977) identify the following 'salient features' of MNCs:

1. MNCs are predominant in certain monopolistic or oligopolistic industries characterized by the importance of marketing and technology.
2. The products of MNCs are new, advanced and cater for consumers who have relatively high incomes and sophisticated tastes, and who are responsive to modern marketing techniques.
3. The techniques of production MNCs use are the most advanced in their respective fields.
4. The expansion of an MNC tends to reproduce the oligopolistic conditions of the MNC's domestic market.
5. The maturing of MNCs may bring with it various commercial practices to bolster market dominance.
6. MNCs are attracted by large and growing economies with reasonably stable political conditions.
7. The organizational evolution of MNCs leads to a centralization of functions such as finance, marketing and research.
8. MNCs prefer complete or majority ownership of subsidiaries.
9. The increasing international role of MNCs has important implications for the structure of socio-political power in developed and developing countries.

Some attempts have been made to measures the extent of being 'multinational' according to a set of indicators. Dorrenbacher (2000) proposes a measure based on the following indicators: (i) structural indicators; (ii) performance indicators; and (iii) attitudinal indicators. Structural indicators include the number of countries where the firm is active, the number of foreign subsidiaries, the number of foreign employees, and the number of stock markets on which the firm's shares are listed. Performance indicators include foreign sales and operating income of foreign subsidiaries. The attitudinal indicators include management style and international experience of top management.

Indices (or composite indicators), which are calculated by combining individual indicators, can also be used as measures of multinationalization. These include the following measures:

1. The transnationality index of the UNCTAD. This indicator, which first appeared in UNCTAD's 1995 *World Investment Report*, aims to capture fully the extent of involvement in the world economy. It is based on three different ratios: (i) foreign sales to total sales; (ii) foreign assets to total assets; and (iii) foreign employment to total employment.
2. The transnational spread index of Ietto-Gillies (1998). This index is calculated by multiplying the average of the ratios used to calculate the transnationality index by the number of foreign countries in which a firm is active, as a proportion of the total number of countries where FDI has occurred minus one (the home country).
3. The degree of internationalization scale, which was suggested by Sullivan (1994). This indicator is based on (i) the ratio of foreign sales to total sales; (ii) foreign assets to total assets; (iii) the number of foreign subsidiaries to total subsidiaries; (iv) the international experience of top managers; and (v) the dispersion of international operations.

Empirical studies of the behaviour and characteristics of MNCs attempt to detect the characteristics that distinguish an MNC from purely domestic firms. The variables that have been found to be significant in the earlier literature are R&D expenditure, size of the firm, and foreign trade intensity, although other variables also appeared to be important. Vaupel (1971) obtained evidence showing that US MNCs (as compared with domestic firms): (i) incurred higher R&D as well as advertising expenditure; (ii) showed more net profit; (iii) had higher average sales; (iv) were more diversified; (v) paid higher wages in the USA; and (vi) recorded a higher export/sales ratio. Vernon (1971) reached a similar conclusion using the same data set. Lall (1980), however, found that R&D, economies of scale and the possession of skill advantages favour exports more than foreign production (FDI) by US MNCs, whereas product differentiation promotes more foreign production than exports. Horst (1972a), on the other hand, came to the conclusion that all of these variables can be accounted for by inter-industry differences, so that size remains the only significant distinguishing factor. A similar conclusion was reached by Bergsten *et al.* (1978). Caves (1971) found strong rank correlation between the extent of product differentiation and the proportion of firms in an industry having foreign subsidiaries.

By using an econometric model of the probability that a firm becomes an MNC, Grubaugh (1987) obtained results supporting the importance of R&D expenditure, product diversity and size as characteristics of MNCs. Grubaugh (1987) tested three hypotheses to explain why firms would choose to become MNCs, based on three views of MNCs. The first view is that an MNC is essentially a firm that engages in capital arbitrage (MacDougal, 1960). The second view is that MNCs are oligopolists that compete by producing in various countries (Hymer, 1976). The third view emphasizes the intangible assets that firms acquire. These views of MNCs imply a certain relationship between whether or not a firm is an MNC and the characteristics of the firm (Dunning, 1977; Rugman, 1981). The capital arbitrage view implies that there is no significant difference between MNCs and domestic firms except the cost of capital and capital intensity. The second view implies the importance of the size of the firm and the diversity of its products. The third view implies the importance of knowledge (hence, R&D expenditure) and goodwill (hence, advertising expenditure). The importance of R&D is emphasized by Petit and Sanna-Randaccio (2000), who show that a firm that invests more in R&D is the one that is an MNC, whereas the rival is an exporter. Hence, they conclude that there is a positive relationship between international expansion and R&D expenditure, and that the latter leads to an increase in the likelihood of international expansion.

What does all of this tell us about the importance of MNCs? Lall and Streeten (1977) answer this question by suggesting that the significance of MNCs lies in the simple fact that they dominate overwhelmingly not only international investment but also international production, trade, finance and technology. They conclude that this domination makes any analysis of the structure of international economic relationships that does not take them into account unrealistic and irrelevant.

APPROACHES TO INTERNATIONAL BUSINESS

FDI is one of several approaches that business enterprises can use to enter foreign markets. The following is a common sequence that firms use to develop foreign markets for their products:

1. Export of the goods produced in the source country.
2. Licensing a foreign company to use process or product technology.
3. Foreign distribution of products through an affiliate entity.
4. Foreign (international) production, which is the production of goods and services in a country that is controlled and managed by firms headquartered in other countries.

Steps 3 and 4 involve FDI. Moving from step 1 to step 4 requires a larger commitment of resources, and in some respects greater exposure to risk. While this sequence may be a chronological path for developing foreign sales, it is not necessary that all four steps are taken sequentially, as some firms jump immediately to step 3 or step 4. UNCTAD (1999) identifies the following characteristics of international production:

1. International production arises when a firm exercises control over an enterprise located abroad, whether through capital investment or through contractual arrangements.
2. Technology flows play an important role in international production.
3. Innovation and research and development are at the heart of the ownership advantages that propel firms to engage in international production.
4. International trade is stimulated by international production because of the trading activities of MNCs.
5. International production generates employment opportunities that are particularly welcome in host countries with high rates of unemployment.
6. Financial flows associated with international production consists of funds for financing the establishment, acquisition or expansion of the foreign affiliates.
7. The capital base of international production, regardless of how it is financed, is reflected in the value of assets of foreign affiliates.

The choice between exporting and FDI depends on the following factors: profitability, opportunities for market growth, production cost levels, and economies of scale. For example, MNCs traditionally have invested in Singapore and Hong Kong because of the low production costs in these countries. For the same reasons, traditionally these countries have exported goods to other countries. Initially, exports precede FDI, but after having become familiar with factor and output markets in the foreign country, a firm will establish a production facility there. Several motives exist for this change. FDI allows a firm to circumvent actual or anticipated barriers to trade. Another motive is the real appreciation of the domestic currency, which reduces the competitiveness of exports.

Step 2 is licensing, which may be defined as the supply of technology and know-how, or it may involve the use of a trademark or a patent for a fee. It offers one way to circumvent entry barriers to FDI. Under these circumstances licensing offers an opportunity to generate revenue from foreign markets that are otherwise inaccessible. Furthermore, the licence owner may often not have the capital, experience or risk tolerance associated with FDI. Firms prefer FDI to licensing in the case of complex technology, or when the risk of leakage of technological advantage to competitors exists.

Franchising is another form of entering a foreign market under contractual agreements. Companies with brand name products (Kentucky Fried Chicken and Burger King, for example) move offshore by granting foreigners the exclusive right to sell the product in a designated area. The parent company provides the technical expertise pertaining to the production process as well as marketing assistance for an initial fee and subsequent royalties related to turnover. UNCTAD (1999) defines royalties and licensing fees as 'receipts and payments of residents and non-residents for (i) the authorised use of intangible, non-produced, non-financial assets and proprietary rights such as trade marks, patents, processes, techniques, designs, manufacturing rights, franchises, etc.; and (ii) the use, through licensing agreements of produced originals or prototypes, such as manuscripts, films, etc.'

FDI may take one of three forms: greenfield investment, cross-border mergers and acquisitions (M&As), and joint ventures. Greenfield investment occurs when the investing firm establishes new production, distribution or other facilities in the host country. This is normally welcomed by the host country because of the job-creating potential and value-added output. Sometimes, the term 'brownfield investment' is used to describe a situation where investments that are formally an acquisition resemble greenfield investment. This happens when the foreign investor acquires a firm but replaces almost completely the plant and equipment, labour and the product line. This concept has been used most to describe acquisitions in transition economies (Meyer and Estrin, 1998).

FDI may occur via an acquisition of, or a merger with, an established firm in the host country (the vast majority of M&As are indeed acquisitions rather than mergers). This mode of FDI has two advantages over greenfield investment: (i) it is cheaper, particularly if the acquired project is a loss-making operation that can be bought cheaply; and (ii) it allows the investor to gain a quick access to the market. Firms may be motivated to engage in cross-border acquisitions to bolster their competitive positions in the world market by acquiring special assets from other firms or by using their own assets on a larger scale. A large number of M&As fail in the sense that the firms engaging in this activity do not produce better results in terms of share prices and profitability than those firms that do not indulge in this activity. However, the extent of failure depends crucially on the success criteria, which means that the failure rate may be high or low, depending on these criteria (Hopkins, 1999).

Whether a firm would choose M&As or greenfield investment depends on a number of firm-specific, host country-specific and industry-specific factors, including the following (UNCTAD, 2000):

1. Firms with lower R&D intensity are more likely to indulge in M&As than those with strong technological advantages.
2. More diversified firms are likely to choose M&As.
3. Large MNCs have a greater tendency to indulge in M&As.
4. There is weak support for the proposition that advertising intensity leads to more acquisitions.
5. Cultural and economic differences between the home country and the host country reduce the tendency for M&As.
6. Acquisitions are encouraged by capital market imperfections and financial crises.
7. MNCs with subsidiaries in the host country prefer acquisitions.
8. The tendency towards M&As depends on the supply of target firms.
9. Slow growth in an industry favours M&As.

McCann (2001) presented a model in which he explained cross-border acquisitions involving UK firms during the period 1987–95 using panel data analysis. He found that models which explain cross-border acquisitions through capital market imperfections are inadequate, but he also found the exchange rate, stock prices and corporate tax differentials to be important determinants. The data on M&As show that acquisitions dominate the scene, as less than 3 per cent of cross-border M&As by numbers are in fact mergers. In reality, even when mergers are supposedly between two equal partners, most are, in reality, acquisitions. For practical purposes, M&As are actually mergers.

Cross-border acquisition of businesses is a politically sensitive issue, as most countries prefer to retain local control of domestic firms. It follows that, while countries may welcome greenfield investments, foreign firms' bids to acquire domestic firms are often resisted, and sometimes even resented. The underlying argument here is that M&As are less beneficial than greenfield FDI, and may even be harmful, because they do not add up to productive capacity but rather represent a transfer of ownership that may be accompanied by layoffs or the termination of some beneficial activities. If mergers and acquisitions take place in some sensitive areas, such as the media, then it may seem (perhaps justifiably) like a threat to the national culture or identity.

Whether or not cross-border acquisitions produce synergetic gains, and how such gains are divided between acquiring and target firms, are important issues from the perspective of shareholders' welfare and public policy. Synergetic gains are obtained when the value of the combined firm is greater than the stand-alone valuations of the individual (acquiring and target) firms. If cross-border acquisitions generate synergetic gains, both the acquiring and the target firms' shareholders gain wealth at the same time. In this case, one can argue, both from a national and a global perspective, that cross-border acquisitions are mutually beneficial and thus should not be thwarted. Moreover, it is sometimes argued that the perceived negative effects of M&As may materialize in the short run only, while several benefits emerge in the long run. The latter include new sequential investments, transfer of new technology, and the generation of employment.[9]

Synergetic gains may or may not arise from cross-border acquisitions, depending on the motive of acquiring firms. In general, gains will result when the acquiring firm is motivated to take advantage of market imperfections such as mispriced factors of production, or to cope with trade barriers. Several studies have investigated the impact of cross-border acquisitions. For example, Doukas and Travlos (1988) investigated the impact of international acquisitions on the stock prices of US bidding firms. The results show that shareholders of the bidding firms experience significant positive abnormal returns when firms expand into new industries and markets. Harris and

Ravenscraft (1991) studied shareholder wealth gains for US firms acquired by foreign firms. They concluded that US target firms experience higher wealth gains than when they are acquired by US firms.

FDI can also take the form of joint ventures, either with a host country firm or a government institution, as well as with another company that is foreign to the host country. One side normally provides the technical expertise and its ability to raise finance, while the other side provides valuable input through its local knowledge of the bureaucracy as well as of local laws and regulations. Buckley and Casson (2000b) present a model that explains the formation of joint ventures in terms of nine distinct factors: (i) market size; (ii) pace of technological change; (iii) interest rates; (iv) cultural distance; (v) protection of independence; (vi) missing patent rights; (vii) economies of scope; (viii) technological uncertainty; and (ix) economies of scale. This model allows them to arrive at detailed predictions about how the formation of joint ventures varies with industries, between industries, across countries and over time.

HISTORY OF FDI

In the nineteenth century, foreign investment was prominent, but it mainly took the form of lending by Britain to finance economic development in other countries as well as the ownership of financial assets. However, a recent article by Godley (1999) analyses some cases of FDI in British manufacturing industry prior to 1890, and shows that from 1890 onwards the bulk of FDI was in the industrial goods sector. Godley also shows that investors in Britain prior to 1890 were primarily in the consumer goods sector, and that they mostly failed because they were narrowly focused and driven entirely by concern about enhancing access to the British market. One exception was the Singer Manufacturing Company. As a result of its enthusiastic commitment to FDI, the company emerged as the world's first modern MNC and was one of the largest firms in the world by 1900.

In the interwar period of the twentieth century, foreign investment declined, but direct investment rose to about a quarter of the total. Another important development that took place in the interwar period was that Britain lost its status as the major world creditor, and the USA emerged as the major economic and financial power. In the post-Second World War period, FDI started to grow, for two reasons. The first was technological – the improvement in transport and communications which made it possible to exercise control from a distance. The second reason was the need of European countries and Japan for US capital to finance reconstruction following the damage inflicted by the war. Moreover, there were some US tax laws that favoured FDI. By the 1960s, all these factors were weakening to the extent that they gave rise to a reversal of the trend towards growth in FDI. First, various host countries started to show resistance to the US ownership and control of local industry, which led to a slowdown of outflows from the USA. Second, host countries started to recover, initiating FDI in the USA, and leading to a decline in the net outflow from the USA. The 1970s witnessed lower FDI flows, but Britain emerged as a major player in this game as a result of North Sea oil surpluses and the abolition of foreign exchange controls in 1979.

The 1980s witnessed two major changes and saw a surge in FDI. The first change was that the USA became a net debtor country and a major recipient of FDI with a negative net international investment position. One of the reasons for this development was the low saving rate in the US economy, making it impossible to finance the widening budget deficit by resorting to the domestic capital market, and giving rise to the need for foreign capital, which came primarily from Japan and Germany. Another reason was the restrictive trade policy adopted by the USA. The other major change in the 1980s was the emergence of Japan as a major supplier of FDI to the USA and Europe. Motivated by the desire to reduce labour costs, Japanese direct investment also expanded in South East Asia.

The surge in FDI in the 1980s is attributed to the globalization of business. It is also attributed by Aizenman (1992) to the growing concern over the emergence of managed trade. Moreover, it is argued that FDI benefits both MNCs and host country, and this is why there has been tolerance towards FDI. Another reason for the surge in FDI is the increase in FDI inflows to the USA as a result of the depreciation of the US dollar in the second half of the 1980s. The total flows of FDI from industrial countries more than quadrupled between 1984 and 1990.

In the period 1990–2, FDI flows fell as growth in industrial countries slowed, but a strong rebound subsequently took place. This rebound is attributed to three reasons: (i) FDI was no longer confined to large firms, as an increasing number of smaller firms became multinational; (ii) the sectoral diversity of FDI broadened, with the share of the service sector rising sharply; and (iii) the number of countries that were outward investors or hosts of FDI rose considerably.

Moreover, the 1990s brought considerable improvements in the investment climate, triggered in part by the recognition of the benefits of FDI.
The change in attitude, in turn, led to a removal of direct obstacles
to FDI and to an increase in the use of FDI incentives. Continued
removal of domestic impediments through deregulation and privatization was also widespread.

Another important feature of the 1990s was the decline in the
importance of Japan as a source of FDI, caused by the burst of the
Japanese bubble economy. The late 1990s were characterized by
cross-border M&As (which were motivated by deregulation and
enhanced competition policy) as the driving force behind FDI. Moreover, the trend towards the liberalization of regulatory regimes for
FDI continued. By the end of 1998, the number of treaties for the
avoidance of double taxation had reached a total of 1871. In 1998 and
1999 some changes were introduced to (host) government policies on
FDI, strengthening the trend towards the liberalization, protection
and promotion of FDI (UNCTAD, 2000).[10] It seems that this trend
will continue for a long time to come, which means that the growth of
FDI will be robust in the foreseeable future.

RECENT TRENDS

In this section we examine briefly the recent trends in FDI. A more
detailed account of the global and regional trends up to 1999 can be
found in the 2000 *World Investment Report* (UNCTAD, 2000). Before
we examine the figures, it may be worthwhile to try to anticipate what
the pattern has been like on the basis of some theoretical considerations. Lipsey (2000) suggests that if FDI flows represented mainly
responses to differences among countries in the scarcity and price of
capital, countries would tend mainly to be sources or recipients of
FDI (capital-surplus and capital-deficit countries respectively). Given
the size of the economy, the levels of outflows and inflows should
therefore be negatively related. This relationship is also obtained by
viewing FDI flows as depending on economic conditions. If the economy is in a boom, FDI inflows will increase and FDI outflows will
decrease. And if the economy is in a slump, then FDI inflows will
decrease and outflows will increase. Hence, FDI outflows and inflows
should be correlated negatively. Lipsey (1999, 2000) shows that this is
not the case. The positive relationship is attributed to the possibility
that economic factors that encourage inward flows also encourage

outward flows. Lipsey also suggests that the coexistence of outward and inward stocks of FDI arises from an alteration between inflows and outflows.

FDI flows comprise the capital provided (either directly or through related enterprises) by a foreign direct investor to an FDI enterprise, or capital received from an FDI enterprise by a foreign direct investor. From the perspective of a particular country, FDI flows may be inward (when a foreign country invests in the country in question) or outward (when the home country invests abroad). FDI flows consist of the following items:

- Equity capital, which is the foreign investor's purchases of shares in an enterprise in a foreign country.
- Reinvested earnings, which comprise the investor's share of earnings not distributed as dividends by affiliates or remitted to the home country, but rather reinvested in the host country.
- Intra-company loans, which refer to short-term or long-term borrowing and lending of funds between the parent company and its affiliates.

FDI inflows and outflows during the period 1994–9 are shown in Table 1.1. These figures are calculated on a net basis; that is, as capital transactions' credits less debits between investors and their affiliates.

Table 1.1   FDI inflows and outflows (US$bn)

Region/country	1988–93*	1994	1995	1996	1997	1998	1999
Inflows							
European Union	78.5	76.9	114.4	108.6	128.6	248.7	305.1
USA	44.8	45.1	58.8	84.5	105.5	186.3	275.5
Japan	0.7	0.9	0.4	0.2	3.2	3.2	12.7
Developing countries	46.9	104.9	111.9	145.0	178.8	179.5	207.6
World	190.6	256.0	331.9	377.5	473.1	680.1	865.5
Outflows							
European Union	107.2	120.7	159.0	182.3	223.7	425.5	509.8
USA	39.3	73.3	92.1	84.4	99.5	146.1	150.9
Japan	32.5	18.1	22.5	23.4	26.1	24.2	22.7
Developing countries	23.5	42.1	50.3	57.8	64.3	33.1	65.6
World	221.4	282.9	357.5	390.8	471.9	687.1	799.9

Note: *Annual average.
Source: UNCTAD (2000).

Net decreases in assets or net increases in liabilities are credits (recorded with a positive sign on the balance of payments), while net increases in assets or net decreases in liabilities are debits (recorded with negative signs on the balance of payments). In this table, the negative signs are deleted for convenience. It is obvious that FDI outflows and inflows are positively correlated, more so in the case of the European Union (EU). During the 1994–9 period, FDI inflows to the EU grew at an average annual rate of 31.7 per cent, whereas outflows grew at a rate of 33.4 per cent. Inflows grew much faster than outflows in the case of Japan and the USA, reflecting the attractiveness of the USA as a destination for FDI. In the case of Japan, however, the disparity between the growth rates of inflows and outflows is a reflection of the fact that Japan traditionally has been a source rather than a recipient country of FDI. Thus, the growth in inflows is measured relative to a very low initial value (US$0.7 billion in 1994). It seems, however, that Japan has more recently become a major recipient country, with inflows totalling US$12.7 billion in 1999. In that same year, the EU accounted for 35.3 per cent of FDI inflows and 63.7 per cent of total outflows, which means that the EU is the largest source region. Japan's economic problems in the 1990s may explain the declining role of Japan as a source of FDI, which in 1999 accounted for 2.8 per cent of total outflows (less than the contribution of developing countries). In 1999, the USA, like the developing countries, was a net recipient of FDI (capital importer), whereas the EU and Japan were capital exporters. While in theory total outflows should be equal to total inflows, this is not the case in practice because of measurement errors. Remember that these statistics were obtained initially from national sources.

Now we turn to FDI stocks, which represent the value of the share of their capital and reserves (including retained profits) attributable to the parent enterprise, plus the net indebtedness of affiliates of the parent enterprise. Like FDI flows, stocks can also be inward or outward. Table 1.2 reports FDI stocks for selected years. FDI stocks are estimated either by cumulating FDI flows over a period of time, or by adding flows to an FDI stock that has been obtained for a particular year from national office sources or the IMF data series on assets and liabilities.

During the period 1980–99, the growth of FDI stocks echoed that of FDI flows. First, there is high correlation between inward and outward stocks. The growth rates of inward and outward stocks during this period were very close. In the case of the EU, the inward stock grew at an annual rate of 12.1 per cent, while the outward stock grew

Table 1.2 FDI inward and outward stocks (US$bn)

Region/country	1980	1985	1990	1995	1998	1999
Inward stocks						
European Union	185.7	236.4	723.5	1050.3	1451.2	1652.3
USA	83.1	184.6	394.9	535.6	811.8	1087.3
Japan	3.3	4.7	9.9	33.5	26.1	38.8
Developing countries	121.2	218.1	377.4	739.5	1241.0	1438.5
World	495.2	763.4	1761.2	2743.4	4015.3	4772.0
Outward stocks						
European Union	212.6	292.7	789.4	1303.2	1920.4	2336.6
USA	220.2	251.0	430.5	699.0	980.6	1131.5
Japan	19.6	44.0	201.4	238.5	270.0	292.8
Developing countries	16.3	32.4	81.9	258.3	403.9	468.7
World	523.2	707.1	1716.4	2870.6	4065.8	4759.3

Source: UNCTAD (2000).

at a rate of 13.4 per cent. Even in the case of Japan, the growth rates were close (13.9 and 15.3 per cent, respectively). In 1999, the EU accounted for 34.6 per cent of the world inward stocks and 49.1 per cent of the world outward stocks. In terms of the net asset value (outward stocks minus inward stocks), the USA and developing countries were in deficit, whereas Japan and the EU were in surplus. Again, the world inward and outward stocks are not equal because of measurement errors.

Table 1.3 reports some statistics on cross-border mergers and acquisitions. These figures are published by UNCTAD based on data provided by KPMG Corporate Finance. By comparing the figures in Table 1.1 with those in Table 1.3, it is obvious that M&As have become the dominant form of FDI. In 1999, M&As accounted for over 80 per cent of total FDI inflows, and over 90 per cent of total FDI outflows. In developing countries, the two ratios were 8.9 per cent and 63 per cent, respectively. For the EU, however, M&As were dominant. This shows that whether FDI takes the form of greenfield investment or M&As depends in part on the level of development in the host country, since this factor determines the supply of target firms.

The statistics that we have considered on FDI flows, stocks and M&As serve to give a general indication as to what is happening, but one should take these statistics with a large pinch of salt. Because of measurement errors and accounting valuation problems, which apply particularly to stocks, individual figures tend to be inaccurate. As we

Table 1.3   Cross-border mergers and acquisitions (US$bn)

Region/country	1993	1994	1995	1996	1997	1998	1999
Sellers							
European Union	38.5	55.3	75.1	81.9	114.6	187.9	344.5
USA	19.9	44.7	53.2	68.1	81.7	209.6	233.0
Japan	0.09	0.8	0.5	1.7	3.1	4.0	15.9
Developing countries	12.8	14.9	16.0	34.7	64.6	80.8	64.6
World	83.1	127.1	186.6	227.0	304.9	531.7	720.1
Purchasers							
European Union	40.5	63.9	81.4	96.7	142.1	284.4	497.7
USA	21.4	28.5	57.3	60.7	80.9	137.4	112.4
Japan	1.1	1.1	3.9	5.7	2.7	1.3	9.8
Developing countries	10.4	10.2	12.8	28.1	32.5	19.2	41.3
World	83.1	127.1	186.6	227.0	304.9	531.7	720.1

Source: UNCTAD (2000), based on data provided by KPMG.

have seen, total inward flows are not equal to total outward flows, and the same is true for stocks. But since planet Earth does not yet have financial relationships with other planets from our solar system or from distant galaxies, inward flows (stocks) should be equal to outward flows (stocks). Moreover, by comparing the figures in Table 1.1 with those in Table 3.1, we find that the value of M&As in EU countries in 1999 was greater than the FDI inflows into the region, which does not make sense. Several other discrepancies can be observed. There are also problems with the measurement of M&As. For example, M&A statistics are compiled either on the basis of announcement or on the basis of completion. The treatment of additional acquisitions may also differ from one collecting agency to another. Moreover, the available data on M&As include portfolio investment, in which case it is necessary to extract transactions corresponding to FDI (in terms of control).[11]

It seems that, as economists, we have to live with the measurement errors problem, but the consolation is that these statistics give a good picture of the general trends in FDI. The next step is to study what determines FDI, and this is the subject matter of Chapter 2.

2 Theories of Foreign Direct Investment

The importance of and growing interest in the causes and consequences of FDI has led to the development of a number of theories that try to explain why MNCs indulge in FDI, why they choose one country in preference to another to locate their foreign business activity, and why they choose a particular entry mode. These theories also try to explain why some countries are more successful than others in obtaining FDI. Thus, some of the theories try to explain outward FDI (why MNCs choose to invest abroad), whereas others try to explain inward FDI (that is, a country's propensity and ability to attract FDI).

Theories of FDI may be classified under the following headings: (i) theories assuming perfect markets; (ii) theories assuming imperfect markets; (iii) other theories; and (iv) theories based on other variables.[1] It must be stated at the outset that this classification, which is suggested by Lizondo (1991) following Agarwal (1980), may result in some overlap. It will be observed that some variables and factors that influence FDI may appear under more than one heading and be used by more than one theory. However, it is felt that this classification is useful for expository purposes. Moreover, theories of FDI can be classified according to other criteria. For example, they can be classified within a range extending between the orthodox neoclassical theories to the Marxist theory of imperialism. They can also be classified according to whether the factors determining FDI are macro factors, micro factors or strategic factors.[2] All these factors and others will be examined under the various theories or hypotheses that will be presented in this chapter.[3] It has to be borne in mind that the common denominator in all this is that the most important reason for undertaking investment is profit-making, and FDI is no exception.

The theories of FDI, classified under the headings suggested above, will be discussed in turn. We shall follow Agarwal (1980, p. 740) by referring to these theories as hypotheses because 'there is not one but a number of competing theories with varying degrees of power to explain FDI'. We start with the theories based on the assumption of perfect markets.

THEORIES ASSUMING PERFECT MARKETS

Three hypotheses fall under this heading: the differential rates of return hypothesis, the diversification hypothesis, and the output and market size hypothesis.

The Differential Rates of Return Hypothesis

The differential rates of return hypothesis represents one of the first attempts to explain FDI flows. This hypothesis postulates that capital flows from countries with low rates of return to countries with high rates of return move in a process that leads eventually to the equality of *ex ante* real rates of return. The rationale for this hypothesis is that firms considering FDI behave in such a way as to equate the marginal return on and the marginal cost of capital (see Chapter 7). The hypothesis obviously assumes risk neutrality, making the rate of return the only variable upon which the investment decision depends. Risk neutrality in this case implies that the investor considers domestic and foreign direct investments to be perfect substitutes, or in general that direct investment in any country, including the home country, is a perfect substitute for direct investment in any other country.[4]

To test this hypothesis, therefore, one may examine the relationship between relative rates of return in a number of countries and the allocation of FDI among them. Most of the empirical studies aimed at testing this hypothesis failed to provide supporting evidence, as documented by Agarwal (1980). For example, Weintraub (1967) tested the hypothesis using US data and failed to find a significant relationship between inter-country differences in the rates of return and the flows of US capital. But while Bandera and White (1968) rejected the differential rates of return hypothesis, they stressed the adequacy of return as a precondition for the movement of capital. This hypothesis has also been investigated by conducting surveys on the motives for, and determinants of, FDI. This approach has also failed to support the hypothesis.

One problem with the differential rates of return hypothesis is that it is not consistent with the observation that countries experience inflows and outflows of FDI simultaneously. This is because a rate of return differential implies capital flows in one direction only, from the low-rate country to the high-rate country, and not vice versa. There is obviously something missing in this hypothesis. However, one must bear in mind that testing this hypothesis entails serious statistical problems pertaining to measurement errors. The hypothesis relates FDI to the expected rate of return, which is invariably calculated as the accounting rate of return on invested capital. The problem is that testing is based on the rate of return calculated from reported profit, which is different from expected profit and actual profit. This is because profit is affected by such factors as transfer pricing (see Chapter 8). In practice, it is rather difficult to obtain evidence on the divergence of reported profit from actual profit, but in general the available evidence indicates that reported profit fails to reflect accurately actual profit (see, for example, Bhagwati, 1967). Furthermore, accounting profit cannot produce a reliable and objective measure of the rate of return, since it can be influenced by many subjective and procedural factors, such as the method used for writing off fixed assets, inventory accounting (FIFO versus LIFO), and inflation accounting. There is also a difference between the profit earned during the whole period under investigation (which is what should be used to test the hypothesis) and the profit realized over the reporting period (say, a year).

The validity of the differential rates of return hypothesis can be questioned on theoretical grounds. First, MNCs may indulge in FDI for reasons other than profit, particularly in the short run and medium run. For example, the objective may be to maximize sales revenue in accordance with market penetration objective. Or the objective may not be purely financial, but rather logistical and operational, such as the desire to circumvent trade barriers. In general, MNCs are faced with a multiplicity of objectives for their international operations, and these objectives are likely to change with the passage of time. More importantly, however, risk aversion implies that the FDI decision does not only depend on return, but also on risk. Instead of maximizing the rate of return *per se*, the objective could be to maximize the rate of return per unit of risk (or to minimize risk per unit of return). This loophole is plugged by the diversification hypothesis, which will be discussed next. Finally, the differential rates of return hypothesis does not explain why a firm indulges in FDI rather than portfolio investment.

Recently, an attempt was made by Yang (1999) to adjust the rates of return on physical capital to allow for differences in human capital as an explanation for why FDI may go to low-return areas. Yang tried to explain why the majority of FDI in China has been flowing to rich coastal areas rather than to poor inland areas, when rates of return are higher in poor areas. After adjusting for human capital, the rate of return differential between rich and poor regions narrows down. Yang concludes that human capital plays an important role in equalizing rates of return on capital in poor and rich regions.

The Portfolio Diversification Hypothesis

When the assumption of risk neutrality is relaxed, risk becomes another variable upon which the FDI decision is made. If this proposition is accepted, then the differential rates of return hypothesis becomes inadequate, in which case we resort to the portfolio diversification hypothesis to explain FDI. The choice among various projects is therefore guided not only by the expected rate of return but also by risk.[5] The idea of reducing risk via diversification that is relevant to portfolio investment is also used here. Because of risk aversion, a rate of return differential will not induce capital flows in one direction until the differential disappears via arbitrage. Rather, capital mobility will be constrained by the desire to minimize or reduce risk, which is achieved by diversification. The theoretical foundations of this hypothesis can be traced back to the theory of portfolio selection of Tobin (1958) and Markowitz (1959).

One way to test this hypothesis is to examine the relationship between the share of FDI going to a group of countries and the two decision variables: the rate of return, and risk as measured by the variance or the standard deviation of the rate of return. The results provided by studies involving empirical testing of this hypothesis offer only weak support, as documented by Agarwal (1980) and Hufbauer (1975). But, once again, problems are encountered in the empirical testing of this hypothesis. The following are some of these:

1. The hypothesis pertains to a trade-off between *ex ante* return and risk (higher risk is accepted only for higher return, and lower return is accepted only if risk is lower). However, available data from which risk and return are calculated are *ex post*. The investigator can either derive a proxy for *ex ante* return and risk (for example, on the basis of scenarios) or by using the rational expectations substitution whereby the expected values of the variables are taken to be equal to the actual values plus or minus a random error term.
2. Risk and return are calculated from reported profit that is unlikely to be equal to actual profit for several reasons, including transfer pricing and accounting procedures.
3. The risk variable cannot be measured accurately from historical data if it is taken to be the (unconditional) variance or standard

deviation. Moosa and Bollen (2002) suggest the use of the concept of realized volatility as a measure of risk in preference to the conventional measures including the conditional variance and related measures.

However, it remains true that the diversification hypothesis, which takes risk into account, is superior to the differential rates of return hypothesis, for the following reasons. First, the diversification hypothesis offers the main advantage that it can be generalized (Prachowny, 1972). Second, it offers a plausible explanation for cross-investment between countries and industries (Agarwal, 1980). Third, it considers risk, which constitutes a very important element in FDI decisions. Like the differential rates of return hypothesis, the portfolio diversification hypothesis does not explain why MNCs are the greatest contributors to FDI, and why they prefer FDI to portfolio investment. One explanation, perhaps, is financial market imperfections (Ragazzi, 1973). In the case of developing countries, financial markets are not only imperfect but also rudimentary, making portfolio investment less attractive than FDI. Another factor, of course, pertains to the very character that distinguishes FDI from portfolio investment: the degree of control. MNCs prefer FDI over portfolio investment because FDI gives more control over foreign investment.

The Market Size Hypothesis

According to the market size hypothesis, the volume of FDI in a host country depends on its market size, which is measured by the sales of an MNC in that country, or by the country's GDP (that is, the size of the economy).[6] This is particularly so for the case of import-substituting FDI. As soon as the size of the market of a particular country has grown to a level warranting the exploitation of economies of scale, the country becomes a potential target for FDI inflows. Balassa (1966) pointed out that a sufficiently large market allows for the specialization of the factors of production, and consequently the achievement of cost minimization.

The relationship between direct investment and output can be derived from neoclassical models of domestic investment. The rationale for the hypothesis that firms increase their investment in response to their sales is based on neoclassical domestic investment theories, the most popular of which is represented by Jorgenson's (1963) model, a generalized form of the flexible acceleration model of Chenery (1952) and Koyck (1954). However, there is no obvious foundation for using the country's GDP. The relevance of GDP as a measure of potential market size does not have much theoretical foundation, but it has been used in empirical studies of FDI.

One way to test the market size hypothesis is to find out whether or not the share of FDI of a given country going to a group of host countries is correlated with the individual income level of the host country. The empirical studies using this testing methodology seem to support the hypothesis that higher levels of sales and the host country's income are related positively to FDI. A number of survey studies have also dealt with market size as a determinant of FDI. Most of the survey studies have produced results supporting the relationship between FDI on the one hand, and the sales of foreign subsidiaries and/or GDP on the other. Agarwal (1980) warns of the hazards of interpreting the significance of this relationship, for the following reasons:

1. The relationship is based on the assumptions of the neoclassical theories of domestic investment that are invariably unrealistic.
2. Market size is likely to influence the FDI undertaken to produce goods for consumption in the host country, and not the FDI aimed at exports. In practice, it is rather difficult to distinguish between various kinds of FDI, for statistical reasons.
3. While GDP and FDI are highly correlated, this says nothing about the direction of causality.
4. Since this hypothesis is based on neoclassical domestic investment theories, investment should be defined as including expenditure on plant and equipment only. But statistics on FDI do not distinguish between expenditure on plant and equipment and other forms of investment such as inventory and financial assets.
5. Statistics on output (GDP and related measures) typically are subject to significant measurement errors, particularly in developing countries.
6. The decisions of a firm regarding initial FDI and expansionary FDI are likely to be guided by different considerations.

The majority of empirical studies of the determinants of FDI include some measures of market size in the host country, typically using real GDP as a proxy. Moore (1993), Bajo-Rubio and Sosvilla-Rivero (1994), and Wang and Swain (1995) all used real GDP in their empirical models and found it to be a significant determinant of FDI. But in a more recent study based on Australian data, Yang *et al*. (2000) failed to find a relationship between FDI flows and either the contemporaneous or the lagged change in GDP. Other proxies for market size have been used, such as the growth rate of real GDP (Wang and Swain, 1995) and GDP per capita (Schneider and Frey, 1985). Yang *et al*. (2000, pp. 47–8) argue that the growth rate of GDP may be regarded as a measure of the future potential of the host country's domestic market, while per capita income may be used to represent the level of the host country's economic development. Lipsey (2000) uses size and growth variables to explain FDI inflows, FDI outflows, and net FDI flows and stocks. The explanatory, size-related variables he uses are nominal GDP, growth in real GDP per capita, real GDP per capita, and gross fixed capital formation as a percentage of GDP. He concludes that inward and outward FDI stocks and flows seem to go together across countries and over time. Love and Lage-Hidalgo (2000) used GDP per capita as an explanatory variable (a proxy for domestic demand) in an equation designed to explain US FDI in Mexico. The variable turned out to be a significant determinant of FDI flows, a result that they took to imply support for the market size hypothesis.

Finally, size does matter, according to a recent survey by A. T. Kearney, the results of which were summarized in *The Economist* issue dated 17 February 2000. This survey is based on the views of 135 executives of the world's 1000 largest companies, who gave marks on a scale of 0–3 for the likelihood of investing in a particular country. The top three countries favoured for investment turned out to be the USA, China and Brazil. Mexico was ranked 6th, while India was ranked 7th. Needless to say, the ranking of countries from the top to the bottom of the list did not exactly match the ranking of countries in terms of size, because of the influence of other determinants of FDI. For example, Japan was 20th, whereas the UK was 4th.

THEORIES ASSUMING IMPERFECT MARKETS

Hymer (1976) was the first economist to point out that the structure of the market and the specific characteristics of investing firms could explain FDI. Kindleberger (1969) refined and publicized Hymer's ideas. Martin (1991) uses cross-sectional analysis to confirm the importance of market structure (concentration and economies of scale) in determining FDI in the USA. Several hypotheses fall under this heading, and these will be discussed in turn.

The Industrial Organization Hypothesis

Hymer (1976) developed the industrial organization hypothesis, which
was extended by Kindleberger (1969), Caves (1982) and Dunning
(1988).[7] According to this hypothesis, when a firm establishes a subsidiary in another country it faces several disadvantages in competing with local firms. These disadvantages emanate from differences in
language, culture, the legal system and other inter-country differences.
For example, MNCs may have to pay higher wages in the host country
than do local firms, because employment with them is regarded by local
workers as being more risky. If, in spite of these disadvantages, the
firm engages in FDI, it must have some advantages arising from
intangible assets such as a well-known brand name, patent-protected
technology, managerial skills, and other firm-specific factors. According to Kindleberger (1969), the comparative advantage has to be firm-
specific, it must be transferable to foreign subsidiaries, and it should be
large enough to overcome these disadvantages. Lall and Streeten
(1977) present a comprehensive list of these advantages that, they
argue, are more significant the more monopolistic the underlying
industry. These advantages are described briefly in Table 2.1.

FDI may arise because it is difficult to sell or lease these intangible
assets. For example, Coca-Cola has invested in bottling plants all over
the world in preference to resorting to the alternative option of licensing foreign firms to produce Coke. The reason for this choice is the
desire of the company to protect the formula used to produce Coke.
In the 1960s, Coca-Cola closed its plants in India because the Indian
government exerted some pressure on the company to reveal the Coke
recipe. Lall and Streeten (1977) argue that the matter is just not one of
the preferences of the MNC, since many of the advantages or the
intangible assets cannot be sold to other firms, either because they
are inherent in the organization or because they are difficult or impossible to define, value and transfer. Intangible assets that cannot be sold,
even though the MNC may want to do so, include the MNC's managerial and organizational capabilities, the experience and the spirit of its
executives, its standing in financial markets, and its contacts with
various officials and other firms (Lall and Streeten, 1977, p. 36).

It is these firm-specific advantages that explain why a firm can
compete successfully in a foreign market. This approach has been
used by Graham and Krugman (1991) to explain the growth of FDI
in the USA. One problem with this approach, however, is that it fails
to explain why the firm does not utilize its advantages by producing in

Table 2.1 Advantages giving rise to FDI

Advantage	Description
Capital	Larger or cheaper cost of capital than local or smaller foreign competitors
Management	Superior management in the form of greater efficiency of operation or greater entrepreneurial ability to take risk or to identify profitable ventures
Technology	Superior technology in the form of ability to translate scientific knowledge into commercial use. This involves the functions of discovering new processes and products, product differentiation and various support activities
Marketing	The functions of market research, advertising and promotion, and distribution
Access to raw materials	Privileged access to raw materials arising from the control of final markets, transportation of the product, processing, or the production of the material itself
Economies of scale	The finance and expertise to set up and operate facilities that enjoy these economies
Bargaining and political power	The ability to extract concessions and favourable terms from the host government

the home country and exporting abroad, which is an alternative to FDI. According to Kindleberger, firms will be inclined to indulge in FDI in preference to exports if they operate with minimum costs at home, in which case additional production for exports would move them into a segment of rising costs. Moreover, lower production costs abroad may be achieved because of the procurement of cheap raw materials, an efficient transportation network, superior managerial skills, non-marketable technology, and substantial investment in R&D in the home country.

Aharoni (1966) suggested another answer to this question based on the behavioural theory of the firm suggested by Cyert and March

(1963). He argued that the three factors affecting the initial investment decision are uncertainty, information and commitment. Uncertainty is normally exaggerated, in which case some initial force (such
as the fear of losing a market) propels the desire to indulge in FDI.
This leads to a search for information relevant to project appraisal.
Once business executives spend time and effort on the project, and if
it is promising, then they will be committed to its implementation.

While the industrial organization hypothesis explains why firms invest
in foreign countries, it does not explain why firms choose to invest in
country A rather than country B. The location hypothesis, which will be
considered shortly, seeks to provide an answer to this question.

The Internalization Hypothesis

According to the internalization hypothesis, FDI arises from efforts by
firms to replace market transactions with internal transactions. This
idea is an extension of the original argument put forward by Coase
(1937), that certain marketing costs can be saved by forming a firm.[8]
For example, if there are problems associated with buying oil products
on the market, a firm may decide to buy a foreign refinery. These
problems arise from imperfections and failure of markets for intermediate goods, including human capital, knowledge, marketing and
management expertise. The advantages of internalization are the avoidance of time lags, bargaining and buyer uncertainty. Indeed, the main
motive for internalization is the presence of externalities in the goods
and factors markets. Buckley and Casson (1976) suggest that if markets in intermediate products are imperfect, firms have an incentive to
bypass them by creating internal markets, such that the activities linked
by the markets are brought under common ownership and control. The
internalization of markets across national boundaries leads to FDI,
and this process continues until the marginal benefits and marginal
costs are equal.

The internalization hypothesis explains why firms use FDI in preference to exporting and importing from foreign countries. It also
explains why they may shy away from licensing. Because of the
significant time lags and transaction costs associated with market
purchases and sales, firms replace some of the market functions with internal processes; that is, with intra-firm transactions. Moreover, the internalization process eliminates uncertainty. For example, a steel firm
may face considerable supply uncertainties and transportation costs
as it has to purchase iron ore in the open market, most probably from

different parts of the world. However, when this firm acquires a foreign mining company, the internalization of the market process, involving the purchase of iron ore and shipping, eliminates uncertainty.

It is sometimes claimed that the internalization hypothesis represents a general theory of FDI, whereas other theories are subsets of the general theory of internalization. Petrochilos (1989) argues that, while it is clear that MNCs do bypass the market for intermediate products through FDI, it is not certain that the motive for internalization is the external market's inefficiency in terms of high transaction costs and longer time lags, or anything else. He further suggests that a stronger argument is the one put forward by Dunning (1977), that firms want to retain the exclusive right of using the innovations generated by their R&D efforts. Buckley and Casson (2000a) present what they call a formal extension of the internalization hypothesis by providing a model that attempts to explain variations in entry mode.

There are two problems with the internalization hypothesis, however. First, Rugman (1980) argues that the hypothesis is so general that it has no empirical content. Second, Buckley (1988) argues that the hypothesis cannot be tested directly. The statistical tests are bound to be based on simplifying assumptions, and boil down to the conclusion that the process of internalization is concentrated in industries with relatively high incidence of R&D expenditure (see, for example, Buckley and Casson, 1976). However, the evidence shows that the pattern of FDI across countries is broadly consistent with this hypothesis. Martin (1991) finds evidence for the effect of transaction costs on FDI in the USA.

The Location Hypothesis

According to this hypothesis, FDI exists because of the international immobility of some factors of production, such as labour and natural resources. This immobility leads to location-related differences in the cost of factors of production. Horst (1972b) used this hypothesis to explain US FDI in Canada.

One form of location-related differences in the costs of factors of production is the locational advantage of low wages. Thus, the level of wages in the host country relative to wages in the home country is an important determinant of FDI. That is why countries such as India attract labour-intensive production (for example, footwear and textiles) from high-wage countries. It is also why MNCs wanting to establish production facilities in North America would choose Mexico in preference to Canada.[9] Of course, high wages may be indicative of high quality of labour, in which case the relationship between low wages and FDI does not hold. For example, activities such as banking and finance, and R&D, are not relocated to countries where people working in these fields earn low wages. What matters in this case is the quality of labour (see, for example, Wheeler and Mody, 1990). It is important to bear in mind that differences in cross-country labour productivity can be so significant that consideration of wage rates alone is not a reliable variable. Petrochilos (1989) points out that cross-country differences in labour productivity can explain partially why the bulk of FDI goes to high-wage industrial countries. After all, an investor may choose to locate in Canada rather than in Mexico.

Evidence on the hypothesis that cheap labour attracts FDI is mixed. Evidence from survey reports is weak, as, for example, in Forsyth (1972). However, the results of some of the time series and cross-sectional studies are favourable. For example, Riedel (1975) found relatively lower wage costs to be one of the major determinants of export-orientated FDI in Taiwan. Goldberg (1972), Saunders (1983), Schneider and Frey (1985), Culem (1988) and Moore (1993) found that a rise in the host country's wages (given wage rates in the source country) would discourage FDI flows. Love and Lage-Hidalgo (2000) investigated whether FDI flows from the USA to Mexico are determined by the cheap labour effect boosted by the Maquiladora industrialization programme (based on the US–Mexican border) or whether the Mexican market itself provides an incentive for forward FDI. They found significant support from the hypothesis that real labour cost differentials between the USA and Mexico have a significant effect on the flow of FDI from one country to another. They concluded that there is support for the 'cheap labour hypothesis'. On the other hand, other researchers found no significant effect or even the reverse effect. These researchers include Nankani (1979), Kravis and Lipsey (1982), and Wheeler and Mody (1990). A similar result was found by Yang *et al.* (2000) using Australian data. Other evidence, indicating that higher unit labour cost leads to higher outward and lower inward FDI, is provided by Cushman (1987), Culem (1988), Lucas (1993), Pain (1993), Bajo-Rubio and Sosvilla-Rivero (1994), Klein and Rosengren (1994), Wang and Swain (1995), and Barrell and Pain (1996).

A possible explanation for the perverse result (negative correlation between FDI and wages) is presented by Lucas (1993), who shows that a rise in the wage rate of the host country means an increase in the costs of production, which should discourage production, and consequently FDI. However, the rise in wages necessarily causes a change in the relative prices of factors of production, leading to a shift to more capital-intensive methods, and therefore to more FDI. An alternative explanation is provided by Yang *et al.* (2000, p. 47) on the basis of changes in productivity. They argue that when markets are imperfect, it is possible that gains in productivity do not fully reflect on labour, in which case wages do not rise in tandem with productivity. Therefore, an increase in the wage rate may be accompanied by a fall in labour costs (that is, wages adjusted for changes in productivity). If a fall in labour costs attracts FDI flows, it would look as if FDI flows and wage rates are negatively correlated.

Another factor that pertains to the labour market is labour disputes, which should have an adverse effect on FDI inflows. The adverse effect on FDI would depend on two characteristics of industrial disputes: incidence and severity. Moore (1993) and Tcha (1998) experimented with variables representing disputes and came up with contrasting results: while Tcha found some support for the importance of this factor in determining FDI outflows from Korea, Moore (using German data) came up with the unexpected finding that FDI is related positively to the severity of a strike as measured by the number of workers involved. Yang *et al.* (2000), who found a similar result for Australia, using the number of working days lost, explain this unexpected result in terms of the arguments on factor price and productivity changes used to explain the negative correlation between FDI and wages.

Of course, a related factor would be the extent of unionization in the host country. It is now conventional wisdom that MNCs prefer flexible non-unionized labour markets and, when unionization is present, decentralized firm-level wage bargaining processes over centralized ones. The underlying idea is that unionization leads to higher labour costs. In fact, it is this very idea that is used as the basis for endorsing legislation aimed at limiting the power of unions, and deregulating the bargaining power in highly-unionized industrial countries. Unfortunately, the interaction between labour market unionization and FDI has received surprisingly little attention in the literature, because the two issues have been studied separately. There are exceptions, however. Zhao (1995, 1998) demonstrates how cross-hauling FDI is generated between two countries with imperfectly competitive product markets and unionized labour markets. Naylor and Santoni (1998) analyze the effects on FDI of union power and the degree of substitutability between products. Contrary to conventional wisdom, Leahy and Montagna (2000b) show that, in the absence of taxes/subsidies, the MNC is less likely to locate in the host country under a decentralized than under a centralized wage setting regime, despite the fact that the latter typically yields higher wages.

Locational advantages not only take the form of low wages; they are also applicable to other factors of production. For example, a firm may indulge in FDI by building a factory in a country where it is cheap to generate hydroelectric power. Similarly, a factory could be located near a copper mine in the host country if copper is an important input in the production process. This is a locational advantage because significant savings can be made on the cost of shipping copper from where it is produced to where it is used. Apart from these savings, the firm can avoid delays in the delivery of copper shipments arising from the time it takes to ship the metal and the red tape that may be involved in this operation. In general, the location hypothesis emphasizes the importance of unavoidable government constraints, such as trade barriers.

Capital may also be the underlying factor of production, particularly if capital markets are segmented. The idea here is that FDI will flow to countries where the cost of capital is low. For example, one of the explanatory variables used by Love and Lage-Hidalgo (2000) to explain FDI flows from the USA to Mexico is the difference between the US and Mexican costs of capital. A perverse result was obtained, showing that the effect of the differential cost of capital runs in the opposite direction from that predicted by theory.

The Eclectic Theory

The eclectic theory was developed by Dunning (1977, 1979, 1988) by integrating the industrial organization hypothesis, the internalization hypothesis and the location hypothesis without being too precise about how they interrelate. The eclectic theory aims at answering the following questions. First, if there is demand for a particular commodity in a particular country, why is it not met by a local firm producing in the same country, or by a foreign firm exporting from another country?

And, second, suppose that a firm wants to expand its scale of operations, why does it not do so via other channels? These other channels include the following: (i) producing in the home country and exporting to the foreign country; (ii) expanding into a new line of business within the home country; (iii) indulging in portfolio invest-ment in the foreign country; and (iv) licensing its technology to for-eign firms that carry out the production. It seems that the answer to these questions is that a foreign subsidiary can out-compete other potential suppliers in the foreign market, and that FDI is more profit-able than other means of expansion. Another question arises: why is this the case? The eclectic theory attempts to answer this question and the related questions.

According to this theory, three conditions must be satisfied if a firm is to engage in FDI. First, it must have a comparative advantage over other firms arising from the ownership of some intangible assets. These are called ownership advantages, which include things like the right to a particular technology, monopoly power and size, access to raw materials, and access to cheap finance. Second, it must be more beneficial for the firm to use these advantages rather than to sell or lease them. These are the internalization advantages that refer to the choice between accomplishing expansion within the firm or selling the rights to the means of expansion to other firms. Third, it must be more profitable to use these advantages in combination with at least some factor inputs located abroad. If this is not the case, then exports would do the job. These are the locational advantages, which pertain to the question of whether expansion is best accomplished at home or abroad.

Let us now see how the eclectic theory explains FDI. Suppose that there is demand for a particular product in which a particular domes-tic firm has an ownership advantage. What happens depends on the internalization and locational advantages. So, there are the following possibilities:

1. If there are no internalization gains, the firm will license its own-ership advantage to another firm, particularly if locational factors favour expansion abroad.
2. If there are internalization gains and if locational factors favour home expansion, the firm expands at home and exports.
3. If there are internalization gains and if locational factors favour foreign expansion, FDI will take place and an MNC will emerge.

The eclectic theory suggests that all forms of FDI can be explained by reference to its conditions. It recognizes that advantages arising from ownership, internalization and location may change over time, and accepts that if country-specific characteristics are important determinants of FDI, it may be invalid to generalize from one country's experience to another.

Casson (1990) seems to have been thinking along similar lines when he put forward his 'integrated theory of FDI', which is the result of integrating the theory of international capital markets, the theory of the firm, and the theory of trade. He argues that the integration of the theory of international capital markets with the theory of the firm is quite straightforward. He also argues that the integration of the theory of international capital markets with the theory of trade poses no major problems in principle. However, he argues that the integration of the theory of the firm with trade theory is more problematic. The integration of these theories, Casson argues, provides answers to a complex set of questions pertaining to FDI.

The Product Life Cycle Hypothesis

This hypothesis was developed by Vernon (1966) to explain the expansion of US MNCs after the Second World War. According to this hypothesis, 'products go through a cycle of initiation, exponential growth, slowdown and decline – a sequence that corresponds to the process of introduction, spread, maturation and senescence' (Vernon, 1971). Petrochilos (1989) points out that this hypothesis is useful because it offers another interpretation of FDI, particularly for manufactured products that are characterized by advanced technology and high income elasticity of demand.

The hypothesis postulates that firms indulge in FDI at a particular stage in the life cycle of the products that they initially produced as innovations. The following three stages are identified:

1. The initial production takes place at home, close to the customers and because of the need for efficient co-ordination between R&D and production units. During this stage of the product life cycle the demand for the new product is price inelastic, and so the innovating firm can charge a relatively high price. As time passes, the product is improved, based on feedback from customers. Up to this point, demand has come from customers living in the home country.

2. The second stage is marked by the maturity and export of the product to countries having the next-highest level of income as demand emerges in these developed countries. As this demand continues to grow and competition emerges, the innovative firm

resorts to FDI in these countries to meet local demand. At this stage, the home country is a net exporter of the product, while foreign countries are net importers.

3. The third stage is characterized by a complete standardization of the product and its production process, which is no longer an exclusive possession of the innovating firm. At this stage, price competition from other producers forces the innovating firm to invest in developing countries, seeking cost advantages. The home country starts to import the product from both domestic and foreign firms based in foreign countries. The home country becomes a net importer, while foreign countries are net exporters.

Hence, FDI takes place as the cost of production becomes an important consideration, which is the case when the product reaches maturity and standardization. FDI is thus a defensive move to maintain the firm's competitive position against its domestic and foreign rivals. Figure 2.1 shows the patterns of production, consumption, exports and imports over time as the product goes through its life cycle.

The product life cycle hypothesis predicts that, over time, the home country where the innovative product first appeared switches from an exporting to an importing country. This prediction is consistent with the pattern of dynamic changes observed for many products. For example, personal computers were first developed by US firms (such as IBM and Apple Computers) and exported to foreign markets. When personal computers became standardized, the USA became a net importer from producers based in Japan, Korea and Taiwan. The exporters include foreign firms as well as subsidiaries of US companies located in these countries.

Agarwal (1980) describes a number of studies that support this hypothesis. Gruber *et al.* (1967) found a strong association between the propensity to invent new products, export performance, FDI, and the ratio of local production to exports on the one hand, and R&D expenditure of the US industries on the other. The association between the ratio of local production to exports and R&D expenditure is interpreted as an indication of the substitution of FDI for exports in host countries in the final stage of a product cycle. Horst (1972b) conducted a similar analysis for US exports to, and FDI in, Canada. He found that the technological intensity of US manufacturing industry was related more closely to the sum of that industry's exports to Canada and its subsidiary sales in Canada than it was to either exports or subsidiary sales taken separately.

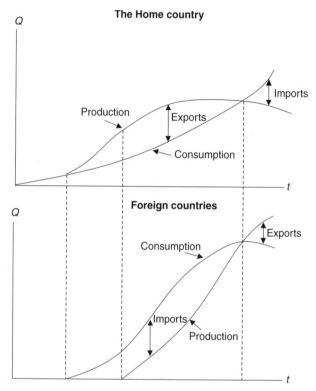

Figure 2.1 Production and consumption during the product life cycle

It is noteworthy that Vernon's original theory was developed in the 1960s, when the USA was the unquestioned leader in R&D and product innovation. Now, product innovation takes place outside the USA, and new products are introduced simultaneously in many advanced countries. Thus, production facilities may be located in several countries right from the beginning, and the international system of production is becoming too complicated to be explained by a simple version of the product life cycle hypothesis. Vernon (1979) admits this by noting that, since the income and technological gaps between the USA and other industrial countries have narrowed, the simple product life cycle hypothesis has become less plausible. This is why the hypothesis has been extended to take into account not only labour costs but also other factors costs, and has been generalized to apply to the FDI of all developed countries. For example, Hirsch (1976) has generalized the model so that the rigid sequential relationship between product innovation, export and FDI is no longer essential for its validity. Furthermore, Vernon (1974, 1977) restated the hypothesis by considering the problems of entropy facing MNCs, which may belong to an innovative, mature or a senescent oligopoly.

One has to admit that the applicability of the product cycle hypothesis is restricted to highly innovative industries (Solomon, 1978), and that it is an oversimplification of the firm's decision-making process (Buckley and Casson, 1976). However, it should be borne in mind that the hypothesis was based originally on the US experience, and offered a useful explanation for the interaction between production, exports and FDI during the 1950s and 1960s.

The Oligopolistic Reactions Hypothesis

Knickerbocker (1973) suggested that, in an oligopolistic environment, FDI by one firm triggers a similar action by other leading firms in the industry in an attempt to maintain their market shares. In their assessment of the motives for Japanese outward FDI, Kreinin *et al.* (1999) conclude that 'securing market share is the most salient motivation [for FDI]'. After all, it is usually firms belonging to monopolistic or oligopolistic industries at home that are better placed and have the necessary incentives to commit resources to R&D. Lall and Streeten (1977) argue that the very structure of oligopolistic competition and equilibrium is such that none of the participants can afford to ignore what the others are doing. For example, a move by one firm to establish production facilities abroad may be interpreted by rivals to imply a threat to the status quo, thus inducing counter-moves. The first move may be prompted by government action or by something else, but, as Lall and Streeten argue, the subsequent pattern cannot be interpreted in terms of the profit-maximizing behaviour of an individual firm independently of the actions of rival firms. Lall and Streeten further argue that this kind of behaviour is consistent with the Marxist view of international capitalism, as put forward by Magdoff (1972) and Barratt-Brown (1974), that it is 'a growing worldwide battle of competing giant firms, forced to extend continually the scope of their activity'. Vernon (1974) discusses three kinds of oligopolies (innovative, mature and senescent) and the different pressures they generate for the firms concerned.

Knickerbocker (1973) suggests that oligopolistic reaction increases with the level of concentration, and decreases with the diversity of the product. On the basis of data on the manufacturing FDI of 187 US

MNCs, he found that the oligopolistic firms try to counter any advantage that the first firm may obtain from its FDI by following it with their own FDI in order to maintain a competitive equilibrium. He concluded that increased industrial concentration causes increased oligopolistic reaction in the field of FDI, except at very high levels. He also found the profitability of FDI to be correlated positively with entry concentration, and that the latter was correlated negatively with product diversity. The hypothesis was also tested by Flowers (1975) on FDI from Canada and Europe in the USA. He found a significant positive correlation between the concentration of FDI in the USA and the concentration in the investing countries.

Agarwal (1980) argues that an implication of the oligopolistic reactions hypothesis is that the process of FDI is self-limiting, since the invasion of each other's home market leads to an increase in competition and a decline in the intensity of oligopolistic reaction. This implication, however, is incompatible with stylized facts. While it has led to increased competition in many industries, this increase has not resulted in a corresponding reduction in FDI. This hypothesis also fails to identify the factors that trigger the initial investment. Yu and Ito (1988) argue that firms in oligopolistic industries do not only consider their competitors' activities but also the same economic factors as firms in a competitive industry.

OTHER THEORIES OF FOREIGN DIRECT INVESTMENT

Four hypotheses are presented under this heading: (i) the internal financing hypothesis; (ii) the currency area hypothesis; (iii) the hypothesis of diversification with barriers to international capital flows; and (iv) the Kojima hypothesis. These hypotheses will be discussed in turn.

The Internal Financing Hypothesis

Here, internal financing refers to the utilization of profit generated by a subsidiary to finance the expansion of FDI by an MNC in the country where the subsidiary operates. This hypothesis, which is based on the 'gamblers' earnings' hypothesis of Barlow and Wender (1955), postulates that MNCs commit a modest amount of their resources to their initial direct investment, while subsequent expansions are financed by reinvesting profits obtained from operations in the host country. It therefore implies the existence of a positive relationship between internal cash flows and investment outlays, which is plausible because the cost of internal financing is lower. According to Froot and Stein (1991), one reason why external financing is more expensive than internal financing is informational imperfections in capital markets. The hypothesis seems to be more appropriate for explaining FDI in developing countries for (at least) two reasons: (i) the presence of restrictions on the movement of funds; and (ii) the rudimentary state and inefficiency of financial markets.

Hartman (1985) provides a tax-based explanation as to why MNCs like internal financing. He argues that, because repatriated earnings and not earnings of the subsidiary are typically the source of the tax liability in the home country, income tax should affect FDI differently, depending on the required transfers of funds from the subsidiary to the MNC. Hence, a firm should finance FDI out of foreign earnings to the greatest possible extent. That is, a firm's required foreign return is set at the point at which desired FDI just exhausts foreign earnings. As a result, Hartman draws a distinction between mature and immature foreign projects (or operations or subsidiaries), the latter being dependent on financing by the MNC without making any remittances.

A number of economists have tested this hypothesis. Stevens (1969) tested it on a sample of 71 US foreign subsidiaries and failed to find supportive evidence. Severn (1972) tested it using data on 68 firms, and concluded that the internally-generated funds are allocated among the parent and subsidiaries by the top management in such a way as to maximize profits from the point view of the whole concern. On the other hand, Brash (1966), Safarian (1969), Kwack (1972) and Hoelscher (1975) have produced supporting evidence. For example, Brash reached the conclusion that 'the most important sources of funds required for expansion are undistributed profits and depreciation allowances'. There is also some survey-based evidence on this hypothesis. Stobaugh (1970) concluded, on the basis of interviews, that the investment behaviour of small companies supported the hypothesis. Reuber *et al.* (1973) suggested on the basis of interviews that a distinction should be made between the cash flows of the enterprise as a whole and those of the subsidiaries alone. It was found that cash flows of the subsidiaries do affect new investment outlays, particularly if there are restrictions on profit repatriation. Agarwal (1980) concludes that there is some empirical support for this hypothesis in the sense that FDI is determined partly by the subsidiaries' internally-generated funds.

The Currency Areas Hypothesis and the Effect of the Exchange Rate

Aliber (1970, 1971) put forward a hypothesis that attempts to explain FDI in terms of the relative strength of various currencies. This hypothesis postulates that firms belonging to a country with a strong currency tend to invest abroad, while firms belonging to a country with a weak currency do not have such a tendency. In other words, countries with strong currencies tend to be sources of FDI, while countries with weak currencies tend to be host countries or recipients of FDI. This hypothesis is based on capital market relationships, foreign exchange risk, and the market's preference for holding assets denominated in strong currencies. Aliber argues that an MNC in a hard currency area is able, based on reputation, to borrow at lower rates in a soft currency country than can local firms. In essence, the crucial assumption is that there is bias in capital markets, which arises because an income stream located in a country with a weak currency is associated with foreign exchange risk. Hence, the view arises that a strong currency firm may be more efficient in hedging foreign exchange risk.

The hypothesis put forward by Aliber can be tested empirically by examining the relationship between the value of the currency and flows of FDI. If the hypothesis is valid, then an overvaluation of a currency is associated with FDI outflows, whereas an undervaluation of the currency must be associated with inflows. There is some support for the hypothesis that an overvaluation of the currency is associated with FDI outflows, and vice versa (Agarwal, 1980). The problem with this hypothesis, according to Lizondo (1991), is that it cannot account for cross-investment between currency areas, for direct investment in countries belonging to the same currency area, and for the concentration of FDI in certain industries. Furthermore, Dunning (1973) suggests that the currency area hypothesis adds to the industrial organization hypothesis, because country risk affects the relationship between the investing firms and their competitors, though it does not supplant it.

Froot and Stein (1991) have come up with a more elaborate theory based on market imperfections. They argue that a weak currency may be associated with FDI inflows resulting from informational imperfections in the capital market, and that these imperfections make the cost of external financing higher than the cost of internal financing. By analysing US data, they show that FDI inflows are related negatively to the real value of the dollar.

Agarwal (1980, p. 757) warns of the hazard of confusing the currency areas hypothesis with the relationship between FDI and changes in exchange rates, even though they are related. The emphasis in the currency areas hypothesis is on overvaluation and undervaluation rather than on appreciation and depreciation. Exchange rates are also important for FDI, because FDI can be viewed as an alternative to exports. Thus, if the domestic currency appreciates against foreign currencies, MNCs based in the home country would find it difficult to export, as domestic goods become less competitive. If the appreciation of the domestic currency persists, the MNC may find it useful to move abroad, resulting in a rise in FDI. In this case, FDI can be viewed as a measure taken to hedge economic exposure to foreign exchange risk. It must be borne in mind, however, that the relevant exchange rate in this case would be the real exchange rate, since it is the rate that determines competitiveness and economic exposure. Moreover, the relationship between FDI and the exchange rate cannot be contemporaneous, as it takes time between the appreciation of the domestic currency and the decision to expand FDI, unless the decision is based on expectation.[10] Given that the real exchange rate is determined by the nominal exchange rate and relative inflation, the latter is a factor that influences FDI flows.

Changes in exchange rates are bound, in theory, to have an effect on FDI. First, a depreciation of the domestic currency makes domestic assets more attractive for foreigners, while foreign assets become more expensive for residents in the home country. Thus, FDI inflows will increase. This, according to Froot and Stein (1991), explains the increase in FDI in the USA as a result of the depreciation of the US dollar that started in March 1985. But this argument can be dismissed as follows. In a world with mobile capital, risk-adjusted expected returns on all international assets will be equalized. For this equality to hold, a depreciation of the domestic currency will result in a rise in the prices of domestic assets. The question that arises here is: if foreigners can buy domestic assets with an appreciating currency, why can't domestic residents with access to global capital markets borrow the foreign currency and take advantage of the situation, just like the foreign investors? However, Froot and Stein (1991) argue that 'the view that exchange rates are irrelevant to FDI is at odds with more than just casual empiricism'. They show empirically that a 10 per cent appreciation of the dollar is associated with additional FDI inflows of about $5 billion.

Caves (1988) argues that the effect of the exchange rate on FDI runs through two channels. First, changes in exchange rates lead to changes in the investor's costs and revenues. The net effect on FDI is ambiguous, depending on certain characteristics of the underlying business activity. The second channel is associated with expected short-term exchange rate movements. A depreciation that is expected to be reversed will encourage FDI inflows to obtain capital gains when the domestic currency appreciates.

The effect of exchange rates on FDI is ambiguous, because the latter is affected by both the level and variability of exchange rates. Moreover, the effect of the level of the exchange rate depends on the destination of the goods produced. If the investor aims at serving the local market, then FDI and trade are substitutes, in which case an appreciation of the currency of the host country attracts FDI inflows. Alternatively, if FDI is aimed at re-exports, then FDI and trade are complements. In this case, appreciation of the currency of the host country reduces FDI inflows through lower competitiveness. The effect of exchange rate variability also depends on the objective of FDI. If the investor aims at serving the local market, then exchange rate variability encourages FDI. If, however, the objective is to re-export, then this benefit vanishes.

Figure 2.2 is a simplified representation of the relationship over time between misalignment (overvaluation and undervaluation), changes in the exchange rate (appreciation and depreciation), and FDI flows. There are two relationships here: the first is that between misalignment and FDI flows, and the second between changes in the exchange rate and FDI flows. Notice that appreciation and depreciation may occur irrespective of whether the currency is overvalued or undervalued. The top part of Figure 2.2 shows the actual level of the exchange rate, S_t, and the equilibrium level of the exchange rate, $\bar{S}_t$, which may be the level implied by purchasing power parity (PPP). When S_t is below $\bar{S}_t$, the currency is undervalued, and when S_t is above $\bar{S}_t$, the currency is overvalued. This is also shown in the middle part of Figure 2.2, in which case the currency is undervalued if $S_t - \bar{S}_t < 0$, and overvalued if $S_t - \bar{S}_t > 0$. Notice that in the third episode (undervaluation) the currency depreciates and appreciates, and the same is true for the fourth episode (overvaluation) in which the currency appreciates, depreciates, appreciates again, and then depreciates, moving towards the elimination of the misalignment. The third part of the diagram shows FDI flows (+ indicates inflows and – indicates outflows). The figure shows that episodes of under-valuation are associated with FDI inflows, whereas episodes of over-valuation are associated with FDI outflows. This is the relationship

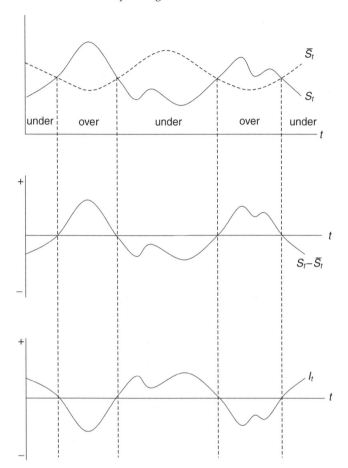

Figure 2.2 Relationship between currency misalignment and FDI flows

between misalignment and FDI flows. But notice in the third episode that, when the currency is undervalued, FDI inflows rise and fall, and when it is overvalued (as in the fourth episode) FDI outflows rise and fall. This is the relationship between changes in the exchange rate and FDI flows.

The relationship between FDI and the exchange rate, as shown in Figure 2.2, can be represented algebraically as follows:

$$I_t = f_1(S_t - \bar{S}_t) + f_2(S_t - S_{t-1}) \tag{2.1}$$

where I is FDI flows, $f_1' > 0$, $f_2' > 0$ and $|f_1(S_t - \bar{S}_t)| > |f_2(S_t - S_{t-1})|$. The term $f_1(S_t - \bar{S}_t)$ represents the dependence of FDI on overvaluation and undervaluation of the currency, whereas the term $f_2(S_t - S_{t-1})$ represents the dependence on currency appreciation and depreciation. Notice that both Figure 2.2 and Equation (2.1) show a contemporaneous relationship between FDI on the one hand, and exchange rate misalignment and changes on the other. This may be unrealistic, since FDI decisions in response to exchange rate variation take a long time to implement. It is therefore more likely that the relationship would be lagged rather than contemporaneous. However, since the length of the lag is an empirical issue, the relationship is portrayed as being contemporaneous. In empirical work, the exchange rate variable may be contemporaneous, lagged, or both. Of course, the choice depends in part on the frequency of the data used.

In general, various studies have produced results showing that FDI is affected by exchange rates. Froot and Stein (1991) obtained results indicating that FDI inflows to the USA are correlated negatively with the real value of the US dollar, although this was not the case for the other three countries examined. Caves (1988) also produced results showing significant negative correlation between the level of the exchange rate (both nominal and real) and inflows of FDI. However, Bajo-Rubio and Sosvilla-Rivero (1994), and Wang and Swain (1995), used an exchange rate variable in their estimated equations without a great deal of success. Similarly, Yang *et al.* (2000) failed to find a significant relationship between the effective exchange rate of the Australian dollar and FDI flows.

The Hypothesis of Diversification with Barriers to International Capital Flows

Agmon and Lessard (1977) argue that for international diversification to be carried out through firms, two conditions must hold: (i) there must exist barriers or costs to portfolio flows that are greater than those associated with direct investment; and (ii) investors must recognize that multinational firms provide diversification opportunities that are otherwise unavailable. They tested the hypothesis that stock prices of firms with relatively large international operations are more closely related to the rest-of-the-world market factors, and less to the domestic-market factors than stock prices of firms that are essentially domestic. Their results were consistent with the second proposition. Errunza and Senbet (1981) developed a model whereby investors demand diversification and MNCs supply diversification services, an activity that is reflected positively in the price of their stocks. The empirical results showed that there was a systematic relationship between the extent of international involvement and excess market value. Furthermore, the relationship was found to be stronger in periods characterized by the presence of barriers to capital flows.

The Kojima Hypothesis

Kojima (1973, 1975, 1985) views direct investment as providing a means of transferring capital, technology and managerial skills from the source country to the host country. This approach is described as being a 'macroeconomic approach' or a 'factor endowment approach', as opposed to the 'international business approach' to FDI. Kojima classifies FDI into two kinds. The first is trade-orientated, which generates an excess demand for imports and an excess supply of exports at the original terms of trade. This kind of FDI leads to welfare improvement in both countries. Moreover, it would normally imply investment in industries in which the source county has a comparative disadvantage. This would promote trade and a beneficial industrial restructuring in both countries. The second kind is the anti-trade-orientated FDI, which has exactly opposite effects to those of the first kind. Thus, anti-trade-orientated FDI has an adverse effect on trade, and it also promotes unfavourable restructuring in both countries. Kojima argues that Japanese FDI has been trade-orientated, but not so the FDI of the USA. Thus, Kojima's hypothesis is based on the complementarity of trade and FDI, and it emphasizes the need for considering comparative costs.

Petrochilos (1989, p. 21) comments on Kojima's hypothesis by arguing that the direction of Japanese outward FDI has been dictated mainly by the lack of raw materials and other basic resources at home, the desire to exploit low wages elsewhere, and by the policy of limiting environmental pollution at home. He concludes that the Kojima hypothesis is not so much a theory explaining FDI, but more like a prerequisite for establishing foreign trade. He also argues that (i) elements of the Kojima hypothesis can be found in other theories such as the product life cycle hypothesis; and (ii) Japanese outward FDI could be explained adequately in terms of the eclectic theory. Buckley (1990) provides further evaluation of the Kojima hypothesis.

THEORIES BASED ON OTHER FACTORS

There are three other factors that have been used to explain FDI. These factors, which will be discussed in turn, are political risk and country risk, tax policy, trade barriers, government regulations, and strategic and long-term factors.

Political Risk and Country Risk

Lack of political stability discourages inflows of FDI. Political risk arises because unexpected modifications of the legal and fiscal frameworks in the host country may change the economic outcome of a given investment in a drastic manner. For example, a decision by the host government to impose restrictions on capital repatriation to the investor's home country will have an adverse effect on the cash flows received by the parent company. Wang and Swain (1995) use dummy variables to capture specific political events that may have an important impact on FDI. Ramcharran (1999) used the *Euromoney* political risk index to examine the effect of political risk on FDI for twenty-six countries.

Although the results produced by studies dealing with this factor have been mixed, Schneider and Frey (1985) concluded that models encompassing economic and political factors perform better than other models that do not contain political variables. These models also perform better than those utilizing indices designed to capture political and economic factors simultaneously. Stevens (2000) makes such an attempt by integrating a number of political and other non-traditional economic variables into a standard theory of FDI based on the maximization of the expected value of the firm. The empirical results show that the generalized model that contains additional variables is superior to the conventional model in explaining US FDI in Argentina, Brazil and Mexico. He found the following non-traditional variables to affect FDI: (i) exchange controls and repatriation restrictions on dividends to the parent firm; (ii) devaluation in a fixed exchange rate system; (iii) specific governments that appear hostile to FDI from the USA; (iv) the number of years a government is in power; (v) pertinent legislation; and (vi) the debt crisis over the period 1982–9. He found no support for the effect of the legality of the government, how it came to power, or even its rhetoric *vis-à-vis* FDI.

Sometimes the wider concept of country risk is used instead of political risk, as the former encompasses the latter, taking into consideration economic and credit indicators (see Chapter 5). In this case, economic factors pose economic risk because adverse developments in economic indicators (such as an acceleration of the inflation rate and a depreciation of the currency) can affect cash flows adversely, and hence discourage FDI. Notice that what is under consideration is the possibility of an adverse economic or political measure, including changes in the 'rules of the game' (such as the possibility of raising the level of taxes). For example, inflation has been used by Schneider and Frey (1985), and by Bajo-Rubio and Sosvilla-Rivero (1994) to proxy the stability of macroeconomic policy. In both studies, a negative relationship was found between inflation and FDI. A similar result was detected from Australian data by Yang *et al.* (2000).

Tax Policies

Domestic and foreign tax policies affect the incentive to engage in FDI and the means by which it is financed. Jun (1989) identifies three channels through which tax policies affect the decisions taken by MNCs. First, the tax treatment of income generated abroad has a direct effect on the net return on FDI. Second, the tax treatment of income generated at home affects the net profitability of domestic investment, and the relative profitability of domestic and foreign investment. Third, tax policies affect the relative cost of capital of domestic and foreign investment (see Chapter 7). Jun shows, by using an intertemporal optimization model, that an increase in the domestic corporate tax rate leads to an increase in the outflow of FDI. Slemrod (1989) examined the effect of host country and home country tax policies on FDI in the USA and obtained results indicating a negative impact of the US tax rate on FDI.

In making his distinction between mature and immature foreign subsidiaries, Hartman (1985) concludes that the domestic tax rate on foreign income and the presence or otherwise of tax credit should be irrelevant to a mature foreign subsidiary. This is because domestic tax acts as an unavoidable cost. This point can be illustrated formally as follows. Let X_t be the subsidiary's earnings, which are taxed at the foreign income tax rate, λ^*, and I_t the extra FDI taken at time t. If the subsidiary uses part of its earnings to finance the extra FDI and transfers the rest to the parent MNC, then the MNC receives $S_t[(1 - \tau^*)X_t - I_t]$ in domestic currency terms, where S_t is the exchange rate (measured as the price of unit of the foreign currency) prevailing at the end of t. If there is full tax credit, in the sense that the

MNC pays the home government its tax liability less the tax paid by the subsidiary, then the MNC's tax bill amounts to:

$$T_t = \tau S_t[(1 - \tau^*)X_t - I_t] - S_t\tau^*X_t \qquad (2.2)$$

in which case it is obvious that:

$$\frac{\partial T_t}{\partial I_t} = -\tau S_t < 0 \qquad (2.3)$$

which means that the MNC can reduce its tax bill by increasing I_t. For the tax bill to become zero, extra FDI must be set at a level given by:

$$I_t = X_t\left(1 - \tau^* - \frac{\tau^*}{\tau}\right) \qquad (2.4)$$

which in the absence of tax credit becomes:

$$I_t = X_t(1 - \tau^*) \qquad (2.5)$$

For an immature subsidiary, Equations (2.4) and (2.5) define the level of FDI undertaken at time t if we assume that no extra funds are required by the subsidiary from the MNC.

Numerous empirical studies have been conducted to examine the effect of international taxation on FDI. Studies based on time series data include those by Hartman (1981, 1984), Boskin and Gale (1987), and Slemrod (1990a, 1990b). Moreover, Hines and Rice (1994) examined the effect of taxation on the cross-sectional distribution of capital and labour employed by US MNCs in their FDI projects. These studies, according to Hines (1996) encountered difficulties in identifying the effects of taxes on the factor demands of MNCs. Hines argues that this is caused by the following factors. First, cross-sectional variation in national tax rates and tax systems may be correlated with a number of observable and unobservable factors that differ between one country and another. Second, time series variation in tax rates may not be adequate to identify tax effects, since tax rates change infrequently, and tax changes may be endogenous to unobservable economic conditions that affect factor demands. Third, it is possible that the tax policy has no effect, or only a trivial effect, on FDI, as suggested by Glickman and Woodward (1989), and by Graham and Krugman (1991).

Moreover, researchers typically find no effect of substantial taxes on the location of business activity. For example, Carlton (1983) found that 'high tax rates do not appear to discourage new firms'. The majority of the studies surveyed in Wasylenko (1981, 1991) report little support for the view that state taxes have important effects on business location within the USA. On the other hand, some studies, including Newman (1983), Bartik (1985), Helms (1985) and Papke (1987, 1991), support the hypothesis that taxes influence significantly the location choices of new businesses. Newman and Sullivan (1988) conclude that the modelling and estimation limitations of existing studies make it difficult, with the available information, to reject the hypothesis that taxes influence business location. Hines argues that 'it is not altogether surprising that it has been difficult for analysts to identify a strong effect of substantial taxes on business activity'. He gives two reasons for his argument. First, there are many (non-tax) attributes that make locations attractive and unattractive for business, some of which are unobservable (for example, tariffs, low wages, industrial relations and proximity to raw materials). Second, tax rates will be correlated positively with business activity if higher rates represent part of a fiscal package that includes greater spending. Helms (1985) offers evidence in support of this hypothesis.

Hines (1996) examined simultaneously the effect of international taxation on FDI, and the effect of substantial taxation on business location. He argued that previous studies had difficulty in finding any effect of state taxation on business location because of the problem of controlling for important unobservable variables. On the basis of survey data obtained from the US Commerce Department, he estimated a model showing that high tax rates have a significantly negative effect on FDI. Specifically, he shows that investors who cannot claim credit for state tax payments reduce their investment shares by 9–11 per cent for every 1 per cent rate of taxation. However, he stresses that it is not possible with the use of cross-sectional data to test directly whether tax factors are an important part of the explanation for the 1980s surge in FDI in the USA.

Swenson (1994) examined empirically how taxes shape FDI, and found that increased taxes boost inward FDI. While simple intuition might suggest that higher taxes should discourage both foreign and domestic investments, Scholes and Wolfson (1990) have shown that the general equilibrium effects on asset returns combined with a careful consideration of foreign tax systems reveals reasons for foreign investors to increase their investments in response to high taxes in the host country. For example, Scholes and Wolfson (1990) have shown that total taxes paid by foreign firms do not necessarily increase when taxes are raised in the host country. Tax reform may simply reallocate the respective amounts paid to the home and host governments. Hence, there is some evidence confirming the surprising connection between US tax increases and increased inward FDI. But Cummins and Hubbard (1995) produced results that, according to them, cast significant doubt on the proposition that taxes do not have an impact upon US firms' decisions. They argue that tax parameters influence FDI in precisely the way indicated by neoclassical models. They further argue that their results also lend support to the application of the tax capitalization model to the study of dividend repatriation and FDI decisions.

Trade Barriers

FDI may be undertaken to circumvent trade barriers such as tariffs because FDI can be viewed as an alternative to trade. This means that open economies without much restriction on international trade should receive fewer FDI flows. A real-life example of a move like this is Honda's establishment of production facilities in Ohio to circumvent the tariffs and quotas imposed by the US government. The surge in FDI in countries such as Mexico and Spain is attributed partly to the desire of MNCs to circumvent the trade barriers imposed by NAFTA and the EU (Eun and Resnick, 1998, p. 394).

Moore (1993) and Wang and Swain (1995) used a trade-weighted tariff rate to represent trade barriers, but it turned out to be an insignificant determinant of FDI. However, Bajo-Rubio and Sosvilla-Rivero (1994) found a significant effect of the tariff rate on FDI. Hufbauer *et al.* (1994) used ratio of trade to GDP as a measure of the openness of the economy. Yang *et al.* (2000) used the same measure of openness and found FDI flows to be related negatively to the degree of openness of the economy, suggesting that FDI is indeed used to circumvent trade barriers. Lipsey (2000) concludes that countries that are more open to trade tend to provide and receive more FDI.

Sometimes, the threat of protectionism by the host government triggers FDI. Blonigen and Feenstra (1996) argue that the literature on *quid pro quo* FDI suggests that FDI may be induced by the threat of protection, and that it may be used as an instrument to defuse protectionist threats. This paper uses a panel data set of four-digit SIC level observations of Japanese manufacturing FDI into the USA in the 1980s to explore these hypotheses empirically. Strong support is found for the hypothesis that threats of protection lead to greater FDI flows. A rise in the expected probability of protection from 5 per cent to 10 per cent means a greater than 30 per cent rise in the next period's FDI flows for an average industry.

Government Regulations

Most governments adopt policies aimed at both encouraging and discouraging inward FDI by offering incentives on the one hand, and disincentives (taking the form of restrictions on the activities of MNCs) on the other. Typically, they offer incentives (such as financial and tax incentives as well as market preferences) while simultaneously placing restrictions on the activities of MNCs. The incentives offered by host governments to investing MNCs include the following:

1. Fiscal incentives such as tax reductions, accelerated depreciation, investment and reinvestment allowances, and exemption from customs duties. It is arguable that fiscal incentives may be successful in attracting the new 'footloose' variety of sourcing investments, but not those of a more long-lived nature.
2. Financial incentives, such as subsidies, grants and loan guarantees.
3. Market preferences, including monopoly rights, protection from competition arising from imports, and preferential government contracts.
4. Low cost infrastructure, fuel and energy.
5. The provision of information by means of agencies located in the capitals of the source countries.
6. A framework for clear, efficiently implemented stable policies with respect to FDI.
7. Flexible conditions with respect to local equity participation.

Indicative of the extent to which governments will go to attract foreign investment is an advertisement that appeared in *Fortune* in 1995. In this advertisement, the government of the Philippines declared that, to attract foreign companies, the government had 'felled [sic] mountains, razed jungles, filled swamps, moved rivers, relocated towns...all to make it easier for you and your business to do business here'. But Leahy and Montagna (2000) suggest that the argument for subsidies for FDI is that unionized labour markets are likely to make the host country less attractive to MNCs. Some observers argue that these policies can distort economic activity severely, and reduce the efficiency of FDI. Moreover, gains from these policies tend to be made at the expense of other countries. There is a certain 'beggar thy neighbour' aspect to all these. It is arguable that incentives usually tend to benefit companies that would have made the investment anyway, so the result is wasteful competitive bidding among host countries. It is the overall environment of a particular country (as constituted by its political, social and economic conditions) that attracts FDI. Incentives and concessions often help only in so far as they indicate a favourable environment. Otherwise, they simply cost the host government a part of the tax revenue and add little new FDI. Moreover, because the host government typically lacks the information needed to assess what incentives have to be offered to secure the underlying investment project, and because of the strong negotiating power of the MNCs, the latter are often in a position to obtain incentives in excess of their needs, and perhaps in excess of the benefits they bring to the host country.[11]

Disincentives include a number of impediments that may range from the slow processing of the required authorization to the outright prohibition of foreign investment in specific regions or sectors. Moreover, MNCs may be required to operate in those sectors that are owned primarily by domestic investors. There are also some requirements such as the ruling that MNCs employ a minimum number of local workers, and restrictions on profit repatriation.

The empirical studies surveyed by Agarwal (1980) show that the incentives have a limited effect on the level of FDI, as investors base their decisions on risk and return considerations. On the other hand, disincentives seem to have a more definite impact than incentives on FDI. For example, Aharoni (1966) concluded from his survey that, at the initial stage of an FDI decision, the incentives are not considered by firms. According to Reuber *et al.* (1973) the incentives may be of some help, particularly for small firms with limited experience, but their overall impact on FDI is marginal at best. They also argue that the variety of incentives granted by developing countries generally adds to the costs of these investments for these countries without increasing their flows effectively, the main reason being that incentives are normally accompanied by disincentives such as various restrictions on ownership and size. It is also important to bear in mind that other factors are more influential for the project under consideration. Since the objective of the incentives is to correct an existing comparative disadvantage of the host country, it is not surprising to find that their effectiveness is circumscribed. Bond and

Guisinger (1985) investigate the effects of incentives on the location decisions of MNCs.

It could happen that a government offers incentives for some kinds of FDI while imposing disincentives for other kinds. This is particularly the case with acquisitions versus greenfield investment. Buckley and Casson (2000a) use their model of entry mode to find an explanation as to why governments so often compete to attract inward greenfield investment while taking a restrictive attitude towards acquisitions. The model reveals that market structure is a crucial factor in the choice between greenfield investment and acquisitions. Governments prefer greenfield investment because, unlike acquisitions, it leads to an increase in the local capacity and an intensification of competition.

One particular case of using incentives to offset disincentives is when the host government uses a package that includes trade-related investment performance (TRIP) requirements, which are seen by some as a significant obstacle to FDI. TRIP requirements can be defined as 'host government policies designed to encourage local purchase of inputs by foreign-owned firms, and policies to encourage these firms to export' (Wallace, 1990). Thus, TRIP requirements include two components: (i) local content; and (ii) export minima. These requirements should be viewed as disincentives to FDI, because the local content requirements may lead to increased cost, and decreased earnings, which makes the underlying project less competitive. Similarly, export minima may lead to lower earnings, adversely affecting the attractiveness of FDI. Normally, TRIP requirements are combined with incentives such as preferential tax status, access to foreign exchange, and import protection. There are reasons why the host country may impose TRIP requirements: (i) they represent an explicit commitment to increasing the supply of foreign exchange; (ii) they can correct market distortions; and (iii) they could be used by the host government as a defensive measure. Wallace (1990) argues that while TRIP requirements are not attractive on economic efficiency grounds, they are not a significant obstacle to FDI. The widespread existence of favourable *quid pro quo* type policies combining incentives and disincentives is the single most important reason for believing that TRIP requirements are not a major impediment for FDI.

Stoever (1999) proposes a schema categorizing different functions performed by different levels of a government in a developing country in formulating its policy towards FDI: (i) examining the mix of government directives and market forces that guide the country's economic activity; (ii) determining priorities for the types of investment the government seeks, and the benefits it hopes to obtain from this investment; (ii) drafting of laws, policies and regulations that govern specific investments; and (iv) employing the tools of input–output analysis, cost–benefit analysis, and balance of payments analysis to evaluate individual investment proposals.

Strategic and Long-Term Factors

There is a set of strategic and long-term factors that have been put forward to explain FDI. Reuber *et al.* (1973) list the following factors as being instrumental to the decision to invest abroad:

1. The desire on the part of the investor to defend existing foreign markets and foreign investments against competitors.
2. The desire to gain and maintain a foothold in a protected market or to gain and maintain a source of supply that in the long run may prove useful.
3. The need to develop and sustain a parent–subsidiary relationship.
4. The desire to induce the host country into a long commitment to a particular type of technology.
5. The advantage of complementing another type of investment.
6. The economies of new product development.
7. Competition for market shares among oligopolists and the concern for strengthening of bargaining positions.

Vaitsos (1976) argues that these factors have indirect, longer-term and wider consequences for FDI. They are also directly relevant to the profitability of the group as a whole through their influence on the streams of future income.

THEORIES OF ENTRY MODES

Theories of FDI deal implicitly with the mode of entry into foreign markets, an issue encountered in Chapter 1. In the 1960s, theories of FDI concentrated on the choice between exports and FDI. In the 1970s, the internalization hypothesis identified other modes of entry into a foreign market, including licensing, franchising and 'arm's-length' arrangements such as subcontracting. In the 1980s, M&As

emerged as an important mode of entry, and so the choice became between acquisitions and greenfield FDI. Buckley and Casson (2000a) distinguish between exporting, foreign licensing and FDI, as follows. Exporting is located domestically and controlled administratively; foreign licensing is foreign-located and controlled contractually; and FDI is foreign-located and controlled administratively. A number of studies have dealt with takeovers as a mode of entry, including Wilson (1980), Zejan (1990), and Agarwal and Ramaswami (1992). The theoretical issues have been surveyed by Svensson (1996) and Meyer (1997). Nitsch *et al.* (1996) relate entry mode to performance.

The issue of advantages of direct investment over exporting has been dealt with extensively in the literature. The question that arises in this respect is: why do large firms exploit the oligopolistic advantages by undertaking the trouble and risk of organizing production abroad rather than by exporting? Lall and Streeten (1977) identify major factors that affect the choice between exports and FDI:

1. Production and transportation costs, as FDI enables them to exploit cost advantages.
2. Government policy in the host country with respect to trade barriers. In general, firms tend to switch from exports to FDI when the destination countries start adopting import-substitution policies. We have seen that the threat of protectionism in the host country induces a shift from exporting to FDI (Blonigen and Feenstra, 1996).
3. The marketing factor, as FDI enables firms to service the destination markets in a better way.
4. Oligopolistic reaction in the sense that a move towards foreign production by one oligopolistic firm induces others to follow. This is indeed the oligopolistic reaction hypothesis presented earlier as a theory of FDI.
5. Product cycle, which triggers FDI along the lines suggested by the product life cycle hypothesis.

Eaton and Tamura (1996) present a simple model of the choice between exports and FDI, showing that it depends on the host country's size, its level of technological sophistication, and the distance from the source country. They find that the importance of FDI relative to exports grows with population, and that distance tends to inhibit FDI much less than it inhibits exports. They also detect a tendency for Japanese exports to rise relative to FDI as countries become more advanced, and the opposite tendency for the USA.

Several factors have also been identified to make FDI more attract-ive than licensing. Licensing is defined by Lall and Streeten (1977) as the sale of technology, brand names, patents, management services, or other similar assets. According to Baranson (1970), McManus (1972), Parker (1974) and Baumann (1975), FDI is preferred to licensing if: (i) the host country is politically stable; (ii) the technology is new and tightly controlled; (iii) the firm is large and more internationally involved; (iv) the firm's sources of power are broadly based; and (v) the absorptive capacity of the licensee is low. Conversely, licensing will be preferred over FDI if: (i) the technology is diffused widely; (ii) the host market is small and risky; (iii) the firm is inexperienced, risk averse or nationally-orientated; (iv) the advantage of the firm is specific; and (v) the potential licensee is big and capable. Of course, the decision does not have to be totally black and white, and many intermediate positions are possible between investment in wholly-owned subsidiaries and licensing.

International joint ventures have also emerged as an important entry mode. Buckley and Casson (1988, 1996) summarize the condi-tions that are conducive to the establishment of joint ventures, includ-ing: (i) the possession of complementary assets; (ii) opportunities for collusion; and (iii) barriers to full integration. The literature has also focused on the selection of joint venture partners, management strat-egy, and performance measurement. Although MNCs prefer to have wholly-owned or majority-controlled subsidiaries, there are reasons why they would agree to take part in joint ventures. First, government policies in many developing countries make joint ventures the only available mode of entry. Second, the joint venture partners may provide complementary skills. Third, because joint ventures can be used as a means of alleviating country risk, particularly the risk of take-over (see Chapter 5). Joint ventures may also be attractive in cases where the project is too big for the MNC.

Buckley and Casson (2000a) present a model of market entry that has three distinctive features. First, it is based on a detailed schematic analysis that encompasses all of the major market entry modes. Second, it distinguishes between production and distribution. Third, the model takes account of the strategic interaction between the entrant and its leading host country rival after entry has taken place. Some of the findings of the Buckley–Casson model are shown in Table 2.2.

On the basis of the model, Buckley and Casson reach the following two conclusions. First, subcontracting is not a very attractive mode of

Table 2.2 Predictions of the Buckley–Casson model of entry mode

Factor	Effect
An increase in transportation costs or loss of economies of scale in domestic production	Licensing and wholly-owned foreign production
Specific type of technology	Greenfield production is preferred to acquisitions and licensing
An increase in the cost of building trust	Greenfield FDI and arm's-length contractual arrangements are preferred to acquisitions
High cost of learning about the foreign market through experience	No inclination towards acquisition, licensing and franchising as well as subcontracting or greenfield FDI in distribution
High transaction costs of intermediate goods	Vertical integration of production and distribution, which can be achieved by exporting to a wholly-owned distribution facility, licensing, or a vertically-integrated joint venture
High transaction costs of arm's length technology transfer	FDI is preferred to arm's length arrangements such as subcontracting
The presence of significant monopoly rents associated with a high cost of competition	Acquisition is preferred to greenfield FDI in either production or distribution. Also, long-term arrangements (such as licensing) are preferred to short-term arrangements (such as subcontracting and franchising)

entry, because it does not give access to the local rival's experience. Second, joint ventures in production do not make much sense as an entry mode unless the production joint venture is part of an integrated joint venture that handles distribution as well.

If FDI is the chosen entry mode, another decision has to be made: whether FDI takes the form of greenfield FDI (the establishment of new production facilities), or mergers and acquisitions (M&As). This issue was discussed in Chapter 1, but more elaboration here will not hurt. Although these two forms of FDI are regarded as alternatives, they are rarely perfect substitutes. Some underlying conditions may leave no choice. The 2000 *World Investment Report* (UNCTAD, 2000) identifies four factors that make a choice between FDI and M&As unattainable. The first of these factors is the level of economic development: the higher the level of development of the host country, the greater will be the likelihood of M&As. Developing countries may not provide suitable target firms while providing attractive investment opportunities. Hence, greenfield investment is more likely to be in the form of FDI in developing countries. The second factor is FDI policy: in a number of countries there are restrictions and perhaps a total ban on M&As, in which case FDI will take the form of greenfield investment. Third, institutional factors play a role in the sense that the use of M&As is affected by differences in corporate governance and ownership structure. It is often the case that M&As are inhibited by rudimentary financial markets and poor accounting standards, which make it difficult to assess the value of corporate assets. Finally, M&As are likely to take the form of FDI when the need arises to rescue ailing companies in the host country as a result of a financial crisis or a similar mishap.

Buckley and Casson (1981) argue that the foreign market servicing decision depends on the cost associated with this function, demand conditions in the market, and host market growth. They distinguish among three types of costs associated with a particular mode of market servicing: (i) non-recoverable set-up cost, which is a one-off cost incurred as soon as the mode is adopted; (ii) recurrent fixed cost (that is, independent of the rate of output); and (iii) recurrent variable cost. Buckley and Casson present a model that is used to specify the optimal timing of a switch in modes of market servicing by reference to costs and other factors.

A FINAL REMARK

The literature on FDI is massive, and there is no alternative here but to be selective. Nevertheless, this chapter has presented a comprehensive survey of the theory of FDI, albeit a less comprehensive survey of the empirical evidence. For this reason, the appendix to this chapter (Table A2.1) summarizes the findings of recent empirical studies of the determinants of FDI. Now that we have dealt with the determinants of FDI, the next task is to examine its effects on the host and home countries. This will be dealt with in Chapter 3.

Appendix

Table A2.1   Summary of selected recent studies of the determinants of FDI

Study	Issue under investigation	Findings
Cleeve (2000)	Factors that determine location of Japanese FDI in the UK	Wage differences are unimportant. Production growth is important
Resmini (2000)	Determinants of FDI by EU in the CEECs	Heterogeneity at sector level
Gray (2000)	Effect of globalization on developing countries	Tendency for virtuous and vicious cycles is magnified
Baumgarten and Hausman (2000)	Location of US FDI in Latin America	FDI decision is complicated, containing variables of political, market and social nature
Pitelis (2000)	Theory of growth of MNCs	Growth results from endogenous factors, and from external opportunities and threats
Moshirian (2001)	FDI in banking	Major determinants include bilateral trade, banks' foreign assets, cost of capital, exchange rates, and other FDI
Sanford and Dong (2000)	Influence of tourism on FDI	Significantly positive relationship between tourism and new FDI in the USA
Lehmann (1999)	Role of country risk	Political and economic risks are deterrents to FDI
Traxler and Woitech (2000)	Labour market regimes as a determinant of location	Investors do not assign high priority to labour market regimes
Schoeman *et al.* (2000)	Impact of fiscal policy on FDI in South Africa	FDI flows are affected by fiscal discipline and tax burden on foreign investors

Table A2.1   (*Continued*)

Study	Issue under investigation	Findings
List and Co (2000)	Relationship between location and environmental regulations	Environmental policies do matter
Cheng and Kwan (2000)	Determinants of the location of FDI in China	Important determinants are regional market size, good infrastructure and preferential policy. Wage cost has a negative effect
Thompson and Poon (2000)	Links between FDI and regulatory change in Asian countries	Significant correlation between reform expectations and FDI flows
Sung and Lapan (2000)	FDI and exchange rate volatility	With sufficient exchange rate volatility, firms can increase profit by opening several plants
Ihrig (2000)	Effect of repatriation restrictions on FDI	Abolishing restrictions encourages FDI inflows
Pistoresi (2000)	Location-specific and policy-related determinants of FDI in Latin America and Asia	FDI depends on economic and political factors
Kosteletou and Liargovas (2000)	Relationship between FDI and real exchange rate	Causality runs from the real exchange rate to FDI in large countries with floating exchange rates. Bidirectional causality in other cases
Clegg and Scott-Green (1999)	Link between FDI and European integration	New FDI is linked to conventional host characteristics whose effects vary considerably between groups of member countries
Kiymaz and Taylor (2000)	Competition for FDI	When a country is not sure that a miserly offer will drive the firm to its rival, it may take the chance and nevertheless make a miserly offer
Marinov and Marinova (1999)	Motives of foreign investors, host governments and host companies in Eastern Europe	Motives are related to the strategic priorities of investing firms

Benacek (2000)	Determining factors of FDI inflows in the Czech Republic	Initially, foreign investors were not motivated by local human capital
Dunning and Dilyard (1999)	Explanations of FDI and portfolio investment	Determinants have common and distinctive characters. They are complementary
Wilkins (1999)	Relationship between FDI and portfolio investment	FDI and portfolio investment ratios have shown no consistency across countries through time
Zhang (2000)	Size of US FDI in China	Small size is a result of US investors' preference for market access, China's export-promotion FDI regime, bilateral relations, and political instability
Ramcharran (1999)	Relationship between FDI and country risk	A significant relationship exists between FDI and country risk (political and economic)
Kreinin *et al.* (1999)	Motives for Japanese FDI	Many motives, but securing market share is the most important
Donnenfeld and Weber (2000)	Choice between FDI and exports	No simple relationship between the size of tariffs and the tendency to engage in FDI
Wei (2000a)	The effect of taxes and corruption on FDI	A rise in either the tax rate or corruption in the host country reduces FDI
Okposin (1999)	FDI by Singapore-based firms	FDI is carried out only by large firms or firms with monopolistic advantage
Konishi *et al.* (1999)	FDI and trade barriers	Firms can jump over trade restrictions by undertaking FDI
Guimaraes *et al.* (2000)	Agglomeration as a determinant of FDI	Agglomeration economies are decisive location factors

Table A2.1 (*Continued*)

Study	Issue under investigation	Findings
Wu (1999)	Intra-urban FDI location in China	Intra-urban FDI location can be explained according to rational economic considerations
Fosfuri and Motta (1999)	The argument that firms embarking on FDI must possess some advantages	Firms might invest abroad to capture local advantages through proximity of plant location
Globerman and Shapiro (1999)	The effect of policy changes on inward and outward FDI	Free trade agreements had a positive effect. Screening of projects had no significant effect
Gyapong and Karikari (1999)	Causal relationship between FDI and economic performance in two African countries	Impact of economic performance on FDI depends on the strategy of the investment
Tuman and Emmert (1999)	Political and economic determinants of Japanese FDI in Latin America	Determinants include market size, economic policies and certain types of political instability
Montiel and Reinhart (1999)	Effect of capital controls on the volume and composition of capital flows	Capital controls influence the composition of flows, but sterilized intervention influences both volume and composition
Mody *et al.* (1999)	The choice of FDI location by Japanese MNCs	Trade barriers do not drive Japanese FDI in Asia
Das (1999)	Choice of entry mode	Riskiness of the project is a factor against joint ventures. In the absence of policy intervention, licensing is dominated by FDI or ventures
Barrell and Pain (1999)	Determinants of location of Japanese FDI	Controlling for size and labour costs, FDI is influenced significantly by trade barriers
Martin and Ottaviano (1999)	Locational factors	High growth rates and transaction costs are associated with FDI

Goldberg and Klein (1997)	Effects of real exchange rate on FDI	A real depreciation of the currencies of Asian countries against the yen leads to an increase in FDI from Japan and a decrease in FDI from the USA
Sin and Leung (2001)	Effect of liberalization on FDI inflows	Policy changes are more important for FDI than GDP growth rate or exchange rate

3 The Effects of Foreign Direct Investment

FDI involves the transfer of financial capital, technology and other skills (managerial, marketing, accounting, and so on) as we have seen so far. This process gives rise to costs and benefits for the countries involved: the investing country (the source of the investment) and the host country (the recipient or the destination of the investment). It is not clear, however, what costs are borne and what benefits are enjoyed by the two countries, at least not quantitatively. There is even a fundamental disagreement on what constitutes the costs and benefits of FDI from the perspectives of the two countries. This disagreement is indicated by the big gap between those holding pro-globalization, free-market views, and those with anti-globalization, anti-market views. Moreover, the division of welfare gains between the host country and the investing country does not only depend on given market prices, but also on the relative strength of the two countries in bargaining over the terms of the agreement governing a particular FDI project. Nevertheless, one country's losses are not necessarily the other country's gains. Kindleberger (1969), for example, argues that the relationship arising from the FDI process is not a zero-sum game. *Ex ante*, both countries must believe (justifiably or otherwise) that the expected benefits to them must be greater than the costs to be borne by them, because an agreement would not otherwise be reached, and the underlying project would not be initiated. However, believing in something *ex ante* is no guarantee that it will materialise *ex post*.

One way to explain the effect of FDI is to use the conventional multiplier process, but an attempt like this will be made more difficult by the qualitative differences between domestic investment and FDI, which are bound to have different effects from each other. One reason for the differences in the effects is that FDI is controlled by parties over which there is limited local jurisdiction. MNCs are less dependent on their host countries or countries of origin than local firms, and this makes them difficult to control. The fact that the investor undertaking an FDI project is foreign to the host country creates economic, political and social effects that impinge upon the costs and benefits of FDI.

The effects of FDI on the host country can be classified into economic, political and social effects. The basic presumption that is found in the literature, based on the principles of neoclassical economics, is that FDI raises income and social welfare in the host country unless the optimum conditions are distorted significantly by protection, monopoly and externalities (Lall and Streeten, 1977). We have to bear in mind that MNCs operate in such a way as to maximize profits worldwide, and in the process they shift resources to areas where returns are high, and buy inputs where their prices are low (after all, they are profit maximizers). On the surface, it would seem that this is some sort of efficiency that should lead to an increase in world welfare. However, the problem is that MNCs exist and operate primarily because of market imperfections, which casts doubt on the validity of the conclusion that FDI leads to an increase in welfare. Unless all markets are perfect, growth in one sector may not be beneficial: improved resource allocation has to be judged against increases in market imperfections. If we assume, for the sake of argument, that markets are perfect and that there are constant returns to scale, then if capital is allowed to move freely, it would flow from a low-return country to a high-return country. This causes the rate of return on capital to fall in the high-return country, and rise in the low-return country, and this would involve a gain in world output (for a diagrammatic illustration, see Winters, 1991, pp. 227–8). But even in this case, some distributional changes occur between labour and capital. In any case, it seems that the conventional wisdom that FDI is always welfare-improving is no longer a conventional wisdom. Leahy and Montagna (2000b) challenge this conventional wisdom, and show that direct product market competition makes welfare losses more likely, because MNCs capture market shares from the indigenous firms.

The economic effects of FDI include the implications for (macro and micro) economic variables such as output, the balance of payments, and market structure. The political effects include the question of national sovereignty, as the sheer size of the investing MNCs may jeopardize national independence (who runs the host country, the prime minister or the CEO of the investing MNC?).[1] The social issues are concerned mainly with the creation of enclaves and a foreign elite in the host country, as well as the cultural effects on the local population (for example, customs and tastes).[2] Naturally, social issues are more likely to arise when there are significant economic, social, and cultural differences between the investing and host countries. For example, it is plausible to think that the social and cultural impact of Australian FDI in New Zealand, if any, will be less than that of Australian FDI in Malaysia, or American FDI in Saudi Arabia.[3] In this chapter (and this book) we are concerned mainly with the economic effects of FDI.

The economic effects of FDI can be classified into macro effects and micro effects. The usual convention in analysing the macro effects of FDI is to treat it as a rise in foreign borrowing. If there is unemployment and capital shortage (as is typically the case in developing countries) such borrowing leads to a rise in output and income in the host country. FDI will, under these conditions, have a beneficial effect on the balance of payments, but an indeterminate effect on the terms of trade (depending on whether the impact of increased output falls on import substitutes or exports). Formal analysis of the macro effects of FDI in a neoclassical framework can be traced back to the analysis by MacDougal (1960), who used partial-equilibrium, comparative-static analysis to show that the host country would gain mainly through taxes on foreign profits. Real wages, the argument goes, would also rise at the expense of profits because of the declining marginal productivity of capital. This kind of analysis has been extended in several ways, including: (i) the analysis of optimum taxes; (ii) dynamic growth models with foreign investment and trade using pure trade theory; (iii) comparative statics general equilibrium models; and (iv) comparative statics trade theory incorporating capital movements.

The micro effects of FDI pertain to structural changes in the economic and industrial organization. For example, an important issue is whether FDI is conducive to the creation of a more competitive environment, or conversely to a worsening of the monopolistic and/or oligopolistic elements in the host economy. In general, the micro effects pertain to individual firms and individual industries, particularly those that are closely exposed to, and associated with, FDI. Markusen and Venables (1997) put forward the idea that the (micro) effects of FDI on the host country may operate through many different channels. They present a simple analysis of two of these channels: product market competition, through which MNCs may substitute for domestic firms, and linkage effects, through which MNCs must be complementary. Hence, it is possible for FDI to act as a catalyst, leading to the development of local industry, which may in turn become so strong as to reduce both the relative and absolute position of MNCs in the industry. This analysis, they argue, fits well with some of the case study literature on South East Asian economies.

While we may consider the costs and benefits of FDI to be borne by, or accruing to, the two countries (the investing country and the host country), we shall refer invariably to the MNC as the 'investing party' and the host country as the 'recipient party'. Furthermore, most of our discussion in this chapter will deal with the effects of FDI on host developing countries, although some reference will be made to the effects on the economy of the investing country. The emphasis on the effects on developing countries results from the ever-increasing importance of FDI in the theory and practice of economic development. Recall that FDI is sometimes hailed as the only salvation for developing countries, and the only way out of the vicious circle of poverty. Our conclusion will not be that sanguine: while FDI has its benefits, it also has its costs, and hence the effects on developing countries may not be favourable in all cases all the time.

We shall now discuss the economic effects of FDI in turn. Just like the theories of FDI, there is a significant overlap in the discussion of these effects. For example, the provision of capital, as performed by FDI, overlaps significantly with the effect on the balance of payments and the effect on output. Moreover, technology is believed to be the main conduit of the effect of FDI on growth and productivity, yet we shall examine the effects of FDI on growth, productivity and technology separately. And the effect on the welfare of the host country encompasses some of the individual effects. While the main body of this chapter contains a brief review of related empirical evidence, the findings of recent empirical studies are tabulated in the appendix (Table A3.1).

THE PROVISION OF CAPITAL

The two-gap model, which is often used in development economics, shows that developing countries typically encounter the problem of increasing their saving to match their investment needs, and that of financing imports through export earnings (see, for example, McKinnon, 1963). The first problem arises from the saving gap (the difference between investment and saving), whereas the second problem arises from the foreign exchange gap (the difference between imports and exports).[4] It is often argued that FDI contributes to filling these two gaps, not only because MNCs have better access to financial markets, but also because: (i) FDI by a particular MNC in a particular project may encourage other MNCs to participate in the same project; (ii) such an action may encourage the flow of official development aid from the investor's home country;[5] and (iii) by offering locals attractive investment opportunities, FDI may mobilize domestic saving. By filling (or contributing to the filling of) the foreign exchange gap, FDI obviously has a positive effect on the balance of payments, which we shall examine shortly. It is arguable, therefore, that the net impact of FDI on the quantum of capital flows to developing countries is usually positive, because it leads to an increase in the inflow of financial resources available for investment. In this respect, FDI offers certain advantages over other sources of foreign finance. First, it is more stable than other financial flows. Second, FDI inflows represent a long-term commitment to the host country.[6] Third, FDI is easier to service than commercial loans, since profits tend to be linked to the performance of the host economy (that is, they are procyclical).

Razin *et al.* (1999a) examined the role of FDI in the financial markets of the host country. They argue that, in the absence of a well-developed domestic credit market (in which case, domestic savings cannot be efficiently channelled into domestic investment) FDI can play a double role. It provides a vehicle for reviving the domestic market through which domestic savings can be channelled to finance domestic investment, and it supplies foreign savings on top of domestic savings to finance domestic investment. The second role provides the traditional gains from trade to the home country. The first role is by no means costless: as the equity market is characterized by asymmetric information, it does not always generate the correct signals about the social rates of return on domestic capital. As a result, Razin *et al.* argue, there are some welfare losses that offset some or all of the gains stemming from the mere channelling of domestic savings into domestic investment. When a well-developed domestic credit market exists (through which domestic savings can be channelled into domestic investment even in the absence of an equity market) then the first role played by FDI does not generate any gain. They conclude that, when FDI can be levered domestically, the traditional gains from trade associated with the second role of FDI is curtailed severely. As a result, the total net effect of FDI on the welfare of the domestic economy could well be negative.

Lall and Streeten (1977) cast doubt on the ability of FDI to perform the function of providing capital, for at least three reasons. First, direct investment is a relatively expensive source of foreign capital.

Second, the actual capital inflow provided by the MNC may not be very large (FDI may be financed by borrowing in the host country). Indeed, MNCs can, through their market power, raise cheap funds and crowd out other socially desirable activities in the host country. Third, the capital contribution of the MNC may take the form of machinery or capitalized intangibles, such as know-how and goodwill. For these reasons, FDI provides little, and expensive, capital.

THE EFFECT OF FDI ON OUTPUT AND GROWTH

One of the most important aspects of FDI is its effect on output and therefore growth in the host country. This effect naturally is more important for developing countries, where inward investment is viewed as a means of boosting economic development. For the effect on output to materialize, a necessary condition is an increase in the capital stock of the host country as a result of the investment or, in the case of a take-over, a more efficient utilization of existing resources. The output effect will be less pronounced if FDI takes the form of a take-over (M&As).

Theories of economic growth and development focus on the increase in real per capita income and relate this increase to certain major factors such as capital accumulation, population growth, technological progress and the discovery of new natural resources. The various ways in which these factors are interrelated have given rise to different theories of economic development. In these theories, however, capital accumulation is seen as the driving force behind faster growth.[7] It is then obvious that FDI, by affecting capital accumulation, ought to be capable of influencing economic development.

Of course, technology (or technological progress) also plays a big role. In contrast to the traditional Solow growth model, where technological change is assumed to be exogenous, the recent growth literature highlights the dependence of economic growth on the state of domestic technology relative to that of the rest of the world. Thus, growth rates in developing countries are in part explained by a catch-up process in the level of technology. In a typical model of technology diffusion, the growth rate of a developing country depends on the extent of the adoption and implementation of new technologies that are already in use in leading countries. According to this view, what matters is the adoption and adaptation of foreign technology, a proposition that is supported strongly by the Japanese experience.

The effect of FDI on output can be explained in terms of the multiplier model, but it is rather difficult to quantify the multiplier associated with FDI. This is because, apart from the leakages associated with domestic investment (such as taxes and imports), FDI has leakages of its own, such as the import content (which represents foreign claims on domestic output) and remittances (in the form of dividends, interest payments, fees and royalties), which again represent claims on local output. On the other hand, FDI may be associated with import substitution, a factor that complicates the matter further.

The effect of FDI on the level, composition and growth of the output of the host country also depends to a large extent on the macroeconomic policy in operation in that country. In general, it seems that FDI can exert an impact on the output of the host country if it is possible to absorb surplus resources and/or improve efficiency through alternative allocations. Specifically, however, the following outcomes are possible:

1. If the host government pursues a macroeconomic policy that always achieves full employment, then inward FDI would not affect the size of output, provided it is as efficient as any domestic means of resource utilization.
2. If FDI absorbs resources that would otherwise remain unemployed, then the output generated by FDI net of remittances represents a net gain to the output of the host country.
3. If FDI is capable of improving the efficiency of domestic resources by shifting them from less efficient to more productive sectors of the economy, then domestic output would rise.

Lall and Streeten (1977) argue that the domination of a developing economy by an MNC may be detrimental economically to growth and development, for at least three reasons. First, the MNC's activity may lead to a lower rate of accumulation domestically, because a proportion of the profits generated by this activity is repatriated rather than invested in the host country. Second, the MNC's presence may lead to some adverse developments, such as a greater incidence of undesirable practices (for example, derogatory transfer pricing), or weaken the control over economic policy.[8] Third, the MNC may affect the market structure adversely, making it less competitive, as we shall see later.

What is the empirical evidence on this issue? We start with the evidence presented by Borensztein *et al.* (1995). This piece of evidence is based on a model of endogenous growth in which the rate of technological progress is the main determinant of long-term economic growth. It is assumed that technological progress takes place through the process of capital deepening that results from the introduction of new varieties of capital goods. MNCs typically are portrayed as possessing more advanced knowledge and to be capable of introducing new capital goods at a lower cost. However, it is argued that the application of more advanced technology requires the presence of a sufficient level of human capital in the host country, which means that if this condition is not satisfied, then the absorptive capacity of the developing host country will be very limited. Hence, the model highlights the role of both the introduction of more advanced technology and the requirement of absorptive capacity in the host country as determinants of economic growth. This line of reasoning brings to the surface the issue of complementarity between FDI and human capital in the process of economic growth.

Borensztein *et al.* (1995) test the effect of FDI on economic growth in a cross-country regression framework, utilizing data on FDI flows from industrial countries to sixty-nine developing countries over two decades. Their results suggest the following conclusions:

1. FDI is an important vehicle for the transfer of technology, contributing relatively more to growth than does domestic investment.
2. For FDI to produce higher productivity than domestic investment, the host country must have a minimum threshold stock of human capital.
3. FDI has the effect of increasing total investment in the economy more than proportionately, which suggests the predominance of complementarity effects with domestic firms.

Feldstein (1994) examines the effect of outward FDI on the national incomes of the home and host countries in the presences of taxes and tax credits (see Chapter 6). He argues that the national income of the home (investing) country depends on the relative importance of two factors acting in different directions: the loss of tax revenue to the foreign (host) government, and the increased use of foreign debt. He develops an analysis of these two factors in the presence of a segmented international capital market, in which most national saving remains in the country where saving arises.

The idea underlying Feldstein's thinking in this respect is very simple. Firms that invest abroad pay taxes on the profit of their foreign subsidiaries to the governments of the host countries, which means that one consequence of outward FDI is the loss of revenue by the home government to the host government. If investing firms receive tax credit for the taxes that they pay to the foreign government, they (the firms) will invariably be indifferent between taxes paid to the host government and those paid to the home government. The tax credit causes the firms to invest abroad until the after-tax rate of return on the foreign investment is equal to the after-tax rate of return on domestic investment. Since the home country receives the full before-tax return on domestic investment (in the form of taxes on the income realized by the investing firms) but only the after-tax return on the investment of foreign subsidiaries, critics of the foreign tax credit argue that it causes an excessive amount of FDI and a reduction in the home country's national income.

Feldstein, however, questions this argument, on the grounds that it fails to take into account the fact that firms that invest abroad increase their use of foreign debt as they increase the extent of their FDI. Although each firm's overall leverage may be unaffected by the extent of its FDI, the home country as a whole benefits from the use of the additional low-cost credit supplied by foreign creditors. While the debt capital may in theory be available to the investing firms (and therefore to the benefit of the home country) through international portfolio investment, the evidence on segmentation of global capital markets implies that this would not occur in practice. For example, Feldstein and Horioka (1980) have shown, in a frequently-cited paper, that the saving generated in a country tends to stay in that country.[9] Hence, the advantage of FDI, according to Feldstein's reasoning, is that it allows the investing firms and the source country of FDI to utilize foreign debt capital without requiring that capital to cross national borders.

But why would firms increase their foreign borrowing as they expand their FDI? Feldstein answers this question by listing a number of reasons. First, such borrowing is one way to hedge the value of foreign profits caused by fluctuations in exchange rates. Second, there may be some restriction on the amount of domestic interest that firms can deduct in calculating domestic taxable income when they have overseas operations. Third, firms may be able to borrow at a lower cost in countries where collateral is available. Fourth, local debt can be used as an anti-expropriation device (see Chapter 5). Irrespective of the relative importance of these factors, foreign borrowing is useful as long as the real after-tax cost of foreign borrowing is less than the after-tax return on the foreign assets acquired with these funds. The net effect of an additional dollar of outward FDI on the national income of the home country thus depends on the relative importance of the tax paid to the foreign government, and the advantage obtained by using foreign debt. The evidence presented by Feldstein shows that the favourable leverage effect is likely to outweigh the loss of revenue to the foreign country. When a firm equates the after-tax rate of return on the domestic investment and investment in a foreign subsidiary, the national rate of return to the home country is higher on foreign investment than on domestic investment. Feldstein's calculations imply that a dollar of cross-border outward FDI raises the present value of US national income by US$1.72.

THE EFFECT OF FDI ON EMPLOYMENT AND WAGES

There is a relationship between investment and employment. In his *General Theory*, Keynes (1936) suggested the existence of a direct relationship between investment and employment. However, there is still considerable divergence in views among economists about the employment effects of FDI (see, for example, Pugel, 1985). Baldwin (1995) argues that this debate encompasses three key issues: (i) the extent to which FDI substitutes for domestic investment; (ii) the extent to which FDI stimulates increases of exports of intermediate goods and capital goods; and (iii) whether FDI involves the construction of new plants or simply the acquisition of existing facilities. In general, the employment effects of FDI may be summarized as follows:

1. FDI is capable of increasing employment directly, by setting up new facilities, or indirectly by stimulating employment in distribution.
2. FDI can preserve employment by acquiring and restructuring ailing firms.
3. FDI can reduce employment through divestment and the closure of production facilities.

The available evidence suggests that the effect of FDI on employment is low. Vaitsos (1976) analysed the employment effects of MNCs with reference to four characteristics: scale, concentration, foreignness, and transnationality. He produced evidence indicating that the overall employment effects of the activities of MNCs on the host countries has been relatively small. Tambunlertchai (1976) evaluated the contribution of foreign firms to the host country by reference to four criteria: (i) contribution to national income; (ii) creation of employment; (iii) utilization of domestic resources; and (iv) earnings and savings of foreign exchange. His empirical evidence suggested that FDI was unable to render a significant contribution to the host country in terms of these criteria because of high capital intensity and import dependency. Feldstein (1994) argues that there is ample evidence that total employment in an economy with a well-functioning labour market will not be affected by the volume or character of FDI. For example, Graham and Krugman (1991) concluded that the net impact of FDI on US employment is approximately zero.

The desirability of FDI with respect to its effect on the demand for labour at home is a controversial issue. The critics of outward FDI argue that such investment destroys jobs at home because the output of foreign subsidiaries becomes a substitute for exports from the home country. Proponents of outward FDI argue that it creates jobs, because domestic firms export more when they have foreign subsidiaries. It is arguable that the technological bias and capital intensive nature of most investment characterizing oligopolistic industries (made possible by their R&D expenditure, and necessitated and supported by their large size) means that investment is unlikely to promote considerable labour usage.

Earlier work on home country employment effects encompasses the important aspect of whether production by foreign subsidiaries of a home country's firms is a substitute or a complement to domestic production by the parent firms or by other home country firms (for a survey, see Blomstrom and Kokko, 1994). Blomstrom *et al.* (1997) argue that the difficulty associated with these studies is the lack of convincing counter-factual situations. They therefore raise the following questions. What would have happened in the absence of foreign production? Would the parent firm have supplied, by exporting, the markets now served by subsidiaries? Would the markets now served by subsidiaries' production, or by some combination of subsidiary and home country production, have been lost to the parent firm?

Evidence from US studies suggest either a positive relationship or no relationship between US-owned production in a market and exports to that market by the parent company and by US companies in general (see, for example, Blomstrom *et al.*, 1988). It has also been found that there is a negative relationship between US-owned production and exports to the host country from other sources. A positive relationship was found across firms between production abroad and firm exports to the world, suggesting that such production had not materialized at the expense of exports to third countries (Lipsey and Weiss, 1981, 1984). Studies of Swedish firms have reported some mixed results, with a long period of findings of positive relationships (Swedenbourg, 1979) and some more recent reports of negative ones, particularly in third-country markets (Svensson, 1996). The main reason for finding a positive relationship is the role of FDI in the rivalry markets. The reason for the ambiguity of the results of most of these studies is that they do not take account of a firm's most important motivation for producing in a foreign country: the opportunity to increase its market share or even the size of the market itself, or to defend its existing market share. This kind of investigation would require data on the size of particular product markets in host countries, which is difficult to obtain.

Other aspects of home country effects that have been studied include competition between home and foreign markets for an MNC's capital resources, the extent to which expansion of offshore production reduces the demand for labour at home, and the relationship between foreign production and home country wage levels. A study of US firms indicated that home and foreign investments were not independent, and that an increase in plant and equipment investment in foreign operations caused a decrease at home because it raised the firm's cost of capital (Stevens and Lipsey, 1992). Brainard and Riker (1997) have concluded that foreign subsidiaries' employment by US MNCs substituted only modestly for US parent employment at the margin. They find much stronger substitution among workers in US foreign subsidiaries located in different low-wage host countries. Furthermore, US wage studies have suggested a positive relationship across firms between foreign activity and home country wage levels (Kravis and Lipsey, 1988). This relationship may reflect an allocation of low-risk activities to foreign operations. Finally, Blomstrom *et al.* (1997) obtained results on the effect of FDI on home country employment using data on US and Swedish manufacturing MNCs. The Swedish experience seems to differ from that of the USA. The results for Sweden show that, given the level of sales by the parent, MNCs with more sales abroad will also have higher employment in the parent company. In sharp contrast to US MNCs, production by Swedish MNCs in both developed and developing counties seems to have positive effects on parent employment.

A related issue is the effect of FDI on relative wages. Feenstra and Hanson (1995) examined the increase in the relative wages of skilled workers in Mexico during the 1980s. They linked rising wage inequality in Mexico to capital inflows, whose effect was to shift production in Mexico towards relatively skill-intensive goods, thereby increasing the relative demand for skilled labour. They also examined the impact of FDI on the share of skilled labour in total wages in Mexico during the period 1975–88. The results they obtained indicated that growth in FDI is correlated positively with the relative demand for skilled labour. Driffield and Taylor (2000) examined the effect of inward FDI on the British labour market, providing evidence indicating that FDI leads to an increase in wage inequality and the use of relatively more skilled labour by local firms.

While there is a general agreement on the proposition that relative wage changes are caused by an increase in relative demand for skilled labour, economists are not in agreement over the reasons for the shift in demand. Two explanations are normally given. One is that the advent of information technology has caused firms to switch towards production techniques that are biased in favour of skilled labour (Davis and Haltiwanger, 1991; Lawrence and Slaughter, 1993; Berman *et al.*, 1994). The other explanation is that an increase in import competition from low-wage countries has shifted resources towards industries that use skilled labour relatively and intensively (Borjas and Ramey, 1993; Leamer, 1993). However, Feenstra and Hanson (1995) argue that the rise in wage inequality across dissimilar countries is consistent with a third explanation: capital flows from North to South, and a corresponding rise in outsourcing by Northern MNCs, have contributed to a worldwide increase in the relative demand for skilled labour. A flow of capital from North to South, which is identified as outsourcing by Northern firms, shifts an increasing portion of input production to the South. These activities are, from the North's perspective, ones that use relatively large amounts of unskilled labour, but from the South's perspective are ones for which the reverse is true. The result is an increase in the relative demand for skilled labour in both countries, which in turn causes the relative wage of skilled labour to rise in both regions. This is called the 'capital-accumulation-outsourcing hypothesis'. Feenstra and Hanson (1995) examined the effect of FDI on the relative demand for skilled labour in Mexico. They found the growth in FDI to be correlated positively with the relative demand for skilled labour. In the regions where FDI was most concentrated, growth in FDI could account for over 50 per cent of the increase in the share of skilled labour in total wages that occurred during the late 1980s. This is consistent with the hypothesis that outsourcing by MNCs has contributed significantly to the increase in the relative demand for skilled labour in Mexico.

The final issue to be discussed in this section is the effect of FDI on factor demand elasticity. Hatzius (2000) argues that the liberalization of FDI has made labour costs more important to domestic investment and long-run labour demand. If higher labour costs induce firms to relocate production abroad, domestic employment will fall. In recent years, this has led some economists to argue that falling barriers to FDI have made wage moderation more important for preserving employment. Unless wages are kept under control, the argument goes, capital will migrate to countries with lower labour costs, thus leading to a rise in unemployment.

In an open economy, rising labour costs tend to reduce labour demand, for three reasons. First, the typical firm produces less total output in response to higher unit costs (the output or scale effect). Second, capital is substituted for labour (the substitution effect). Third, some firms may move abroad (the location effect). With high FDI barriers, a given small change in production costs will push only a small number of firms to relocate. As FDI barriers fall, the same production cost change will induce more firms to move. Hence, the elasticity of the capital stock and labour demand with respect to production costs rises as relocation costs fall.

Hatzius (2000) presents a simple equation relating FDI to unit labour costs and other control variables, as suggested by Cushman (1987), Culem (1988), Lucas (1993), Moore (1993), Pain (1993), Klein and Rosengren (1994), Bajo-Rubio and Sosvilla-Rivero (1994), Wang and Swain (1995), and Barrell and Pain (1996). Control variables include the deviation of output from trend in the source and host countries, which is used to control for short-term business cycle fluctuations, the relative number of days lost to strikes and lockouts to control for the industrial relations climate, and the relative real long-term interest rate to control for differences in the return on financial assets across countries. Dummy variables are also included to control for unobserved factors that drive the international propensity to invest abroad. Hatzius obtains evidence from British and German data that suggests the following conclusions. First, high unit labour costs encourage FDI outflows and discourage FDI inflows. Second, the effect of unit labour cost on domestic manufacturing investment was more negative in the high-FDI 1980s

Foreign Direct Investment

than in the low-FDI 1970s, and this change was concentrated in high-FDI industries. The estimates suggest that the long-run labour demand elasticity may have risen substantially.

What can we conclude from the discussion of the employment effect so far? While FDI may have positive employment effects under certain conditions, it can certainly have adverse effects on employment and industrial relations in the host country. This is probably what prompted the OECD to issue its guidelines on how MNCs should deal with the employment and industrial relations issue. These guidelines boil down to urging MNCs, *inter alia*, to (i) respect the rights of their employees represented by trade unions; (ii) contribute to the abolition of child labour; (iii) avoid discrimination against employees; (iv) encourage the development of collective agreements; (v) provide a true picture of the performance of the firm; and (vi) take into account the livelihood of their employees when they consider changes in operations.

THE BALANCE OF PAYMENTS EFFECT

The balance of payments effect is more important for developing countries than for developed countries. This is because foreign exchange is regarded as a scarce resource affecting growth through the foreign exchange gap. Hence, any effect of FDI may mitigate or worsen the constraints imposed by the balance of payments on the attainment of macroeconomic objectives pertaining to growth and employment. In general, FDI is often blamed for its balance of payments effect: the investing country faces a sudden deficit when the FDI occurs, while the host country faces a small perpetual deficit as a result of profit repatriation. After all, a profitable FDI project with profits repatriated in foreign currency must necessarily result in greater balance of payments outflows than a similar project financed locally.

The balance of payments effect has certain features. First, there is a distinction between direct and indirect balance of payments effects. Hence, the effect of FDI must be examined in terms of (i) the absorption of the host country's factor input in the production process; (ii) the proportions of output sold in the host country and abroad; and (iii) the distribution of the value of output between the host country's factor inputs, the host government (in the form of tax revenue), and the retained share. The direct effect, which is reflected immediately in the foreign exchange gap, results from the flows associated with the investment. Inflows include (i) exports and inflows of equity capital; and (ii) loans from abroad net of capital and loans repatriated. Outflows include: (i) value of capital goods imported; (ii) the value of raw materials and intermediate goods imported; (iii) royalties and technical fees paid abroad after tax; and (iv) net after-tax profits and interest accruing abroad. The direct effect does not tell the whole story, and it is deficient in two important respects. First, it does not show what would have happened had the foreign investment not occurred. Second, it does not give an idea of the effect of FDI on the balance of payments via domestic sales and the use of local resources. The latter is the indirect effect.

The second feature of the balance of payments effect is that it takes two forms. The initial, one-off, effect leads to an improvement in the capital account of the host country by the amount of the investment less the value of any imported machinery. The second form is the continuing effect, which is by far the most important.

The third and final feature is that the balance of payments effect is the result of (i) the export effect; (ii) the import substitution effect; (iii) the import effect; and (iv) the remittances effect. The first two effects lead to an improvement in the balance of payments, whereas the remaining two lead to its deterioration.

The empirical evidence on the balance of payments effect of FDI indicates that there is a difference between developed and developing countries, particularly with respect to investment in manufacturing industries. In assessing the impact of US FDI in Britain, Dunning (1961, 1969) estimated a positive effect of around 15 per cent of the total capital invested. However, Dunning only dealt with the direct effect of FDI, which results in observable flows in the balance of payments. He did not consider the indirect effect arising from changes in the income of residents, or changes in consumption patterns.

There is evidence indicating that the balance of payments of developing countries benefit from FDI in extraction, but not in manufacturing (for example, Vaitsos, 1976). Investment in manufacturing seems to have detrimental effects on the balance of payments of developing countries because of the high import content of the investment as well as the mechanism of transfer pricing of MNCs. The high import content of the output of MNCs results from the unavailability of local products and materials, the uncompetitiveness of local prices, and inferior quality.

THE EFFECT OF FDI ON TRADE FLOWS

Romer (1975) makes a very interesting observation about the relationship between the involvement of countries in FDI and their involvement in trade, based on the economic history of four industrial countries: the UK, Germany, Japan, and the USA. He puts forward the proposition that an industrial country passes through the following four stages, characterized by the country's shares of trade and FDI: (i) the share in world exports of manufactured goods rises; (ii) the trade share stabilizes, while the share in FDI starts rising; (iii) the trade share starts to fall; and (iv) the FDI share starts to fall. More recently, attempts have been made to integrate the theory of FDI with the theory of international trade (see, for example, Markusen, 2000).

Concern has been expressed over the effect of FDI on trade flows. Although it may appear that MNCs are trade-intensive firms, this is more a reflection of the activities in which they indulge rather than their own behaviour. Solomon and Ingham (1977) suggest that MNCs export fewer engineering products than do domestic firms, while Panic and Joyce (1980) suggested that MNCs' exports were stagnant over the 1970s. More recently, Goldberg and Klein (1997) have shown that FDI directed into developing countries affects their trade flows with industrial countries even after controlling for the effect of the exchange rate. There is also some evidence indicating that subsidiaries tend to import parts and capital equipment from the parent MNC, located in the home country. Hence, it seems that by indulging in FDI, MNCs affect the size and direction of trade flows. In a study of US FDI in developing countries, Rock (1973) found a significant correlation between the trade of these countries in the USA and FDI in these countries.

The most critical issue about the relationship between FDI and trade is whether they are complements or substitutes. In other words, to what extent do production and sales by subsidiaries in a foreign market replace or help to increase exports to the same market? One reason we should believe that FDI and trade are substitutes is that they are two alternative modes of entry, as we have seen. However, there are reasons to believe that FDI does not replace exports, but rather stimulates them. One reason for this is that FDI enables firms to establish a larger distribution base, thus enlarging the line of products sold in the foreign market over and above what could be achieved via exports. Moreover, production in the foreign country invariably requires the import of intermediate products from the home country (and hence exports). This argument also applies to imports by the home country. If a foreign subsidiary can produce goods more cheaply abroad and export them to the home country, this obviously means that FDI leads to increasing imports by the home country.

There is now a consensus that whether trade and FDI are complements or substitutes depends on whether FDI is horizontal – as in Markusen (1984), or vertical – as in Helpman (1984). Whether FDI is horizontal or vertical depends on various country characteristics. For example, if countries have significantly different factor endowments, then vertical FDI dominates. On the other hand, horizontal FDI dominates if countries are similar in size and relative endowments, and if trade costs are moderate to high. Markusen *et al.* (1996) tried to predict the relationship between FDI and country characteristics. Naturally, it seems that the same criteria would determine whether FDI and trade are complements or substitutes.

But why would this relationship exist? In horizontal FDI, firms serve foreign markets by setting up plants there to provide identical goods (Markusen, 1984). Hence, exports from the source country to the host country will decline, implying that they are substitutes. In vertical FDI, MNCs separate different production stages geographically across countries, to take advantage of lower factor prices (Helpman, 1984). Specifically, the unskilled-labour-intensive stages of production are located in a low-wage country. In this case, there will be an increase in the exports of final products from the host country (the cheap labour country), while there is also an increase in the exports of intermediate products by the MNC (from the source country) to the host country where the subsidiary is located. Hence, FDI and trade are complements in this case. The question really boils down to the relationship between the sales of MNCs and the volume of trade.

The available empirical evidence is mixed. Most empirical studies based on cross-sectional industry and firm level data indicate a positive relationship. For example, Lipsey and Weiss (1981, 1984) and Blomstrom *et al.* (1988) found a predominantly positive relationship. Pain and Wakelin (1998) considered a time series relationship between manufacturing exports and FDI for eleven OECD countries, with mixed results. Blonigen (1999) argues that most of the empirical studies of the relationship between trade and FDI indicate complementarity (for example, Belderbos and Sleuwaegen, 1998). He attributes this finding to aggregation bias and shows that the substitution effect is easy to identify in product level data. Finally, Amiti *et al.* (2000) explain why the evidence is mixed in terms of country characteristics, hence attributing the difference to whether FDI is horizontal or vertical.

THE EFFECT OF FDI ON PRODUCTIVITY

Productivity is likely to rise and unit cost likely to decline if: (i) FDI is export-promoting and the products of the subsidiary are destined for the large world markets; and (ii) the underlying conditions and policies allow the installation of plants designed to achieve full economies of scale. On the other hand, if FDI is import-substituting and the size of the market is too small to allow the installation of the optimum plant size, then productive efficiency may not be achieved. There are, however, some reasons for believing that productive inefficiency may not be important. First, the empirical evidence indicates that unit costs of operating a plant smaller than the optimum size are not significantly higher than those of the most efficient scale. Second, even if investment was mainly import-substituting, any scope for some exports leads to an increase in the size of the market and allows for the utilization of a higher capital intensity technology.

Petrochilos (1989) argues that productivity is likely to be affected by a host of other factors that are not necessarily exclusively applicable to FDI. The general factors include: (i) the full utilization of the firms' resources; (ii) the quality of existing manpower; (iii) the climate of industrial relations; and (iv) the existence or otherwise of restrictive practices. The effect of FDI on productivity is channelled through technology diffusion, an issue we shall deal with next.

FDI AND TECHNOLOGY

Technology diffusion plays a central role in the process of economic development (see, for example, Nelson and Phelps, 1966; Jovanovic and Rob, 1989; Segerstrom, 1991). The interaction between FDI and technology is considered to be of great and critical importance in the discussion of FDI. Indeed, the transfer of technology has perhaps become the predominant issue around which discussions of MNCs and their dealings with developing countries evolve. This is because technology is believed to be a vital source of economic growth, capital accumulation, trade, and even changes in the organization of social relations and the relations of production. Particular problems in this respect take the form of how foreign technology is transferred to, and absorbed by, the host country and how it affects that country's economy. It is because of problems like these that the anticipated positive effects of technology on developing countries may not materialize. The importance of technology, particularly for developing countries, has prompted the OECD to issue guidelines urging MNCs to: (i) ensure that their activities are compatible with the technology plans of the host countries; (ii) adopt practices that allow the transfer and rapid diffusion of technology; (iii) address local market needs in an exercise pertaining to technology; (iv) license technology on reasonable terms and conditions; and (v) develop ties with local universities and research institutes. As we shall discover from the following discussion, it is doubtful whether MNCs' practices are consistent with these guidelines.

Technology is the product of R&D, aiming at the invention of new products or techniques of production, or both (Petrochilos, 1989, p. 36). Johnson (1970) considered the transfer of technology to be the crucial element of the FDI process. Any new technology confers an advantage on its owner, the original investor in R&D. In the case of new products, the advantage comes in the form of monopoly power. The owners of a particular type of technology have the options of selling the technology, licensing it, or exploiting it directly in production. The first option is unlikely to be considered by large firms engaged in R&D, but it may appeal to a sole inventor. On the other hand, licensing is considered as a suitable form of transfer to firms in the host country, but it may be limited because of the need of the owners to maintain control over business secrets, patents and trademark rights. Reasons for licensing may involve external factors, such as the prohibition of FDI by the host country, and internal factors such as the desire to receive a return on a sunk cost asset, technology or a product approaching obsolescence. If FDI cannot take place, for whatever reason, the transfer of technology can be accomplished through a technical assistance agreement.

Technology diffusion can take place through a variety of channels, including imports of high-technology products, adoption of foreign technology, and acquisition of human capital through international study. FDI by MNCs is considered to be a major channel for the access to advanced technologies by developing countries. In addition to its effects on technological progress, FDI contributes to growth by increasing capital accumulation in the host country. Knowledge transferred from the MNC to its subsidiaries may leak out to the host country, giving rise to an externality known as the spillover effect from FDI. Various channels for spillover have been suggested: labour turn-over from MNCs to local firms; technical assistance and support to suppliers and customers; and the demonstration effects on local firms in issues such as choice of technology, export behaviour, and managerial practices.

It appears that the benefits of foreign technology accruing to the investing firm and the source country are substantial (for example, increased monopoly power). However, the corresponding benefits of foreign technology accruing to the host country may not be so obvious, and may turn out to be negligible or even negative. This may be caused partly by the inability of the host country to absorb the foreign technology properly. The main reason seems to be the fact the technology is created to suit a particular environment of factor endowments but it is then used indiscriminately in different environments, in which case it may work against the interests of the host country. Technology may also have a detrimental effect on employment: new foreign technology can destroy jobs in existing industries, render obsolete human skills, and necessitate retraining of the redundant labour force, thus accentuating further the difficulties on the employment front.

Lall and Streeten (1977) cast doubt on the proposition that FDI plays an important role in technology diffusion. First, they consider the appropriateness of technology with respect to the products that are made with the technology transferred, and to the factor endowments of host countries. It is not only that the products are developed in high-income countries, but Lall and Streeten also argue that it is in the nature of MNCs that their products are excessively sophisticated in relation to the needs of developing countries (will Rolex allow the production of cheap versions of its watches to suit low-income consumers, for example?). Winters (1991, p. 229) agrees with this argument, stating that MNCs frequently pass on old technologies, which can be too capital-intensive for the local economy. Such a technology transfer, according to Winters, would create a 'dualistic structure' in the host country containing a small advanced industrial sector linked to the outside world, surrounded by a large, capital-starved sector. If the technology is capital-intensive in relation to factor endowment in the host country, then technology transfer would result in: (i) worsening employment; (ii) worsening income inequality; (iii) distorting influences on the technology used by other firms; and (iv) bias in production towards sophisticated and differentiated products. It is by no means controversial that much of modern technology cannot be adapted to suit developing countries. Reuber *et al.* (1973) found, in a survey of the issue of adapting foreign technology, that most foreign firms generally introduce their production technologies in the host country intact. If adaptation takes place then it must be in response to (i) the need to scale down the volume of production in keeping with the size of local markets; (ii) the difficulty of achieving and maintaining acceptable standards of quality control; and (iii) the local customs and legal regulations of the host country.

Lall and Streeten (1977) further argue that, even if we disregard the appropriateness of the technology, the role played by MNCs and FDI in the transfer of technology may be limited, for the following reasons. First, there are several sources of technology besides MNCs (such as small consultants who are not interested in FDI). Second, the relative importance of MNCs in transferring technology depends on several factors, including the commercialization of the technology. Third, FDI may not be the only way of acquiring technology from an MNC. Fourth, and perhaps more importantly, the price set for the transfer of technology depends on the form of transfer and the bargaining skills of the parties (the MNC and the host country). There is ample evidence that MNCs have greater bargaining power than the developing host countries ('money talks'). Narula and Dunning (1999) argue that the balance in bargaining power has shifted in favour of MNCs. Furthermore, the conditions attached to the transfer of technology may restrict the freedom of the party acquiring the technology to buy and sell commodities related to the technology. Finally, the patent system as embodied in the Paris Convention and national laws imposes further constraints in the form of restrictive clauses, and the sale of intermediate and capital goods on which transfer pricing can be used.[10] Winters (1991) argues that MNCs are very skilled and powerful negotiators, which enables them to strike a very favourable bargain in a bilateral negotiation with the government of a poor country. This is particularly the case because the negotiating poor country has little information about the underlying technology. As a result, the MNC will be in a position to demand high royalties and impose severe licensing restrictions. In summary, while FDI may in theory be the fastest and most efficient way of gaining access to the latest technology, some costs arise because the monopolistic power of MNCs allows them to extract rents.

Work on economic growth has highlighted the contribution of FDI to the technological progress, and hence growth, of developing countries.

However, the evidence is rather mixed. Findlay (1978) postulates that FDI boosts the rate of technical progress in the host country through a contagion effect from the more advanced technology and management practices used by foreign firms. Wang (1990) incorporates this idea into a model more in line with the neoclassical framework, by assuming that the increase in 'knowledge' applied to production is determined as a function of FDI. There are a number of studies examining spillovers from FDI. Positive spillovers were found in Australia (Caves, 1974b), Canada (Globerman, 1979), and Mexico (Blomstrom and Persson, 1983). No positive spillovers were found in Morocco (Haddad and Harrison, 1993) or Venezuela (Aitken and Harrison, 1999).

The difference in the results suggests that the ability to benefit from foreign technology is not automatic as it is affected by various economic and technological factors. Findlay (1978) presents a dynamic model of technology transfer through FDI from developed to developing countries. He concludes that spillovers are greater, the wider the technology gap. However, it is also arguable that wide gaps may constitute an obstacle to spillovers. Wang and Blomstrom (1992) take competition into account, arguing that the greater the extent of competition, the greater will the transfer of technology also be, from the MNC to subsidiaries, and this is likely to leak out to local firms. A high technology gap combined with a low degree of competition tends to prevent spillovers. Sjoholm (1999) examines spillovers from FDI in the Indonesian manufacturing sector. The results show that high competition tends to increase the degree of spillovers from FDI, because the degree of competition affects the choice of technology transferred from the MNC to subsidiaries. It also seems that domestic competition rather than competition from imports affects spillovers from FDI. The fruits of technology transfer are therefore by no means certain, or they may be too sour to be enjoyed.

FDI AND TRAINING

Foreign investors, much as they dislike to spend on the training of locals, realize that such expenditure may be crucial for the success of their investment. Therefore, expenditure on training becomes part of the initial investment and another sunk cost. While it is true that foreign subsidiaries can rely on expatriate personnel, at least at the beginning of operations, they have a strong incentive to limit the number of such personnel working in the host countries, and so they start to use more local people as soon as they can. This is partly because of cost considerations, since the remuneration of an expatriate tends to be higher than that of a local employee. Using local people may also result from pressure from the host government.

The effects of FDI on the training of local employees are difficult to quantify. For example, the extent to which subsidiaries use an appropriate combination of local and foreign personnel is difficult to know. The capital-intensive nature of most FDI implies that the number of local workers who are likely to be involved in training is not large. Reuber *et al.* (1973) reached the conclusion that, even allowing for the fact that training costs could not be identified properly, costs of training local people are not large enough to make a significant contribution to the improvement of the skills of these people.

Training may sometimes be considered under the general heading of 'organization and management', in the sense that the host country will benefit from the 'managerial superiority' of MNCs, and these benefits would show up as lower costs and prices. Lall and Streeten (1977) consider three kinds of managerial benefits: (i) managerial efficiency in operations arising from better training and higher standards; (ii) entrepreneurial ability in seeking out investment opportunities; and (iii) externalities arising from training received by employees (technical, executive, accounting, and so on). However, Lall and Streeten (1977) cast doubt on the proposition that the practices of MNCs are necessarily more efficient than those of smaller firms. They also argue that the practices of MNCs may be irrelevant to the host country, in which case the training will be useless and may even be harmful. Furthermore, they argue that the hierarchical structure of MNCs may entail costs to the host countries. These costs are: (i) dependence and subordination; (ii) transfer pricing; and (iii) the suppression of local entrepreneurship.

FDI AND INTER-INDUSTRY LINKAGES

FDI can influence the economy of the host country via inter-industry linkages. To the extent that foreign subsidiaries establish links with local suppliers for locally-produced materials and parts, FDI can help to provide local firms with increased opportunities that in turn affect their employment and income positions. These are called backward linkages. Forward linkages can also be established for distribution purposes.

Assuming that they have the choice, there is no reason to assume that the subsidiaries have a preference for locally-produced materials and parts compared to importing them. If these materials are produced by the parent firm or other subsidiaries, there is less scope for inter-industry linkages, particularly if the locally-produced goods are of inferior quality. Baranson (1966) cites evidence showing that supplies from the car industry in Mexico and the steel industry in India have a greater cost and are of a lower quality than the components produced in the US.

Petrochilos (1989, p. 44) warns of the hazard of exaggerating the importance of inter-industry linkages for the developing economies. Most MNCs operating abroad in the manufacturing sector are sufficiently vertically integrated or have incentives to engage in inter-subsidiary transactions that limit the scope for developing strong and extensive ties with local suppliers. Risk considerations may indicate that extensive ties are imprudent, while the state of industrial relations in certain host countries may be particularly significant in this respect. Also, for the subsidiary to minimize risk there is the option of a take-over of the local supplier.

THE EFFECT OF FDI ON MARKET STRUCTURE

FDI is likely to affect the structure of the industries it is directed towards. It may be responsible for improving the competitive forces or for worsening the monopolistic or oligopolistic elements in the host economy. Caves (1971, 1974b) argues that the entry of a foreign subsidiary into local markets can force more active rivalry and an improvement in performance than would a domestic entry at the same scale. This is because FDI is thought of as a vehicle for disseminating the transfer of technology, including a higher level of technical efficiency. On whether or not this will materialize depends the actual practice of MNCs, and this is what has prompted the OECD to issue some relevant guidelines for MNCs, with the aim of encouraging behaviour that is conducive to boosting competition. According to these guidelines, MNCs should (i) refrain from entering into or carrying out anti-competitive agreements such as price fixing; (ii) conduct their activities in a manner that is consistent with local competition laws; and (iii) co-operate with the competition authorities.

On the grounds of allocative efficiency, it is arguable that FDI can provide a significant increase in competition in the host country. Kindleberger (1969) suggests that the main impact of FDI is widening the scope for competition. This is because it is typical that foreign subsidiaries, backed up by strong parents, can compete effectively with local oligopolists and break the latter's grip on the local market. By reducing monopolistic/oligopolistic distortions, FDI can improve the allocation of resources in the host country.

The preceding discussion presupposes the existence of large local firms dominating local markets that can only be challenged by equally powerful rivals. If small local firms cannot provide this rivalry, MNCs will act as a catalyst for more competitive behaviour. However, if this condition is not satisfied, the danger is that foreign subsidiaries may dominate local markets. Reuber *et al.* (1973) argue that FDI may 'preempt the development of indigenous firms and managers capable of establishing and maintaining a strong countervailing influence'. In this case, there would be a worsening of market concentration and the possibility that monopolistic or oligopolistic practices might arise, leading to worsening industrial performance. Moreover, Reuber *et al.* argue that the entry of foreign subsidiaries might raise the level of concentration in the host country because their presence might exert pressure for mergers among local firms. Lall and Streeten (1977) argue that MNCs may induce a very high degree of oligopolistic concentration, imposing diminished price competition. Newfarmer and Mueller (1975) present evidence from Mexico and Brazil supporting the proposition that the entry of MNCs significantly speeds up the process of oligopolization in developing host countries.

FDI AND THE ENVIRONMENT

It is arguable that, because MNCs have significant financial, political and negotiating power, they can get away with causing a lot of damage to the environment, particularly in developing countries that are trying to attract FDI. Indeed, one of the reasons why MNCs choose to locate production facilities in developing countries is that these countries have less stringent environmental damage requirements. Indeed, the governments of these countries may even inflict damage on the environment in an attempt to attract FDI. Recall our earlier reference in Chapter 2 to the 1995 advertisement in *Fortune*, in which the government of the Philippines declared its willingness to 'fell [sic] mountains', 'raze jungles', 'fill swamps', 'move rivers' and 'relocate towns' to please foreign investors.

Some work has been done on the environmental effects of FDI, again without reaching a consensus view on whether FDI is good or bad for the environment. A recent publication by the OECD (1999) deals with the effect of FDI on the environment, and explores the role of host countries in developing and implementing coherent policies to ensure that proposed projects are environmentally sound. It also considers the strengths and weaknesses of voluntary corporate environmental management. One of the arguments put forward by the OECD is that FDI can be either 'a boon or a bane for the environment', depending on the specific circumstances. It seems, however, that it is more likely that FDI is a boon for the environment in a developed country and a bane for it in a developing country. A major motivation for the anti-globalization movement is the environmental damage believed to be inflicted by FDI and the operations of MNCs in developing countries.

There is obviously some concern about the environmental effects of FDI that has prompted the OECD to issue some guidelines as to how MNCs should tackle environmental issues. The OECD urges MNCs to 'take due account of the need to protect the environment, public health and safety' and to 'conduct their activities in a manner contributing to the wider goal of sustainable development'. Specifically, the OECD's guidelines on the environment encourages MNCs, *inter alia*, to: (i) provide information on the potential environmental impact of their activities; (ii) consult with the communities affected directly by the environmental policies; and (iii) maintain contingency plans for preventing, mitigating and controlling serious environmental damage.

It is interesting to note that, in its 8 February 1992 issue, *The Economist* reported a World Bank internal memo in which, by using three arguments, a bank official allegedly advocated the idea of exporting more pollution to developing countries. The first argument was that a given amount of health-impairing pollution should be done in a country with the lowest cost; that is, the country with the lowest wages. The second was that the costs of pollution are likely to be non-linear, as the initial increments of pollution probably have very low costs. Finally, the third argument was based on the idea that demand for a clean environment for health reasons is likely to have very high income elasticity. No wonder, then, that anti-globalization demonstrations are directed against the World Bank and the IMF as much as they are directed against MNCs.

MODELLING THE EFFECTS OF FDI

Most of the empirical work that has been done on the effects of FDI is based on the single equation approach using time series or cross-section aggregated or disaggregated data. Typically, the underlying model would consist of an equation in which the dependent variable is the variable hypothesized to be affected by FDI, while FDI, whatever the measure may be, appears as an explanatory variable. Other explanatory variables are used to control for the effect of other variables on the dependent variable. For example, Borensztein *et al.* (1995) investigated the effect of FDI on economic growth by specifying a relationship of the form:

$$g = f(I^F, H, Y_0, X) \tag{3.1}$$

where g is the growth rate, I^F is foreign direct investment, H is the stock of human capital, Y_0 is the initial level of output, and X is a vector of variables that are frequently used as determinants of growth, such as government expenditure, and variables representing foreign exchange and trade restrictions. The implication of Equation (3.1) is that the growth rate is determined by FDI and other factors, and in this sense causality runs from FDI to growth. Now, compare this with models of FDI determination, such as the model used by Yang *et al.* (2000) to study FDI in Australia. This (time series) model is written as:

$$I_t^F = \alpha_0 + \alpha_1 \Delta i_t + \alpha_2 \Delta E_t + \alpha_3 \Delta Y_t + \beta_4 \Delta W_t$$
$$+ \beta_5 O_t + \beta_6 D_t + \beta_7 \pi_t \tag{3.2}$$

where i is interest rate, E is the effective exchange rate, Y is output, W is the wage rate, O is openness, D is a measure of industrial disputes, and π is the inflation rate. The implication of Equation (3.2) is that output (which is a proxy for market size) determines FDI, and hence causality runs from output to FDI.

It is more plausible, however, to postulate that both output and FDI are endogenous variables that affect each other within a macroeconomic system. Hence, a simultaneous equation model may be more appropriate as a representation of both the determination and the effects of FDI.[11] Unfortunately, most of the empirical work on FDI is based on the single equation approach, but one notable exception is

Petrochilos (1989), who specified and estimated a simultaneous equation econometric model designed to show the effect of capital formation on the growth of output in general, and the influence of FDI in particular. In this model, FDI is an endogenous variable which is determined within the system while affecting the other variables. A simultaneous equation model makes a lot of sense, since FDI affects and is affected by the other variables, and because postulating bi-directional causality is highly plausible. In a sense, this model can be used to test hypotheses concerning the determinants and the effects of FDI at the same time. The model consists of ten behavioural equations and three identities which can be written as follows (the notation is explained in Table 3.1).

Table 3.1 Notation for the simultaneous equations model

Endogenous variables		Exogenous variables	
Variable	*Definition*	*Variable*	*Definition*
C	Private consumption	F^H	Long-term housing finance
I^D	Gross private domestic investment in manufacturing industry	D	Tariffs
I^F	Gross private foreign investment in manufacturing	I^G	Gross public investment
I^H	Gross private residential investment	N	Employment in manufacturing
I^O	Other gross private investment	R	Discount rate
I	Total gross investment	S	Political dummy
M^C	Imports of capital goods	T	Payments for foreign technology
M^R	Imports of raw materials and intermediate goods	Z	Residual (government consumption + exports + subsidies + change in stock − indirect taxes)
M^O	Other imports	K	Difference between gross domestic product and personal disposable income
Y^M	Manufacturing output		
Y^O	Non-manufacturing output		
Y^D	Personal disposable income		
Y	Gross domestic product		

$$C_t = F_1(Y_t^D, C_{t-1}) \tag{3.3}$$

$$I_t = F_2(Y_t^D, F_{t-1}^H) \tag{3.4}$$

$$I_t^D = F_3(Y_{t-1}, I_{t-1}, D_t) \tag{3.5}$$

$$I_t^F = F_4(Y_{t-1}, D_t, R_{t-1}, S_t) \tag{3.6}$$

$$I_t^O = F_5(Y_{t-1}^D, I_{t-1}^O) \tag{3.7}$$

$$M_t^C = F_6(I_{t-1}^D, I_{t-1}^F, T_t) \tag{3.8}$$

$$M_t^R = F_7(I_{t-1}^D, I_{t-1}^F, Y_{t-1}^D) \tag{3.9}$$

$$M_t^O = F_8(Y_t^D, C_{t-1}) \tag{3.10}$$

$$Y_t^M = F_9(I_{t-1}^D, I_{t-1}^F, N_t, T_t) \tag{3.11}$$

$$Y_t^O = F_{10}(Y_{t-1}, I_{t-1}^O) \tag{3.12}$$

$$I_t = I_t^H + I_t^D + I_t^F + I_t^O + I_t^G \tag{3.13}$$

$$Y_t = Y_t^M + Y_t^O = I_t + C_t + Z_t - M_t^C - M_t^R - M_t^O \tag{3.14}$$

$$Y_t^D = Y_t^M + Y_t^O - K_t \tag{3.15}$$

The model was estimated using linear and log-linear specifications and Greek data by employing more than one estimation method. The main findings are as follows:

1. FDI in manufacturing is explained by the factors typically found in the literature, such as the size of the market (proxied by GDP), tariffs, political stability, and the discount rate.
2. Manufacturing output is determined primarily by domestic investment in manufacturing, imports of foreign technology and employment in large-scale industry and, to a lesser extent, by investment in manufacturing by foreign subsidiaries.
3. Capital formation played an important role in the development process of the Greek economy during the period 1953–78.
4. The direct employment effect arising from the operations of foreign subsidiaries is not significant.
5. The contribution of FDI to the balance of payments is difficult to evaluate because of data problems.

A FINAL REMARK

In this chapter we discussed the effects of FDI, a highly controversial and contentious issue. There is no doubt that FDI affects both home and host countries. In theory, the effects on the host country can be highly positive, but the benefits are not realized automatically. There are certain conditions that have to be satisfied for a positive effect to materialize, and these conditions are more likely to be satisfied by a developed rather than by a developing host country. The empirical evidence (more of which is presented in the appendix to this chapter) is so mixed that it cannot resolve the underlying issues.

So far we have dealt with the characteristics, determinants and effects of FDI. In the following six chapters we shall deal in more detail with some aspects of FDI and the behaviour of MNCs that we have encountered in the book so far. There is no doubt that MNCs are not charities and that they are profit-seeking firms. Therefore, FDI is triggered, first and foremost, by the profitability (or anticipated profitability) of the underlying projects, at least in the long run. In Chapter 4 we shall study international capital budgeting, which tells us how MNCs determine the financial feasibility of FDI projects.

Appendix

Table A3.1   Summary of selected recent studies of the effects of FDI

Study	Issue under investigation	Findings
Zukowska-Gagelmann (2000)	Examining the effect of FDI on productivity growth	FDI has a negative impact on the performance of the most productive local firms
Driffield and Taylor (2000)	The labour market impact of inward FDI in the UK	FDI leads to an increase in wage inequality and the use of skilled labour in domestic firms
Kearns and Ruane (2001)	Relationship between FDI and growth in Ireland	FDI has been beneficial to Ireland. R&D-active firms provide greater benefits
Fan and Dickie (2000)	Contribution of FDI to growth and stability in Asian countries	FDI accounts for 4–20 per cent of GDP growth
Xu and Wang (2000)	International trade and FDI as channels for technology diffusion	No evidence that FDI is a significant channel for technology diffusion

Nachum (1999)	Impact of FDI on international competitiveness	FDI weakens the link between location advantages and ownership advantages
Asafu-Adjaye (2000)	Effect of FDI on Indonesian economic growth	FDI has a significant positive effect on growth
Jarolim (2000)	Role of FDI in the economic transition of the Czech Republic	FDI's spillover effect is statistically insignificant
Henneberger and Ziegler (2000)	Effect of Swiss FDI on employment	Negative correlation between variations in levels of domestic and foreign employment
Leahy and Montagna (2000a)	The welfare implications of using union legislation to attract FDI	The host government may ban unions in the short run to extract higher rents in the future
Barrel and Holland (2000)	Effects of FDI on manufacturing sector in central Europe	FDI has led to increasing labour productivity in most manufacturing sectors
Figlio and Blonigen (2000)	Effects of FDI on local communities in the USA	FDI raises local real wages more than domestic investment but lowers per capita local government expenditure
Berthelemy and Demurger (2000)	Relationship between FDI and growth in China	FDI plays a fundamental role in provincial growth
Zhang (1999a)	Relationship between FDI and economic growth in Asian countries	FDI enhances growth in the long run
Chen and Ku (2000)	Effect of FDI on firm growth	FDI is beneficial to the survival of firms
Braunerhjelm and Oxelheim (2000)	Substitutability between FDI and domestic investment	Substitutability exists for R&D intensive production
Djankov and Hoekman (2000)	Relationship between FDI and productivity in Czech enterprises	FDI has a positive impact on total factor productivity of recipient firms
Hsu and Chen (2000)	Effect of FDI on labour productivity in Taiwan	FDI enhances productivity of small and medium-sized firms. It has negative spillover on large firms
Zhang (1999b)	Effect of FDI on economic growth in China	Long-run link and two-way causality between FDI and growth
Walkenhorst (2000)	Spillovers from FDI to related industries in transition economies	FDI brings not only capital but also managerial and technological skills

Table A3.1   (Continued)

Study	Issue under investigation	Findings
Bosworth and Collins (1999)	Implications of financial flows for saving and investment in host country	Little correlation among FDI, portfolio investment and loans. FDI has close to one-to-one effect on investment
Glass and Saggi (1999a)	Consequences of FDI in a general equilibrium setting	FDI raises wages and lowers profits in the host country, and vice versa
Yabuuchi (1999)	Effects of FDI on welfare and unemployment	An increase in FDI leads to an increase in welfare and a decrease in unemployment if capital is also used in the domestic manufacturing sector
Fung *et al.* (1999)	Effects of FDI on national welfare	FDI can affect national welfare positively or negatively
Saggi (1999)	Implications of licensing and FDI for technology transfer	Relative to licensing, FDI limits technology spillovers to local firms, but dissipates more rents in the product market
Bonelli (1999)	Links between FDI and industrial competitiveness in Brazil	FDI has contributed to increased productivity and competitiveness in Brazil
Roling (1999)	German job export through FDI	Empirical basis for German job export is weak
Driffield (1999)	Employment consequences of inward FDI in the UK	FDI generates employment substitution away from local firms
Okamoto (1999)	Effect of FDI on production efficiency	FDI has a positive effect through the enhancement of competitive pressure and technology transfer
Chuang and Lin (1999)	Effect of FDI on productivity	FDI has a positive spillover effect on productivity
Elahee and Pagan (1999)	The role of FDI in Asia and Latin America	FDI plays an important role in fostering economic growth
De Andrade-Castro and Teixeira (1999)	FDI, technology transfer and growth	FDI may have a positive effect on long-run growth, eventually helping the recipient country to catch up with the investing country

Aitken and Harrison (1999)	Effect of FDI on domestic firms in Venezuela	FDI affects the productivity of domestic firms negatively. Net impact of FDI is small
De Mello (1999)	Direct investment-led growth	The extent to which FDI is growth-enhancing depends on the degree of complementarity and substitution between FDI and domestic investment
Glass and Saggi (1999b)	FDI and technology	The role FDI plays in technology transfer depends on whether substitute channels are available for transfer to the host country
Heinrich and Konan (2000)	Impact of PTAs on horizontal FDI	PTA welfare increases regardless of changes in FDI
Stone and Jeon (2000)	Relationship between FDI and trade in Asia-Pacific economies	Significant and positive relationship between FDI and trade
Mucchielli *et al.* (2000)	Relationship between intra- or inter-firm trade and FDI	Complementarity for global trade is explained by complementarity for intra-firm trade and substitutability for inter-firm trade
Castilho and Zignago (2000)	Relationship between FDI, trade and regional integration	Positive link between FDI and trade flows mitigated by the impact of integration on FDI
Ellingsen and Warneryd (1999)	FDI and protectionism	An import-competing industry may not want maximum protection because it may encourage FDI, which could be less desirable
Wilamoski and Tinkler (1999)	The effect of FDI on exports and imports	FDI leads to increased exports and imports
Gopinath *et al.* (1999)	FDI and trade	Small substitution effect between foreign sales and exports
Chen (2000)	Relationship between FDI and intra-industry trade	Positive and strong link between FDI and intra-industry trade

4 International Capital Budgeting

An MNC's decision to invest abroad (which is often based on strategic, economic or behavioural motives) may be defensive or aggressive, aiming at strengthening the company's position. Although the decision to invest abroad may be taken for non-financial reasons, it is imperative that the underlying project is financially viable because the MNC will not otherwise survive in the long run. Capital budgeting (also called investment appraisal and project evaluation) is used for evaluating the financial viability of a project.

Capital budgeting is a process of investigation and analysis that leads to a key financial decision for both purely domestic firms and MNCs. More broadly, capital budgeting is defined as the process of analysing capital investment opportunities and deciding which, if any, to undertake. The process involves the creative search for investment opportunities, the collection of data and the generation of forecasts, the economic analysis, the decision and the implementation. Thus, the process consists of (i) determination of alternatives and strategic analysis; (ii) economic analysis of the remaining alternatives; and (iii) implementation of chosen alternatives (including performance assessment). In making capital budgeting decisions it is normally assumed that the managers attempt to maximize the value of the firm to existing shareholders. Given this objective, managers need some way to estimate the value that a project is capable of providing.

International capital budgeting is more complicated than domestic capital budgeting because MNCs are typically large and capital intensive, and because the process involves a larger number of parameters and decision variables. In general, international capital budgeting involves a consideration of more risk than domestic capital budgeting. But like domestic capital budgeting, international capital budgeting involves the estimation of some measures or criteria that indicate the feasibility or otherwise of a project (a capital budgeting evaluation measure) such as the net present value (NPV). However, certain factors that are not considered in domestic capital budgeting should be taken into account in international capital budgeting because of the special nature of FDI projects. The estimation of NPV and similar criteria requires (i) the identification of the relevant expected cash flows to be used for the analysis of the proposed project; and (ii) the determination of the proper discount rate for finding the present value of the cash flows.

International capital budgeting involves substantial spending (capital investment) in projects that are located in foreign (host) countries, rather than in the home country of the MNC. Foreign projects differ from purely domestic projects with respect to a number of factors: the foreign currency dimension, different economic indicators (such as inflation) in different countries, and different risk characteristics with which the MNC is not as familiar with as those pertaining to domestic projects. All these differences lead to a higher level of risk in international capital budgeting than in domestic capital budgeting.

Many studies have surveyed the practices of MNCs with respect to international capital budgeting (for example, Stanley and Block, 1983). The prime finding of these studies is that a typical MNC employs various techniques for evaluating international projects. One reason for the diversity of the techniques is that the decision process involves a number of management groups with different backgrounds (for example, the engineering group, the finance group, and the legal affairs group).

International capital budgeting involves a number of issues that do not appear in domestic capital budgeting. These issues include the following:

1. Should the project be evaluated from the perspective of the MNC or that of the subsidiary?
2. How should taxation be treated, given the presence of both foreign and domestic taxes?
3. How should future exchange rates be forecast for the purpose of converting expected cash flows from foreign to domestic currency?
4. Is the foreign exchange exposure resulting from cash flows a risk factor that requires additional expected return as a compensation?

These issues and others will be dealt with in this chapter. We start with the first issue, which is discussed in the following section. But before moving on to the following section it may be worthwhile to reiterate the convention used to identify nationality. The word 'domestic' is used to refer to the home country, where the parent MNC is located. Hence, the home government is the government of the home country and the domestic currency is the functional currency of the MNC. On the other hand, the word 'foreign' refers to the foreign or host country, where the subsidiary and the project are located. Hence, the foreign government is the government of the foreign country and the foreign currency is the functional currency of the subsidiary.

WHICH PERSPECTIVE?

The first issue to be encountered in international capital budgeting is whether the project under consideration is assessed from the perspective of the subsidiary or that of the parent MNC. Measures of project feasibility, such as the NPV, can be calculated from either perspective, depending on whether the calculation is based on the cash flows received by the subsidiary or those remitted by the subsidiary to the MNC. One view is that it should be from the subsidiary's perspective, since the subsidiary will eventually be in charge of administering the project. It is also argued that projects should be evaluated from the subsidiary's perspective because the subsidiary belongs to the MNC, which means that what is good for the subsidiary should be good for the MNC.

One counter-argument is that since the MNC is financing the project, it should be assessed from its perspective. This is more the case if the subsidiary is wholly owned by the MNC. After all, the MNC's objective is to enhance its net worth, which is what is expected by its shareholders. Hence, for a project (domestic or foreign) to be accepted by the MNC, it must have a positive net present value from the MNC's perspective. An exception would be when the subsidiary is not wholly owned by the MNC. In this case, the subsidiary would also have the objective of increasing its net worth as expected by the shareholders who are not shareholders of the MNC. Hence, the acceptability, or otherwise, of a project is determined by negotiation between the MNC and the subsidiary.

Another argument for evaluating projects from the MNC's perspective is that there is a tendency for the subsidiaries not to appreciate fully the ways in which a project may benefit the MNC. This tendency is reinforced by the practice of rewarding the subsidiary's management on the basis of its net income, not on its contribution to the consolidated performance of the MNC.

What makes this matter important is that the net after-tax cash flows that accrue to the MNC can be substantially different from those accruing to the subsidiary. The earnings of the subsidiary are subject to corporate income tax and withholding tax in the host country, and part of the after-tax earnings are kept by the subsidiary as retained earnings. Sometimes the whole amount is retained, in which case the parent company gets nothing. This normally happens when the host country encounters balance of payments problems, as happened in many Latin American countries following the international debt crisis of the 1980s. The amount remitted to the MNC is then converted to its functional currency (the domestic currency), and these earnings are subsequently taxed once more by the home government. Hence, what may look like an attractive project from the point of view of the subsidiary may be utterly unattractive to the MNC. Several reasons explain the difference between the cash flows accruing to the MNC and to the subsidiary. Remember that the net present value and other measures of the feasibility of projects are calculated from the net after-tax cash flows.

The first reason for the difference between the cash flows received by the subsidiary and those received by the MNC is tax differentials, that is, when there is a difference between the tax rates in the host country and the home country. If the host government imposes a lower tax rate on earnings than does the home government, then the project may be feasible from the perspective of the subsidiary but not from the perspective of the MNC.

The second reason is restricted remittances. This occurs when the host government requires a certain percentage of the subsidiary's earnings to remain in the host country. Sometimes the earnings generated by the subsidiary are required to be reinvested in the host country for some years before they can be remitted to the MNC, giving rise to so-called 'blocked funds'. If there are restrictions on remittances, the MNC will not have access to these funds, and hence its after-tax cash flows will be lower than those of the subsidiary. Again, the project may not be feasible from the MNC's perspective, but is viable from the subsidiary's perspective.

The third reason is excessive remittances. This occurs when the MNC charges the subsidiary high administrative fees, making the cash flows accruing to the subsidiary lower than those accruing to the MNC. In this case, the project may be feasible from the MNC's perspective but not from the perspective of the subsidiary. There are obviously differences between the revenue/cost configurations of the MNC and the subsidiary: what is regarded as revenue by the MNC is regarded as cost by the subsidiary. The same conclusion would be valid if the MNC charged the subsidiary high transfer prices, a subject that will be dealt with in Chapter 8.

The fourth reason for differences in cash flows is exchange rate movements. If the domestic currency appreciates against the foreign currency, then the cash flows received by the MNC will be reduced in value measured in terms of the domestic currency. Remember that the subsidiary and the MNC calculate the net present value and other measures of the feasibility of the project on the basis of cash flows denominated in terms of two different currencies. Fluctuations in exchange rates lead to fluctuations in the cash flows received by the MNC in terms of the domestic currency for a given amount received from the subsidiary denominated in the foreign currency.

The fifth reason is differences in the discount rates used by the MNC and the subsidiary to calculate the present value of future cash flows arising from the project. From the subsidiary's perspective, the appropriate discount rate should relate to the cost of funds facing the subsidiary's local competitors. For the MNC, the discount rate should be related to the cost of capital pertaining to its worldwide operations. Obviously, the two rates can diverge significantly.

THE NET PRESENT VALUE

The net present value (NPV) is a project evaluation criterion based on cash flows, taking into account the time value of money by discounting future cash flows at an appropriate discount rate.[1] NPV measures the absolute financial benefit of a project, and leads consistently to an absolute financial gain by adding to the shareholders' net worth. A project is considered to be acceptable if the NPV is positive. To choose between two mutually exclusive projects, the one that is picked must have a higher NPV.

The NPV is the difference between the initial investment outlay (the capital cost) and the sum of the discounted cash flows realized from the project. If the initial investment is X_0 and the cash flows resulting from the projects over years $1, 2, \ldots, n$, are $X_1, X_2, \ldots, X_n$, then the NPV is given by the equation:

$$\text{NPV} = -X_0 + \sum_{t=1}^{n} \frac{X_t}{(1+k)^t} + \frac{V_n}{(1+k)^n} \qquad (4.1)$$

where k is the discount rate, n is the project's lifetime, and V_n is its salvage value (also called the terminal or liquidation value). The discount rate is normally taken to be (or closely related to) the cost of capital or the required rate of return on the investment (we shall deal with the determination of the cost of capital in Chapter 7). The underlying idea here is that, for a project to be financially acceptable, it must attract a rate of return that is at least equal to the cost of obtaining the funds required to finance it.

One has to be precise about the meaning of the cash flows represented by X_t. Specifically, X_t represents the incremental change in the subsidiary's or the MNC's cash flow (depending on the perspective from which the NPV is calculated) for year t resulting from the project. Hence,

$$X_t = (R_t - C_t - D_t - I_t)(1 - \tau) + D_t + I_t(1 - \tau) \qquad (4.2)$$

where R_t is sales revenue, C_t represents costs or expenses, D_t is depreciation, I_t is interest payments, and τ is the tax rate. The term $(R_t - C_t - D_t - I_t)(1 - \tau)$ is net income accruing to the shareholders, which is calculated after tax by applying the factor $(1 - \tau)$ to the gross amount, $(R_t - C_t - D_t - I_t)$. The second term, D_t, represents the fact that depreciation is a non-cash expense, removed from the calculation of net income only for tax purposes. It is added again because it is not an actual cash flow. The last term, $I_t(1 - \tau)$, represents the after-tax interest payments. Equation (4.2) can be written as:

$$X_t = (R_t - C_t - D_t)(1 - \tau) + D_t \qquad (4.3)$$

where the term $(R_t - C_t - D_t)(1 - \tau)$ is the after-tax operating income. Equation (4.3) can be manipulated to obtain:

$$X_t = (R_t - C_t)(1 - \tau) + \tau D_t \qquad (4.4)$$

where the term τD_t represents the tax saving resulting from D_t being a tax deductible item. Finally, Equation (4.4) can be rewritten as:

$$X_t = O_t(1 - \tau) + \tau D_t \qquad (4.5)$$

where $O_t = R_t - C_t$ is the operating cash flow. Hence, X_t consists of the after-tax operating cash flow and tax savings from depreciation. The difference between the total cash flow and the operating cash flow is that the former represents the total change in the MNC's cash account (as recorded on the cash flow statement), whereas the latter is a measure of funds generated by the MNC's operations.[2]

In order to implement the NPV formula, some forecasts must be made to estimate the variables implied by Equation (4.1), including the cash flows and the salvage value. For this purpose, a large number of factors must be taken into account. These factors will now be considered in turn.

The Initial Investment

The initial investment includes not only the funds required to start the project but also the working capital needed to support it over time. The working capital is needed to finance inventory, wages and similar items until the project starts to generate revenue.

A major complication in international capital budgeting arises when the MNC sets up part of the initial investment as equipment or inventory. Clearly, this should be considered as part of the initial investment. The problem here concerns the valuation of these items. One way to do this is by using the concept of deprived value, which can be defined as the value of the entire loss, direct or indirect, resulting from the surrender of the underlying asset. The valuation can be based on three measures: (i) the replacement cost (*RC*), which is the current purchase price of an asset in a comparable state of wear and tear; (ii) the net realizable value (*NRV*), which is the current net disposable value; and (iii) the present value (*PV*) of the expected future earnings stream from the asset. Given these three valuation criteria, several possibilities will arise. These possibilities and their interpretation are presented in Table 4.1.

Consumer Demand

Forecasting consumer demand for the products generated by the project is required to estimate the future cash flows. Since there are competing products, a market share must be estimated, and this is not an easy task. Forecasting the total size of the market is normally based on historical data, and may involve the use of univariate or multivariate models. If univariate models are used, the market size (or total consumer demand) is specified as a function of its own previous values, using ARIMA modelling. Otherwise, some other techniques may be used, including smoothing methods, time series decomposition, and structural time series modelling. If a multivariate model is used, demand is specified as being a function of several variables, including own price, prices of competing goods, population and income. Once the model is estimated from historical data, it can be used to forecast or project consumer demand in the future.[3]

Table 4.1 Valuation of assets surrendered to subsidiaries

Possibility	Course of action	Interpretation	Correct basis
$NRV > PV > RC$ $NRV > RC > PV$	Dispose of the asset	RC (not NRV), since the firm can restore the opportunity to obtain NRV by acquiring an asset of the same type. RC is the correct basis for valuation	RC
$PV > RC > NRV$ $PV > NRV > RC$	Use the asset in the business to realize its present value	If the firm was deprived of the asset it could replace it to achieve the PV. The replacement cost is the relevant deprival value alternative	RC
$RC > PV > NRV$	Do not replace the asset if it is surrendered	Since the PV of future cash flows exceeds the NRV, there would be no point in replacing it. Hence, RC is irrelevant	PV
$RC > NRV > PV$	Do not replace the asset if it is surrendered	If the asset is surrendered, the firm loses the NRV, not the PV	NRV

Price

The revenues that the project generates during its lifetime depends on the volume of sales and the selling price. Thus, the selling price must be forecast. The simplest way to do this is to start with a price that reflects the prices of competitive products, provided that this price is viable for the firm considering the project. Starting from this price, the prices over each year of the project's lifetime may be estimated in relation to inflation in the host country where the project is located. A decision must be made as to whether the price is going to move exactly in tandem with the inflation rate, or that it will move at a faster or a slower pace. This necessarily means that a forecast of the future inflation rate is needed. Again, inflation may be forecast from univariate or multivariate models.

Variable Costs

Variable costs depend on the units of factors of production used (such as labour) and the cost per unit (such as the hourly wage rate). The cost per unit is related closely to the inflation rate, while the number of units used depends on production, and therefore on consumer demand.

Fixed Costs

Fixed costs are easier to estimate than variable costs because they do not depend on consumer demand. Again, fixed costs are determined by inflation, and for this purpose a forecast of inflation is required.

Project Lifetime

The lifetime of the project may be easy or difficult to determine. In some cases, the project lifetime is determined in advance, by stating when the project will be liquidated. In other cases, the project keeps running as long as it is profitable, and so it would be difficult to say when it will no longer be profitable and hence terminated. Sometimes the MNC has no control over the life of the project because of political risk, specifically the risk of take-over by the host government, as we shall see in the following chapter.

Salvage Value

Salvage value is also known as the terminal or liquidation value, and is invariably measured after tax. This item is difficult to forecast because it depends on the success of the project, as well as on political risk. For example, the salvage value will be zero if the host government confiscates the project (that is, takes it over without compensation).

Even if a project is expected to continue indefinitely, it is still necessary to pick a finite period over which to analyse it. The appropriate period depends on the nature of the project, its size and complexity and the amount of time the management wishes to devote to its analysis. If the project is expected to continue to generate cash flows beyond the terminal point of the analysis, the salvage value should represent these cash flows.

When the salvage value is uncertain, the MNC may want to experiment with several salvage values. Sometimes, the concept of a break-even salvage value is introduced: it is the salvage value that makes the NPV of the project equal to zero. The break-even salvage value is calculated by setting the NPV at zero then solving the equation for V_n. Hence:

$$-X_0 + \sum_{t=1}^{n} \frac{X_t}{(1+k)^t} + \frac{V_n}{(1+k)^n} = 0 \qquad (4.6)$$

or:

$$V_n = (1+k)^n \left[X_0 - \sum_{t=1}^{n} \frac{X_t}{(1+k)^t} \right] \qquad (4.7)$$

Restrictions on the Transfer of Funds by the Host Government

Restrictions on remittances are related to political risk. This factor is important because it affects the cash flows received by the MNC, which are used to calculate the NPV. If the percentage of cash flows that is allowed to be transferred to the MNC is known in advance, this information can be used to forecast the cash flows received by the MNC. However, regulations concerning the transfer of funds may be changed by the host government any time in the future for an unanticipated reason. For example, the host government may impose a total ban on the transfer of funds because of a currency or a balance of payments crisis. This will reduce the cash flows received by the MNC to zero.

Tax Laws

Again, changes in tax laws may be introduced by the governments of the home and the host countries. This item is difficult to forecast because these laws could change, both with or without a reason. For example, the home government may change the tax law in such a way as not to grant the MNC credit for taxes paid by the subsidiary in the host country. Such a change will reduce the cash flows received by the MNC.

Let the cash flow generated by the project at time t be X_t, the foreign tax rate be τ^* and the domestic tax rate τ. In this case, the subsidiary pays $\tau^* X_t$ to the host government, and if there are no retained earnings, blocked funds or withholding tax, then the MNC receives $X_t(1 - \tau^*)$. Assuming that the MNC gets full credit for taxes paid by the subsidiary and that $\tau > \tau^*$, then the amount of tax paid by the MNC is $X_t(\tau - \tau^* - \tau\tau^*)$. Hence, the after-tax cash flow that is used by the MNC to calculate the NPV is $X_t(1 - \tau + \tau\tau^*)$. If there is no tax credit then the cash flow becomes $X_t(1 - \tau^*)(1 - \tau)$. And if there is only a partial tax credit, then the cash flow becomes $X_t[(1 - \tau^*)(1 - \tau) + \theta\tau^*]$, where $\theta < 1$.[4] Forecasting in this case pertains to which of these expressions is to be used for calculating the NPV, as well as to the values of τ, τ^* and θ.[5]

Exchange Rates

Exchange rates are difficult to forecast. This is particularly the case with the exchange rates of the so-called exotic currencies, which are currencies that are not actively traded. Forecasting exchange rates for a long time into the future is rather difficult, although it could be based on purchasing power parity (PPP); that is, on inflation rates. Even fixed exchange rates do not alleviate this problem, as these rates may be corrected (via devaluation or revaluation) with the passage of time. If it is believed that PPP holds then the exchange rate at time t, S_t, may be determined by adjusting the exchange rate at time 0, S_0, by a factor that reflects the inflation differential. Hence:

$$S_t = S_0 \left[\frac{1 + \pi_t}{1 + \pi_t^*}\right] \tag{4.8}$$

where π_t is the domestic inflation rate and π_t^* is the foreign inflation rate between 0 and t. A similar relationship that can be used to forecast the exchange rate is uncovered interest parity (UIP), which can be written as:

$$S_{t+1} = S_t \left[\frac{1 + i_t}{1 + i_t^*} \right] \tag{4.9}$$

where i and i^* are the domestic and foreign interest rates respectively. This relationship, however, may not be a proper forecasting model in this case because normally it is viewed as a short-term relationship, whereas capital budgeting covers a long period of time.

Otherwise, exchange rate forecasts may be generated from a univariate time series model or a model that contains explanatory variables. It is even possible to use long-term forward rates as forecasts if they are available. An example of a forecasting model containing two explanatory variables can be obtained if it is believed that the exchange rate is determined by the inflation differential and interest rate differential. This model, which takes into account both short-term and long-term factors, may be specified as:

$$S_t = \alpha_0 + \alpha_1 (\pi_t - \pi_t^*) + \alpha_2 (i_t - i_t^*) \tag{4.10}$$

It is also possible to forecast exchange rates by using the global asset pricing model, as we shall see in Chapter 7. For a comprehensive survey of the techniques of exchange rate forecasting, see Moosa (2000a).

Sometimes it is possible to eliminate the effect of fluctuations in exchange rates by hedging exposure to foreign exchange risk. For example, it is possible to lock in the domestic currency value of the cash flows by entering into a forward contract whereby the foreign currency cash flows received from the subsidiary are converted into the domestic currency. In international capital budgeting, this is not so straightforward, for (at least) two reasons. The first reason is that the foreign currency cash flows will not be known in advance, in which case the MNC will not know what to hedge. Of course, the MNC can hedge the forecast of the cash flows, which typically will be different from the actual cash flows. Second, because some cash flows may arise too far in the future, this exposure cannot be hedged because of the unavailability of long-term forward contracts. Although there are other instruments and techniques for hedging long-term exposure, such as swaps, it still remains true that hedging over a long period of time is difficult (see Moosa, 1998). Thus, the MNC must depend on exchange rate forecasting for the purpose of converting the foreign currency cash flows remitted by the subsidiary from the foreign currency into the domestic currency.

The Discount Rate

In order to calculate the present value of the future cash flows, a discount rate, k, must be used. This discount rate is normally the required rate of return on the project, which may or may not be equal to the MNC's cost of capital. Whether or not the required rate of return is equal to the project's cost of capital depends on the riskiness of the project.

If the discount rate is nominal (that is, unadjusted for inflation) then consistency requires that cash flows be estimated in nominal terms as well. There is nothing wrong with discounting real cash flows at the real discount rate, although this is not normally done. However, it can be shown that if real cash flows are discounted at the real discount rate, an NPV will be obtained which is the same as that by discounting nominal cash flows at the nominal discount rate. Consider a two-year project costing X_0 and generating cash flows X_1 and X_2 in years 1 and 2, respectively. If the general price level at time 0 is 1, and assuming a constant inflation rate of π, then the price levels at times 1 and 2 will be $(1 + \pi)$ and $(1 + \pi)^2$, respectively. In nominal terms the NPV will be given by:

$$\text{NPV} = -X_0 + \frac{X_1}{1+k} + \frac{X_2}{(1+k)^2} \tag{4.11}$$

If the NPV is calculated by discounting the real cash flows at the real discount rate, then:

$$\begin{aligned} \text{NPV} &= -X_0 + \frac{X_1(1+\pi)^{-1}}{(1+k)(1+\pi)^{-1}} + \frac{X_2(1+\pi)^{-2}}{(1+k)^2(1+\pi)^{-2}} \\ &= -X_0 + \frac{X_1}{1+k} + \frac{X_2}{(1+k)^2} \end{aligned} \tag{4.12}$$

which gives an identical result. This is because the real discount factor (1 plus the real discount rate) is equal to the nominal discount factor $(1 + k)$ divided by one plus the inflation rate $(1 + \pi)$.

It follows, therefore, that discounting real cash flows at the nominal discount rate and vice versa is a big mistake. Consider first discounting real cash flows at the nominal discount rate, which gives:

$$
\begin{aligned}
\text{NPV} &= -X_0 + \frac{X_1(1+\pi)^{-1}}{(1+k)} + \frac{X_2(1+\pi)^{-2}}{(1+k)^2} \\
&= -X_0 + \frac{X_1}{(1+k)(1+\pi)} + \frac{X_2}{(1+k)^2(1+\pi)^2}
\end{aligned}
\tag{4.13}
$$

which obviously underestimates NPV if $\pi > 0$, as is usually the case. If the NPV is calculated by discounting the nominal cash flows at the real discount rate, then:

$$
\begin{aligned}
\text{NPV} &= -X_0 + \frac{X_1}{(1+k)(1+\pi)^{-1}} + \frac{X_2}{(1+k)^2(1+\pi)^{-2}} \\
&= -X_0 + \frac{X_1(1+\pi)}{(1+k)} + \frac{X_2(1+\pi)^2}{(1+k)^2}
\end{aligned}
\tag{4.14}
$$

which obviously overestimates NPV if $\pi > 0$, as is usually the case.

Now, if the discount rate is taken to be equal to the cost of capital, then the question is: which cost of capital? In this case, we distinguish between the MNC's cost of capital and the project's (or subsidiary's) cost of capital. The MNC's cost of capital is the expected return on the MNC's total assets and operations, given its total risk. The project's cost of capital is the minimum acceptable expected rate of return on the project, given its risk. The project's cost of capital depends on the use to which that capital is put. It therefore depends on the risk of the project, not that of the MNC. The discount rate should be the project's cost of capital. Cooper and Kaplanis (2000) explain how the required rate of return differs for companies raising capital in partially-segmented markets. They also explain how these differences can be consistent with general equilibrium, and the effect they have on incentives for FDI.

Depreciation

Depreciation is normally determined by the accounting standards used in the host country. This item applies to plant and equipment (including buildings). Cash flows are affected by the length of time it takes to write off an asset completely.

Depreciation can be calculated using the straight-line method or the accelerated method. According to the straight-line method, the cost of an asset is allocated equally over a period of time by dividing the historical cost of the asset by the number of years and allocating that equal fraction of the cost to each year in the period. According to the accelerated method, the cost of an asset is allocated over the period according to a schedule that allows a greater fraction of the historical cost to be allocated for later years.

THE ADJUSTED PRESENT VALUE (APV)

For the purpose of the following discussion, it is assumed that k is equal to the cost of capital; that is, the underlying project is as risky as what is implied by the capital structure of the MNC. We start by substituting Equation (4.5) into Equation (4.1) to obtain:

$$\text{APV} = -X_0 + \sum_{t=1}^{n} \frac{O_t(1-\tau)}{(1+k)^t} + \sum_{t=1}^{n} \frac{\tau D_t}{(1+k)^t} + \frac{V_n}{(1+k)^n} \qquad (4.15)$$

Modigliani and Miller (1963) have shown that:

$$V_\ell = V_u + \tau B \qquad (4.16)$$

where V_ℓ is the market value of a levered firm (whose capital structure includes debt financing), V_u is the market value of an equivalent unlevered firm (capital consists of equity only), and B is the value of debt ($B = 0$ in the case of an unlevered firm). Assuming that the debt is perpetual, Equation (4.16) can be written as:

$$\frac{O(1-\tau)}{k} = \frac{O(1-\tau)}{k_u} + \frac{\tau I}{i} \qquad (4.17)$$

where i is the levered firm's borrowing rate, $I = iB$ and k_u is the cost of equity for an all-equity financed firm. The average cost of capital is given by:

$$k = (1-\lambda)k_\ell + \lambda i(1-\tau) \qquad (4.18)$$

where k_ℓ is the cost of capital for a levered firm and λ is the optimal debt–equity ratio. Modigliani and Miller (1963) have shown that:

$$k = k_u(1 - \tau\lambda) \tag{4.19}$$

This is because:

$$k_\ell = k_u + (1 - \tau)(k_u - i)\lambda^* \tag{4.20}$$

where λ^* is the actual debt/equity ratio.

Recall that Equation (4.2) can be simplified to Equation (4.4), which means that regardless of how the firm is financed, it will earn the same after-tax operating income. From Equation (4.19), if $\lambda = 0$, implying an all-equity financed firm, then $k = k_u$ and $I = 0$. Thus, Equation (4.16) reduces to $V_\ell = V_u$. For Equation (4.17) to hold, it is necessary to add the present value of the tax savings received by the levered firm. The main result of the Modigliani–Miller theorem is that the value of a levered firm is greater than the value of an equivalent unlevered firm earning the same after-tax operating income, because the former has tax savings from the tax deductibility of interest payments.

Following a similar line of argument, Equation (4.15) can be converted into an adjusted present value (APV) equation that takes the form:

$$\text{APV} = -X_0 + \sum_{t=1}^{n} \frac{O_t(1 - \tau)}{(1 + k_u)^t} + \sum_{t=1}^{n} \frac{\tau D_t}{(1 + i)^t} + \sum_{t=1}^{n} \frac{\tau I_t}{(1 + i)^t} + \frac{V_n}{(1 + k_u)^n}$$

$$\tag{4.21}$$

Just like the NPV, a project is accepted if the APV is positive, and a project is chosen from two mutually exclusive projects if it has a higher APV.

It is obvious from equation (4.21) that each cash flow that is a source of value is considered individually and discounted at a discount rate consistent with the risk inherent in that cash flow. Operating cash flows and the salvage value are discounted at k_u because the firm would receive these cash flows irrespective of its capital structure. The tax savings resulting from interest payments, τI_t, are discounted at the borrowing rate, i. The tax savings due to depreciation, τD_t, are also discounted at i because these cash flows are less risky than the operating cash flows.

Equation (4.21) can be used by an MNC considering a domestic project or a subsidiary considering a project in the host country. It does not take into account factors such as currency conversion (from the foreign currency to the domestic currency, or vice versa), blocked funds and different tax rates.

Lessard (1985) developed an APV formula that recognizes explicitly currency conversion and special cash flows that are encountered in the analysis of foreign projects. This formula takes the form:

$$
\text{APV} = \sum_{t=1}^{n} \frac{S_t^e O_t (1 - \tau)}{(1 + k_u)^t} + \sum_{t=1}^{n} \frac{S_t^e \tau D_t}{(1 + i)^t} + \sum_{t=1}^{n} \frac{S_t^e \tau I_t}{(1 + i)^t} + \frac{S_t^e V_n}{(1 + k_u)^n}
$$

$$
- S_0 X_0 + S_0 F_0 + S_0 L_0 - \sum_{t=1}^{n} \frac{S_t^e P_t}{(1 + i)^t} \tag{4.22}
$$

The following points are explanatory notes pertaining to Equation (4.22):

1. The cash flows are assumed to be denominated in a foreign currency, which is the functional currency of the subsidiary. They are converted into the domestic currency at S_t^e, the spot exchange rate expected to prevail at time t. Cash flows arising at time zero are converted at the current spot rate, S_0.
2. The equation assumes that the MNC gets credit for the taxes paid by the subsidiary in the host country. Hence, τ is the larger of the two corporate tax rates imposed on the subsidiary in the host country and imposed on the MNC in the home country.
3. The discount rates are the domestic rates because the cash flows are converted into the domestic currency.
4. O_t represents only a portion of the operating cash flows available for remittance that can be legally remitted to the MNC. Hence, it excludes blocked funds.
5. Only incremental revenues and costs are included. For example, the project may cause a crowding out of the sales of a subsidiary or those of the MNC itself (when production in the host country replaces exports by the MNC).
6. The term $S_0 F_0$ is the domestic currency value (converted at the current spot rate) of the restricted funds that are freed by the project, F_0. Examples are funds whose use is restricted by exchange controls, which can be used to offset part of the project's capital cost.

7. The term $S_0L_0 - \Sigma[S_t^e P_t/(1+i)^t]$ is the domestic currency present value of the benefits of foreign currency concessionary loans. The host country may offer such loans to attract investors from other countries. The benefit is measured as the difference between the domestic currency value of the concessionary loan, S_0L_0 and the present value of the payments, $\Sigma[S_t^e P_t/(1+i)^t]$, all measured in domestic currency terms.

Thus, the APV of a foreign project can be estimated as the capital cost (cash outflow) plus the present values of the following items: (i) remittable operating cash flows; (ii) tax saving from depreciation and capital allowances; (iii) subsidies to the project; (iv) other tax savings; (v) the project's effect on corporate debt capacity; and (vi) other cash inflows and outflows that result directly from the project. Booth (1982) shows that under certain circumstances the NPV and APV are equivalent.

FURTHER EXTENSIONS OF THE APV FORMULA

Consider the term $\Sigma[S_t^e O_t(1-\tau)]/(1+k_u)^t$ in Equation (4.22). The numerator, $S_t^e O_t(1-\tau)$, is the expected domestic currency value of the cash flow arising at time t. Hence, k_u is the domestic nominal discount rate, which reflects the project's systematic risk and all-equity financing. By applying the Fisher equation we obtain:

$$(1+k_u)^t = (1+\rho+\pi^e)^t \tag{4.23}$$

where ρ is the domestic real rate of return and π^e is the expected domestic inflation rate. More precisely, Equation (4.23) can be written as:

$$\begin{aligned}(1+k_u)^t &= (1+\rho+\pi^e+\rho\pi^e)^t \\ &= (1+\rho)^t(1+\pi^e)^t\end{aligned} \tag{4.24}$$

Let us assume that the exchange rate changes at a steady expected rate, $\dot{S}^e$. Hence:

$$S_t^e = S_0(1+\dot{S}^e)^t \tag{4.25}$$

Furthermore, if we assume that foreign currency cash flows grow at the foreign inflation rate, it follows that:

$$O_t = O_1(1 + \pi^{*e})^{t-1} \tag{4.26}$$

where π^{*e} is the expected foreign inflation rate. Therefore,

$$\sum_{t=1}^{n} \frac{S_t^e O_t(1 - \tau)}{(1 + k_u)^t} = S_0 \left[\frac{O_1}{1 + \pi^{*e}} \right] \sum_{t=1}^{n} \frac{(1 + S_t^e)^t(1 + \pi^{*e})^t(1 - \tau)}{(1 + \rho)^t (1 + \pi^e)} \tag{4.27}$$

Let us now invoke the *ex ante* purchasing power parity (PPP) condition, which tells us that the expected change in the exchange rate is determined by the expected inflation differential. In a precise (rather than an approximate) form, this condition can be written as:

$$\pi^e = \pi^{*e} + \dot{S}^e(1 + \pi^{*e}) \tag{4.28}$$

which can be manipulated to produce:

$$\frac{(1 + \dot{S}^e)(1 + \pi^{*e})}{(1 + \pi^e)} = 1 \tag{4.29}$$

By substituting Equation (4.29) into Equation (4.27), we can write the cash flow term in the APV equation as:

$$\sum_{t=1}^{n} \frac{S_t^e O_t(1 - \tau)}{(1 + k_u)^t} = S_0 \left[\frac{O_1}{1 + \pi^{*e}} \right] \sum_{t=1}^{n} \frac{(1 - \tau)}{(1 + \rho)^t} \tag{4.30}$$

which means that all we need to evaluate this expression is the initial exchange rate, S_0; the initial cash flow at today's prices, $O_1/(1 + \pi^{*e})$; the tax rate, τ; and the real discount rate that reflects systematic risk, ρ. This result depends on three assumptions: (i) cash flows can be expected to grow at the overall inflation rate; (ii) PPP holds; and (iii) the Fisher equation holds.

ADJUSTING PROJECT ASSESSMENT FOR RISK

International capital budgeting involves the consideration of more risk than domestic capital budgeting. Both domestic and international projects are subject to market risk, which is specific to industries and may involve the likely evolution of markets and competitor behaviour. The MNC may perceive the market risk for international projects as exceeding that associated with domestic projects. This may be attributed to the relative lack of knowledge about foreign markets.

International capital budgeting also involves a consideration of country risk, which is the risk of an adverse outcome arising from economic and political factors in the host country. For example, inflationary policies in the host country are an adverse factor for a subsidiary that depends on local supplies while exporting its products if there is no offsetting depreciation of the currency. Country risk would also be present if the government of the host country imposed import controls when a subsidiary depends on imported raw materials. It also involves changing the 'rules of the game', such as changes in tax laws and the regulations governing the repatriation of capital.

From the previous discussion, it is obvious that a typical project evaluation process consists of the following steps:

1. Estimating the incremental cash flows arising in the host country, taking into account any tax effects.
2. Estimating remittable cash flows to the MNC and translating these cash flows into the domestic currency at the spot exchange rates expected to prevail in each future time period.
3. Incorporating into the remitted cash flows any indirect costs and benefits, which arise as a result of undertaking the project. All tax effects applicable to the MNC must be considered at this stage.
4. Discounting the MNC's incremental cash flows at a rate that reflects the risk associated with the project or the particular cash flow.

When an MNC uses either the NPV or the APV method to evaluate foreign investment projects, typically a problem is encountered as to the accuracy of the cash flows that are expected to materialize in the future as a result of operating the project. Risk means that cash flows generated by the project may fluctuate far away from the expected value that would normally be used to calculate the NPV and the APV. If it is felt that this is the case, then some adjustment may be made to account for risk. There are three methods to deal with risk in situations like these.

The Risk Adjusted Discount Rate

The greater the risk associated with future cash flows, the greater should be the discount rate used to calculate the present value of the future cash flows, which is why the discount rate may differ from the cost of capital. This is also the reason why different discount rates are used in the APV formula, as more risky cash flows are discounted at higher rates. For example, cash flows associated with tax saving from depreciation and interest payments to creditors are less risky than operating cash flows, and this is why the latter is discounted at a higher rate.

This approach to the adjustment for risk is easy to implement, but it is criticized as being somewhat arbitrary. Furthermore, it does not take into account changes in the riskiness of cash flows from one time period to another, since the discount rate is assumed to be constant over time for a class of cash flows with a particular degree of risk. An example of changes in the riskiness of cash flows over time is changes in blocked funds and tax laws in a country with a high degree of political risk. Despite these shortcomings, the method of adjusting the discount rate is used because of its simplicity. It is also arguable that this technique is more appropriate for dealing with country risk than with market risk.

Risk Adjusted Cash Flows

Some economists argue that adjusting the cash flows is more appropriate than adjusting the discount rate, particularly if the project involves market risk. This approach, it is argued, allows the MNC to reflect more specifically the impact of the risk during the investment. Shapiro (1992) also argues that better information is available on the effect of risk on cash flows than on the discount rate.

This approach is normally known as the 'certainty equivalent approach', as it is based on a reduction of risky future cash flows to a lower level that is accepted by the market. This adjustment is made separately for each period of the project's life. The adjusted risk-free cash flows are then discounted at the risk-free discount rate to estimate the NPV of the project. The difference between this method and the adjusted discount rate method is that this method considers time and risk separately, whereas the previous method treats them jointly. Although this method is theoretically more appealing, it is not widely used because there are practical problems in identifying the equivalent risk-free cash flows.

In this case, the NPV formula is modified to the following:

$$\text{NPV} = -X_0 + \sum_{t=1}^{n} \frac{\theta_t X_t}{(1+k)^t} + \frac{\phi V_n}{(1+k)^n} \tag{4.31}$$

where $0 \leqslant \theta_t \leqslant 1$ is the certainty equivalent factor applicable to cash flow X_t, and $0 \leqslant \phi \leqslant 1$ is the certainty equivalent factor applicable to the salvage value, V_n. Because it is invariably the case that risk rises the further into the future the cash flow is, it follows that $\theta_1 > \theta_2 > \cdots > \theta_n$.

Sometimes, a problem arises as to accounting for risk by adjusting cash flows or adjusting the discount rate. The likelihood of a bad outcome should be allowed for in the calculation of the cash flows rather than by adjusting the discount rate. Suppose, for example, that there are two possible outcomes – good and bad. If the cash flow under the good and bad outcomes are $X_{i,t}$ and $X_{j,t}$, arising with probabilities p and $(1-p)$ respectively, then the cash flow $pX_{i,t} + (1-p)X_{j,t}$ should be discounted at the unadjusted discount rate. It would be wrong in this case to discount $X_{i,t}$ at a higher discount rate to reflect the possibility of a bad outcome.

Sensitivity Analysis

Sensitivity analysis entails the use of 'what if' scenarios, which are implemented by changing the input variables, including the exchange rate. If the NPV or APV remains positive for several scenarios, then the MNC should become more comfortable with the project. Sensitivity analysis can be applied to the discount rate or rates as well.

Simulation

Simulation can be used to generate a probability distribution for the NPV or the APV based on various combinations of the values of input variables. Consider, for example, a situation in which the exchange rate is forecast to be within a certain range, such that any value within this range can materialize with equal probability. A large number of iterations are performed; and in each iteration the value assumed by the exchange rate is picked randomly. This value is then used to calculate the cash flows and subsequently the NPV or APV. Each iteration produces a value for the NPV or APV, and after a large number of iterations there is an eventual probability distribution for

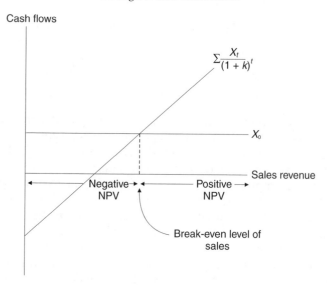

Figure 4.1   Break-even analysis in capital budgeting

the APV or the NPV. From this probability distribution it is possible to estimate the probability with which the NPV or APV will be positive.

Break-even Analysis

In break-even analysis, focus is placed on the point at which the NPV or the APV switches from positive to negative. In Figure 4.1, cash flows generated by a project are represented as depending on sales revenue. The initial cash flow, X_0, is represented by a horizontal line because it does not depend on sales revenue, whereas the present value of subsequent cash flows is a positive function of sales revenue. The point of intersection of the lines representing the initial cash flow and the present value of subsequent cash flows defines the level of sales that generates a zero NPV, the break-even level of sales. Below this level, the NPV is negative, and above it, the NPV is positive.

OTHER PROJECT EVALUATION CRITERIA

The NPV (and APV) are the most widely used project evaluation criteria. However, other criteria or measures of feasibility are available. These criteria are discussed briefly in turn.

The Accounting Rate of Return

The accounting rate of return is the percentage return on capital invested in the project, normally (but not necessarily) the average annual percentage profit before taxation relative to the average amount of capital invested in the project. This method is criticized because it is based on profit, which is an accounting concept, rather than on cash flows, which are more appropriate for a resource allocation decision-making problem such as capital investment. Another problem with this technique is that it takes no account of the size of the project or the time value of money. Moreover, the accounting rate of return is affected by accounting conventions such as the choice of the depreciation method. Simply stated, there is no 'correct way' of measuring the accounting rate of return.

It is cash flows, and not accounting profits, that should be discounted when NPV is calculated. Income statements, in which accounting profits are reported, are used to show how well the firm has performed, but they do not track cash flows. In principle, the profit figure is intended to measure changes in value, albeit imperfectly. (Operating) cash flows are funds generated by the firm's operations and are available for spending. The funds may be used to expand investment in fixed assets, to pay dividends, to expand working capital, to retire debt, or for a variety of other purposes.

Consider a project that costs X_0, producing X_t in year t, where $t = 1, \ldots, n$. Assuming a zero salvage value, the project's NPV is given by:

$$\text{NPV} = -X_0 + \sum_{t=1}^{n} \frac{X_t}{(1+k)^t} \tag{4.32}$$

If we calculate the NPV on the basis of accounting profits, the capital cost is depreciated over the life of the project. Hence, accounting profit for year t is $X_t - X_0/n$. In this case, the NPV will be given by the equation:

$$\text{NPV} = \sum_{t=1}^{n} \frac{X_t - X_0/n}{(1+k)^t} \tag{4.33}$$

which can be manipulated to produce:

$$\text{NPV} = -X_0 \sum_{t=1}^{n} \frac{1}{n(1+k)^t} + \sum_{t=1}^{n} \frac{X_t}{(1+k)^t} \tag{4.34}$$

which is obviously larger than in the original case. Hence, accounting profits give a misleading picture if project evaluation is based on them. This difference depends on whether investment expenditure is recognized when it occurs (the first case) or when it shows up as depreciation (the second case). The first case is more logical: projects are financially viable because of the cash flows they generate, either for distribution to shareholders or for reinvestment. One reason for the difference between cash flows and accounting profits is that accountants recognize profit when it is earned, not when it is realized.

The Payback Period

The payback period measures how quickly the initial outlay in an investment is paid back from after-tax cash flows generated from the investment. Only the projects that are paid back within a period of time that is acceptable to the investor will be undertaken. The payback period method is preferable to the accounting rate of return method because it is based on cash flows. However, it also ignores both the time value of money and the cash flows that occur after the initial investment has been paid back. Moreover, setting a maximum acceptable payback period is essentially an arbitrary decision: there is no easy way to relate the payback period to more general criteria, such as profit maximization or value maximization.

Because the risk associated with international projects increases as years into the future are considered, the payback period is often used as a 'shorthand' way of incorporating risk. Although this method is incomplete from the standpoint of financial theory, it has the advantage of providing a concrete cash-orientated measure of risk because it helps to answer the question: how long will the investor's funds be tied up in the project under consideration? It is because of this 'risk-bounding interpretation' of the payback period that this analysis is used as a constraint which needs to be satisfied before accepting the project. Of course, it is possible to adjust this method to take into account the time value of money by discounting the cash flows. However, the discounted payback criterion still takes no account of the cash flows arising after the cut-off date.

The Internal Rate of Return

The internal rate of return (IRR) is the discount rate that makes the NPV of a project equal to zero. It is calculated by solving for r the equation:

$$-X_0 + \sum_{t=1}^{n} \frac{X_t}{(1+r)^t} + \frac{V_n}{(1+r)^n} = 0 \qquad (4.36)$$

Thus, the IRR on a project with a zero NPV is equal to the discount rate or the cost of capital. A project will have a positive NPV if the IRR is greater than the cost of capital, and vice versa. The problem with the IRR, however, is that its calculation is based on the assumption that cash flows can be reinvested at the same rate, and this is not necessarily the case. Hence, it may be in conflict with NPV when competing projects have different sizes or time horizons. Moreover, under certain circumstances, a project will have multiple IRRs, which creates difficulty in interpreting the simple decision rule whereby a project is selected if the IRR is greater than the cost of capital. For example, how can we implement this rule if one of the values of the IRR is lower than the cost of capital?

In general, the NPV and IRR criteria may lead to conflicting conclusions when mutually exclusive projects have different scales, or when the time patterns of the cash flows are different. If such a conflict arises, the decision should be based on the NPV criterion.

The Profitability Index

The profitability index is calculated by dividing the present value of cash flows by the initial investment, X_0. Hence the profitability index (ignoring the salvage value) is given by:

$$PI = \frac{\sum_{t=1}^{n} \frac{X_t}{(1+k)^t}}{X_0} \qquad (4.37)$$

A project is undertaken if its profitability index is greater than one. To choose between two mutually exclusive projects, we pick the project that has a higher profitability index. A conflict may arise between the NPV and the PI in the case of mutually exclusive projects because of differences in the project size. In this case, the conflict should be resolved in favour of the NPV if the MNC is not under a capital rationing constraint (see Ross *et al.*, 1996, Chapter 6).

Which Criterion?

The NPV (and hence APV) is preferred to all the other criteria for (at least) three reasons:

1. The NPV recognizes the time value of money, which is important.
2. It is an objective criterion, depending mainly on the future cash flows and the discount rate. Criteria that depend on subjective factors (such as the manager's taste and accounting methods and standards) lead to inferior decisions.
3. Because the NPVs are measured in current monetary units, they can be added up. The additivity property is important, because it precludes the possibility that the decision-maker may be misled into accepting a poor project just because it is packaged with a good one.

CAPITAL BUDGETING FOR INTERNATIONAL ACQUISITIONS AND DIVESTITURES

MNCs assess constantly whether their volume of international business should be adjusted by resorting to international acquisitions or divestitures. We start by describing the methods used for assessing the feasibility of international acquisitions.

Assessing the Feasibility of International Acquisitions

An international acquisition of a firm is similar to other international projects in that it requires an initial outlay and is expected to generate cash flows whose present value will exceed the initial outlay. MNCs may view international acquisitions as being a better form of FDI than establishing a new subsidiary. This proposition is substantiated by the fact that FDI flows now predominantly take the form of mergers and acquisitions, as we saw in Chapter 1. However, there are distinct differences between them. By acquiring an existing firm in another country, the MNC can expand its international business immediately, since the target is already in place. Establishing a new subsidiary takes time. In terms of cost–benefit analysis, acquisitions are more expensive, but they are also more beneficial because (i) the acquired firms have established customer relationships; and (ii) they generate quicker and larger flows than new subsidiaries. International acquisitions also require the integration of the parent company's management style with that of the foreign target firm. The project evaluation criteria described earlier can be used for evaluating acquisitions.

A problem of valuation arises when the acquisition is directed at a privatized business in an emerging economy or an economy in transition. There are several reasons why this is the case. First, it is difficult to forecast cash flows because privatized businesses operate in an environment with little or no competition prior to privatization. Second, if the privatized business is located in a country whose currency is not floating, it would be extremely difficult to forecast the exchange rate factor. This is because privatization is normally coupled with other measures of financial liberalization and deregulation that impinge on the exchange rate arrangement. Eventually, the host country may decide to float its currency, making exchange rate movements significantly uncertain. Third, the existence of capital controls in these countries may make it difficult to determine the cost of capital, and hence the discount rate. Finally, the absence of established stock markets in these countries prevents an MNC from deriving a value for a business based on comparable public shareholding companies.

Divestiture Analysis

Divestiture analysis is needed when a decision as to whether to divest (dispose of) a project is being considered. Foreign projects that have been accepted must be assessed regularly in order to determine whether they should be continued or divested. Many divestitures occur as a result of a revised assessment of industry or economic conditions, or other factors. Divestiture analysis is conducted by comparing the after-tax proceeds from a possible sale of the project (in domestic currency terms) to the present value of the expected cash flows that the project will generate if it is not sold.

The decision to divest depends on the NPV of the divestiture, $(NPV)_d$, which is calculated as the difference between the selling price (the cash flow resulting from the divestiture) and the present value of the future cash flow. Suppose that an n-year project with a salvage value of V_n is taken at time 0 because it has a positive NPV. At the end of year m, there is an opportunity to sell the project at a price C. The NPV of the divestiture is calculated as:

$$(NPV)_d = C - \sum_{t=m+1}^{n} \frac{X_t}{(1+k)^t} + \frac{V_n}{(1+k)^n} \qquad (4.38)$$

The decision rule in this case is straightforward: accept the divestiture if $(NPV)_d > 0$.

WHERE TO GO FROM HERE?

This chapter has dealt with the methods or criteria used to determine the financial feasibility of FDI projects. For MNCs, profitability is a prime factor to be considered in FDI-related decisions. We have seen that the project evaluation criteria, as calculated from the expected cash flows, are affected by three important factors: political risk, taxation, and the cost of capital. This is why these terms arise frequently in the discussion. It is therefore obvious where we should go from here: we should go on a tour to explore these three factors. Thus, Chapter 5 will deal with country risk and political risk, Chapter 6 will investigate international taxation, and Chapter 7 will explore the area of international cost of capital.

5 Country Risk and Political Risk

Country risk represents a potentially adverse impact of a country's environment on the cash flows generated by an FDI project. Country risk analysis is important for a number of reasons. First, the MNC can use it as a screening device to avoid investing in countries with excessive risk. A second reason is that it can be used to monitor countries where the MNC is currently engaged in international business. In this case, a decision to divest (which may involve a change of the location of the production facilities) may be taken if it is felt that country risk has become excessive. A third reason why the study of country risk is important for MNCs is the need to assess particular forms of risk for a proposed project considered for a foreign country. These forms of risk may be general, such as economic risk and political risk, or they may be more specific, such as the risk of a take-over by the host government. Of course, all these problems can be avoided by keeping away from international business, but this strategy would preclude potentially profitable opportunities. Furthermore, it is the antithesis of being a multinational firm.

Apart from the general risks associated with any kind of investment (domestic or foreign), such as market risk and credit risk, investing outside a country's national frontiers entails more and different kinds of risk. These additional risks, which include currency risk and country risk, arise as a result of the nature of the foreign market. Investing abroad generally implies additional costs apart from the normal costs resulting from lack of knowledge about the foreign market. For example, currency risk arises because foreign investment necessarily means that the underlying assets are denominated in a foreign currency, whereas country risk arises because of economic and political factors that are specific to the country where the investment takes place. The result is a greater exposure to a more diversified set of risks.

COUNTRY RISK, SOVEREIGN RISK AND POLITICAL RISK

Considerable conceptual confusion surrounds the idea of country risk. The concepts of 'country risk', 'sovereign risk' and 'political risk' are often regarded, wrongly, as being interchangeable, when in fact they mean different things. Country risk is wider than either sovereign risk or political risk. We shall now describe the three concepts, but political risk will receive a more extensive treatment in subsequent sections because of its special relevance to FDI.

Country risk may be defined as exposure to a loss in cross-country transactions, caused by events in a particular country that are, at least to some extent, under the control of the government, but definitely not under the control of a private enterprise or individual. Country risk is a broader concept than sovereign risk. Any cross-border transaction is subject to country risk, whether this transaction is conducted with the government, with a private enterprise, or with an individual. Sovereign risk is limited to transactions (mainly lending) to the government of a sovereign country. Since this book is about FDI, not about bank lending, we shall not consider sovereign risk any further.

Only events that are, at least to some extent, under the control of the government can lead to the materialization of country risk. For example, a possible bankruptcy of a subsidiary is country risk if the bankruptcy is caused by a mismanagement of the economy by the government; but is commercial risk if it is the result of mismanagement by the firm. Consider also the case of national calamities. If they are unforeseeable, they cannot be considered to be country risk. But if past experience shows that they have the tendency to occur periodically, then the government can make preparations for such a contingency in order to minimize their harmful effects.

Country risk arises from political risk factors, and economic or financial risk factors. Hence, political risk is a subset of country risk arising from political risk factors. These include war, occupation by a foreign power, riots, disorder, attitude of consumers in the host country, attitude of the host government, changes in the rules and regulations governing FDI, blockage of fund transfers, currency inconvertibility, and bureaucracy. All these factors can obviously have adverse effects on the cash flows arising from FDI projects. In general, political risk refers to potential losses to a firm resulting from adverse developments in the host country. Events whereby political risk materializes range from the outright expropriation of assets to unexpected changes in the tax laws that hurt the profitability of FDI projects.

Economic factors pertain to the current and potential state of the economy. An MNC that exports to a country or establishes a subsidiary in a country should be concerned about the demand for its products in that country. This demand, naturally, is influenced strongly by the state of the country's economy. A recession in the country could reduce demand significantly because lower income leads to lower demand for all goods and services, including those that are imported. However, one has to be careful about the contribution of recession to economic and country risk. If the recession is worldwide and the government applies appropriate countercyclical policies, it is not country risk. But if the recession occurs in one country in isolation, or if it is aggravated by improper government policies, then it is country risk.

Because the state of a country's economy depends on several factors, an MNC should consider all these factors. Some of the obvious ones are interest rates, exchange rates, and inflation. High interest rates normally depress the economy and reduce the demand for the MNC's products, while low interest rates have the opposite effects. Exchange rates determine the country's demand for exports as well as the domestic currency value of the MNC's costs and revenues. This is why MNCs tend to establish production facilities in countries where currencies are undervalued, and sell their products in countries where currencies are overvalued. The problem is that the state of undervaluation or overvaluation may change over time. Inflation affects the purchasing power of consumers and can be an adverse factor for economic growth. Moreover, these three factors are intricately related. Interest rates and exchange rates are related, not only because higher interest rates attract capital flows and lead to currency appreciation, but also because uncovered interest parity (UIP) implies a direct relationship between the expected change in the exchange rate and the interest rate differential. Interest rates and inflation rates tend to move together, because they are related by the Fisher equation (stipulating a proportional relationship between the two variables), and because central banks tend to raise interest rates when inflation rises or is expected to rise. Finally, exchange rates and inflation rates are related by the purchasing power parity relationship, so that the higher the domestic inflation rate, the weaker will be the domestic currency.[1]

Consider, for example, an MNC operating in a country with a high inflation rate and a depreciating currency. Currency weakness threatens the long-term hard currency value (that is, the value in hard currency terms) of local profit and cash flows. High inflation, on the other hand, poses difficult operating problems, such as the problem of pricing products, and the inflation-induced financial accounting problems. The objective behind measuring country risk arising from these factors is to decide whether an investment in a country with these characteristics is worthy of being undertaken, and if it is, what kinds of measures should be taken to reduce their adverse effects. For example, the MNC may choose to export a substantial part of production to combat currency weakness. Another measure is to maximize the local content of the production process to reduce the problems of foreign currency costs. To reduce the effect of inflation, the MNC may choose to minimize cash and other asset holdings subject to the risks of inflation and hence declining real values.

Thus, country risk is broader than calculating the probability that a subsidiary will be taken over by the host government. The latter is one kind of political risk, which is a subset of country risk. The assessment of country risk includes the assessment of political risk and economic risk that can influence cash flows. Furthermore, one has to bear in mind that political risk events are often triggered by economic factors. Political risk is thus not always entirely independent of economic risk. For example, a persistent trade deficit may induce the host country's government to delay or stop interest payments to foreign lenders, erect trade barriers, or suspend the convertibility of the currency, causing major difficulties for MNCs. Severe inequality in income distribution and deteriorating living standards can cause major political disturbances. For example, in 1977, Egypt witnessed popular revolt against a massive rise in the price of bread resulting from the implementation of some IMF-prescribed economic policies that included the abolition of subsidies. In this chapter we deal more extensively with political risk rather than economic risk, since it is more relevant to FDI.

COUNTRY RISK ASSESSMENT

Although there is no consensus on how country risk can best be assessed, some guidelines have been developed for this purpose. The first step is to recognize the difference between macro-assessment and micro-assessment of country risk. Macro-assessment refers to the overall risk assessment of a country without consideration of the specific characteristics of the MNC's business. Micro-assessment, on the other hand, refers to the risk assessment of a country as related to the particular characteristics of the business in which the MNC indulges.

Macro-assessment involves a consideration of all the variables that affect country risk except for those that are unique to a particular industry. This type of assessment is convenient, because it remains the same for a given country, regardless of the firm or industry under consideration. This is the assessment underlying the country risk ratings found in financial magazines such as *Euromoney* and *Institutional Investor*. Thus, macro-assessment of country risk is not ideal for an individual MNC because it excludes relevant information that could lead to an improvement in the accuracy of the assessment. However, macro-assessment could serve as a foundation that can be modified to reflect the particular business in which the MNC is involved. In this case, the macro-assessment may be carried out by an external party, such as *Euromoney* magazine, whereas the micro-assessment is carried out by the MNC.

Macro-assessment involves a consideration of both political and economic indicators of the country under examination.[2] Political factors include, *inter alia*, the relationship between the host government and the MNC's home country's government, the historical stability of the host government, the probability of war, the probability of changing the rules of the game, and so on. The economic factors should include the main macroeconomic indicators, both current and projected, such as economic growth, inflation, the fiscal balance (budget deficit or surplus), interest rates, unemployment, the extent to which the country relies on export income, the balance of payments and its components, and so on.

There is normally some subjectivity in identifying each of the relevant political and economic factors for the macro-assessment of country risk. There is also some subjectivity in determining the weights assigned to each factor. Furthermore, there are some differences in predicting these factors. However, it seems that as far as FDI is concerned, political risk factors are more important than economic ones. A study by Petry and Sprow (1993) has identified the factors with the greatest potential impact on the profitability of large MNCs. In order of importance, these factors are: (i) restrictive practices; (ii) tariffs or regulations; (iii) unstable currencies; (iv) foreign government subsidies; (v) shaky government; and (vi) national debt.[3]

Micro-assessment of country risk involves the evaluation of micro-political risk and microeconomic risk. Micro-political risk can be best illustrated with the following example. Suppose that a country has received a very good score for macroeconomic risk. The government of that country is, however, sensitive to foreign ownership of mining operations of uranium, but not to other operations, mining or otherwise. If this government is considering some legislation curtailing foreign ownership of uranium mining operations, then there is high (micro) country risk for an MNC considering starting uranium mining operations there. However, other MNCs will not be subject to this kind of risk. Microeconomic risk results from the sensitivity of the MNC's earnings to changes in the economic environment. Consider, for example, two MNCs operating in the same country: one of them produces electricity, while the other produces luxury clothing. Since the demand for electricity is less cyclical than the demand for luxury clothing, the first MNC's earnings will be less sensitive to economic growth and the business cycle than the earnings of the second MNC. Hence, a country with a good evaluation in the macro-assessment may end up with a low overall evaluation when the micro-assessment is taken into account, and vice versa.

Once the macro and micro factors have been identified, a number of techniques can be used to evaluate these factors. These techniques, which can be used in conjunction with each other, include the following:

The Checklist Approach

The checklist approach involves judgement on all the political and economic factors that are believed to contribute to country risk. Some of these factors (such as the current growth rate or inflation rate) are readily available. Others (such as the future growth rate and inflation rate, and the probability of a civil war) have to be assessed on a judgemental basis. These factors are then assigned weights and used to calculate a score.

The Delphi Technique

The Delphi technique involves the collection of independent opinions on country risk with no group discussion by the assessors who provide the opinions. The advantage of this technique is that the individual assessors (who may be the MNC's employees, external consultants, or both) will not be subject to group pressure when they form their opinions. The project leader has the task of collecting the individual views of the participants to come up with a 'consensus' view. The degree of disagreement can also be assessed by measuring the dispersion of opinions.

Quantitative Analysis

Quantitative analysis involves the use of statistical techniques to analyse data on the factors contributing to country risk. For example, discriminant analysis can be used to distinguish between a country with tolerable risk and another with intolerable risk. Regression analysis can also be used for this purpose, since it can measure the sensitivity of one variable against another. For example, regression analysis can give us an idea about the quantitative effect of changes in the growth rate, inflation rate and interest rate on an MNC's earnings. The problem with quantitative analysis is that the conclusions derived from it are based on historical data. Naturally, there is no guarantee that a relationship that has held so far will hold into the future. But it is the future we are interested in, since the outcome of a decision taken now is contingent upon what will happen in the future. In fact, there is no guarantee that the relationship will remain stable during the historical period over which it is estimated.[4] Another problem with quantitative analysis is that some important risk elements are not quantifiable. For more details on the general problem of trying to generate forecasts from a regression model, see Moosa (2000a).

The Old Hands Method

The old hands method amounts to collecting information from diplomats, journalists, economists, financial analysts and other professionals who have some expert knowledge of the country in question. These professionals typically are external to the firm. Two drawbacks of this method are its unsystematic character, and the fact that it is based on the judgement of outsiders. However, Rummel and Heenan (1978) point out that the old hands method is capable of providing firms with an improved understanding of developments in the country under discussion.

Inspection Visits

Inspection visits involve travelling to a country and meeting government officials, business people and consumers. Meeting these parties helps to clarify opinion about the country. The same task can be accomplished via a representative office in the country. Major banks and other MNCs establish representative offices in other countries for the purpose of following up political and economic developments. All the information that is gathered is then analysed and evaluated.

A shortcoming of this method is what Rummel and Heenan (1978) call an 'overdose of selective information'.

QUANTIFYING COUNTRY RISK

Once the political and economic risk factors have been evaluated, two things can be done with them: (i) the construction of a foreign investment risk diagram; and (ii) quantifying overall country risk. We start with a description of the foreign investment risk diagram.

A foreign investment risk diagram is shown in Figure 5.1, where economic risk is measured on the horizontal axis and political risk is measured on the vertical axis. The scale for risk ranges from zero (no risk) to 100 (maximum risk).[5] The firm's risk preferences are represented in the diagram. The firm can accept economic risk up to 70, is not sure for levels of economic risk between 70 and 80, and certainly will not accept a level of economic risk above 80. As far as political risk is concerned, the firm accepts a level up to 60, is not sure about levels between 60 and 70, and definitely will not accept a level above 70. The points marked on the horizontal and vertical axes are connected by

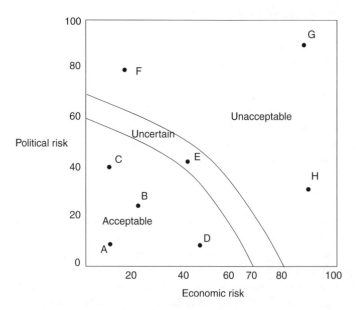

Figure 5.1   Foreign investment risk diagram

concave curves that reflect the trade-off between economic risk and political risk. The diagram is divided into three zones. Countries A, B, C and D fall into the acceptable zone. All these countries are acceptable, but given the choice between countries A and B, the firm will choose country A because it has both a lower political risk and a lower economic risk. The choice between countries C and D is not quite as clear, as it depends on the firm's preferences. Country C has more political risk, whereas country D has more economic risk. Countries F, G and H fall into the unacceptable zone because they have unacceptable political risk (F), unacceptable economic risk (H), or both (G). Finally, there is the uncertain zone where country E falls. This country has a level of economic risk between 70 and 80, and a level of political risk in the range 60–70. This case may be re-examined to find out if country E can be reclassified to fall into the acceptable zone.

The foreign investment risk diagram reflects the importance of political risk relative to economic risk. The shallower the curves representing the trade-off between political and economic risk, the lower the maximum amount of political risk and the greater the maximum amount of economic risk the firm is willing to bear. Figure 5.2 shows that a reduction in the level of political risk from P_1 to P_2 is accepted for a large increase in economic risk (from E_1 to E_2).

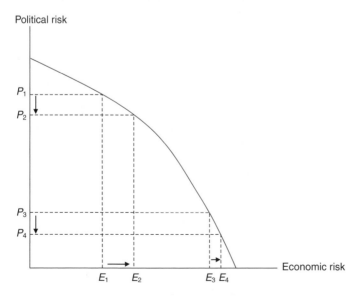

Figure 5.2 The trade-off between political risk and economic risk

However, if we start from a lower level of political risk, say P_3, then the same reduction in political risk as before (from P_3 to P_4, which is equal to the reduction from P_1 to P_2) will be acceptable at the cost of a smaller increase in economic risk (from E_3 to E_4, which is smaller than the reduction from E_1 to E_2). Thus, the foreign investment risk diagram is firm-specific, and this should be the case because the relative importance of the two kinds of risk varies from one firm to another. If an MNC wants to indulge in FDI to attract demand in a foreign country then it must be highly concerned about economic risk. If, on the other hand, another firm has the objective of locating an FDI in the country under consideration to exploit low production costs and export the products, then political risk would be more important. The first firm has more tolerance for political risk than for economic risk, whereas the second firm has more tolerance for economic risk. These two firms have foreign investment risk diagrams that look like diagrams A and B in Figure 5.3. Some firms have high tolerance for both kinds of risk, while others have low tolerance for both. These two cases are represented by diagrams C and D in Figure 5.3. There are also firms that are willing to accept the maximum amount of political risk if they are compensated by low economic risk (diagram E), and those that are willing to accept the maximum amount of economic risk if they are compensated by low political risk (diagram F). Finally, there are firms that are willing to accept the maximum amount of either kind of risk if they are compensated by a lower amount of the other kind of risk (diagram G).

While a foreign investment risk diagram may be useful for an MNC, it does not quantify the overall risk rating for an individual country, which requires the combination of political and economic risk factors. Suppose that there are m political risk factors: $P_1, P_2, \ldots, P_m$, and n economic risk factors: $E_1, E_2, \ldots, E_n$. Let us assign the weights $v_1, v_2, \ldots, v_m$ to the political risk factors, and $w_1, w_2, \ldots, w_n$ to the economic risk factors. The political risk score, P, and the economic risk score, E, are given, respectively, by:

$$P = \sum_{i=1}^{m} v_i P_i \tag{5.1}$$

and:

$$E = \sum_{i=1}^{n} w_i E_i \tag{5.2}$$

141

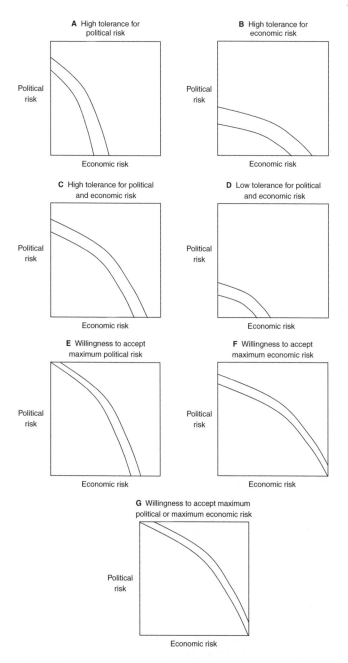

Figure 5.3 Risk tolerance as represented by the foreign investment risk diagram

If political risk and economic risk are assigned the weights λ_P and λ_E, respectively, then the overall country risk score, S, is given by:

$$S = \lambda_P P + \lambda_E E = \lambda_P \sum_{i=1}^{m} v_i P_i + \lambda_E \sum_{i=1}^{m} w_i E_i \qquad (5.3)$$

It should be emphasized at this stage that country risk assessors have their individual procedures for quantifying country risk, which may differ from the one described in this section. In fact, it is often the case that the system is designed in such a way that a high score implies low risk, and vice versa. Here, the system is designed so that a high score means higher risk, which is easier to understand. In the following section, we describe a system that is used in practice, whereby the lowest risk country has the highest score, and vice versa.

AN EXAMPLE OF MACRO-ASSESSMENT: THE *EUROMONEY* METHODOLOGY

Periodically, *Euromoney* magazine publishes tables of country risk ratings. These ratings are based on country risk scores ranging from 100 (risk free) to zero (ultimate risk). The overall score is calculated as the sum of the individual scores corresponding to each of nine indicators, that is:

$$S_j = \sum_{i=1}^{9} S_{ij} \qquad (5.4)$$

where S_j is the country risk score of country j and S_{ij} is the jth country's score corresponding to factor or indicator i, where $i = 1, \ldots, 9$. The individual scores are calculated by assigning a weight, w_i (expressed as a percentage, not as a decimal), to indicator i, such that $0 \leqslant S_i \leqslant w_i$. The exact formula that is used to calculate S_{ij} is:

$$S_{ij} = w_i - \left[\frac{w_i}{\ell - h}\right](x_{ij} - h) \qquad (5.5)$$

where ℓ is the lowest value in the range, h is the highest value and x_{ij} is the value of the ith factor for country j. Table 5.1 reports the nine indicators and the maximum scores (which are equal to the weights, w_i) on each of these indicators. Ramcharran (1999) uses the *Euro-*

Table 5.1 Elements of the *Euromoney* country risk scores

Indicator	Max (w_i)	Description
Political Risk	25	Defined as the risk of non-payment or non-servicing of payments for goods, services, loans, trade-related finance and dividends, and the non-repatriation of capital.
Economic performance	25	Based on income per capita and economic forecasts
Debt indicators	10	Calculated from three ratios: debt to income; debt service to exports; and current account balance to GNP
Debt in default or rescheduled	10	Based on the ratio of rescheduled debt to debt stock
Credit rating	10	Based on the ratings of Moody's, Standard & Poor's, and Fitch IBCA
Access to bank finance	5	Calculated from disbursements of private long-term unguaranteed loans as a percentage of GNP
Access to Short-term finance	5	Based on the views of the OECD and the US Export Import Bank
Access to capital markets	5	Based on surveys of debt syndicates
Discounts on forfeiting	5	Reflects the average maximum tenor for forfeiting and the average spread over riskless countries

Source: *Euromoney*, September 1999, p. 254.

money risk measures to study the relationship between FDI and country risk over a period of three years.

Obviously, this system is different from the system described in the previous section, not only because a high score implies low risk, but also because other factors are taken into account as well as political risk and economic risk. Indeed, political risk and economic risk combined command half the total weight, whereas measures of indebtedness comprise the other 50 per cent of the weight. These measures of indebtedness are important for banks whose transactions are mainly cross-border lending, but not so important for FDI. Indeed, even political risk is defined (for the purpose of this measure) as the risk

Table 5.2   Country risk scores

Country	S_1	S_2	P	E	S(P)	S(E)
Switzerland	24.74	23.05	1.04	7.80	3.07	5.77
Japan	23.26	19.31	6.96	22.76	11.70	18.02
Greece	18.61	13.61	25.56	45.56	31.56	39.56
Egypt	13.08	8.04	47.68	67.84	53.73	61.79
Brazil	10.37	8.35	58.52	66.60	60.94	64.18
Vanuatu	10.09	9.85	59.64	60.60	59.93	60.31
Senegal	6.54	6.70	73.84	73.20	73.65	73.39
Belarus	3.06	3.81	87.76	84.76	86.86	85.66
Somalia	0.59	4.52	97.64	81.92	92.92	86.64
Cuba	2.02	3.97	91.92	84.12	89.58	86.46

Source: *Euromoney*, September 1999, pp. 251–3.

of non-payment and non-servicing of payment, which is rather different from what we have seen so far.

But let us for the time being assume that political risk is political risk no matter how it is defined. We can then convert the scores obtained from the *Euromoney* system to the scores that can be obtained from the system suggested in the previous section, which is based on economic risk and political risk only. Table 5.2 illustrates an example for ten countries with varying degrees of country risk.

Let us now figure out what Table 5.2 tells us. The first two columns report the political and economic country scores, S_1 and S_2, according to the *Euromoney* system as at September 1999.[6] These scores are out of 25, with a high number indicating low risk. Thus, Switzerland has both the lowest political risk and the lowest economic risk, Somalia has the highest political risk, and Belarus has the highest economic risk. P and E are the political and economic risk scores calculated by converting the *Euromoney* scores to match the system described in the previous section. The conversion is based on the formulae $P = 4(25 - S_1)$ and $E = 4(25 - S_2)$. Now, the higher the score, the higher the risk.

We can use Equation (5.3) to calculate the country risk scores by assigning values to the weights λ_P and λ_E. We obtain the country risk scores under $S(P)$ if we let $\lambda_P = 0.7$ and $\lambda_E = 0.3$, that is for MNCs assigning greater weight to political risk. Alternatively, we obtain the country risk scores under $S(E)$ if we let $\lambda_P = 0.3$ and $\lambda_E = 0.7$, that is for MNCs assigning greater weight to economic risk. According to $S(P)$ and $S(E)$, Switzerland has the lowest country risk, whereas Somalia has the highest country risk.

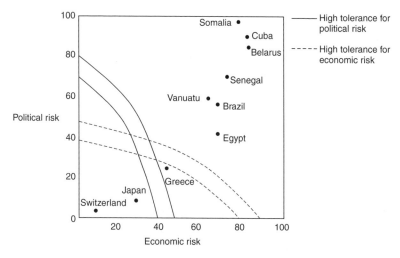

Figure 5.4 Foreign investment risk diagram with actual scores

We can use the data on P and E to draw investment risk diagrams for a firm with a high tolerance of political risk and for a firm with a high tolerance of economic risk. These are shown in Figure 5.4. The firm with the high tolerance of political risk accepts a maximum amount of political risk of 70 with an uncertain range of 70–80, while accepting a maximum amount of economic risk of 40, with an uncertain range of 40–50. The firm with the high tolerance for economic risk accepts a maximum amount of economic risk of 80 with an uncertain range of 80–90, while it accepts a maximum amount of political risk of 40, with an uncertain range of 40–50. For the first firm, only two countries fall in the acceptable zone: Switzerland and Japan. For the second firm, a third country is acceptable, namely, Greece.

THE USE OF COUNTRY RISK ANALYSIS

Once the degree of country risk has been determined, the next step is to decide whether or not the risk is tolerable. If it is felt that the risk is too high then the firm does not need to analyse the feasibility of a project to be undertaken in that country. Of course, it may be argued that no risk is too high if the rate of return on the underlying project is high enough to compensate for the risk. However, in some cases, the risk is considered to be so high that the country is deemed to be off limits. This would be the case if, for example, the country has a tendency to experience civil war or kidnapping of foreign personnel for ransom. This would also be the case if the probability of confiscation is too high as judged from historical experience.

Country risk analysis can also be incorporated in capital budgeting analysis, as suggested by Robock (1971), Kobrin (1979), Raddock (1986), Sethi and Luther (1986) and Clark (1997). One way to do this is by adjusting the discount rate or the cash flows. The higher the country risk, the higher the discount rate applied to the project's cash flows. If, for example, blocked funds are anticipated, then the discount rate may be raised from 10 per cent to 13 per cent. The problem with this procedure is that there is no precise formula for adjusting the discount rate for country risk, which makes adjustment rather arbitrary. The use of a shorter payback period can be used for the same purpose. However, Haendel (1979) argues that neither of these two methods provides a detailed examination of the risk involved, or a true reflection of the investor's fear. This is why it may be preferable to incorporate country risk analysis by adjusting the cash flows, as suggested by Shapiro (1992).

Suppose that a project is analysed under three scenarios derived from country risk analysis: (i) that nothing will happen; (ii) that the host country will block a certain percentage of the funds to be transferred to the parent firm; and (iii) that the project will be confiscated after few years. Suppose also that these scenarios produce three net present values (NPV_1, NPV_2 and NPV_3) with probabilities of p_1, p_2 and p_3 respectively. The NPV of the project in this case should be calculated as the expected NPV, which is the weighted average of NPV_1, NPV_2 and NPV_3, where the weights are the probabilities. Hence:

$$NPV = \sum_{i=1}^{3} p_i NPV_i \qquad (5.6)$$

Levi (1990) has suggested the following formalization of the process whereby country risk is allowed for in capital budgeting. Let X_t be the cash flow expected to arise from a project in the absence of country risk. Assume that country risk is present, so that the project would cease to exist (for example, because of a take-over by the host government) at year t with a probability p. Hence the probability that a cash flow arises in each individual year is $1 - p$. This means that the probability that cash flows arise for t years is $(1 - p)^t$. The expected value of the cash flow in year t is $X_t(1-p)^t$. If X_t is constant so that $X_t = \bar{X}$, then the present value of the cash flow is given by:

$$PV = \sum_{t=1}^{n} \frac{(1-p)^t X_t}{(1+k)^t} = \bar{X} \sum_{t=1}^{n} \frac{(1-p)^t}{(1+k)^t} \tag{5.7}$$

As $n \to \infty$, we obtain:

$$\sum_{t=1}^{n} \frac{(1-p)^t}{(1+k)^t} = \frac{1-p}{k+p} \tag{5.8}$$

Hence:

$$PV = \frac{\bar{X}(1-p)}{k+p} \tag{5.9}$$

In the absence of country risk, we have:

$$PV = \frac{\bar{X}}{k} \tag{5.10}$$

It is obvious that the present value of the cash flows in the absence of country risk is greater than that obtained when country risk is present.

Agmon (1985) has suggested a workable and comprehensive way to integrate country risk into capital budgeting. Agmon's method is based on the proposition that the potential dependence of a project on the external environment is divided into two components: vulnerability and cost. Vulnerability is expressed in terms of the probability that an event that is likely to affect the project (such as tax changes) will occur. Vulnerability is also defined in terms of a probability distribution, and for simplicity it is assumed that the distribution can be described fully by its first and second moments. Cost, on the other hand, is measured as the actual impact on the cash flows of the project if a given event occurs. The distinction between vulnerability and cost is crucial, because firms do not need to be concerned with all possible events. Only the non-trivial effects on cash flows have to be weighted by the probabilities that they will take place.

In general, there are three approaches to the integration of country risk into capital budgeting. The first is the approach suggested by Shapiro (1992), which involves the adjustment of the expected cash flows to account for losses caused by country risk. Buckley's (1996) approach is a refinement of Shapiro's approach in the sense that

Buckley attempts to devise a general formula for integrating country risk into capital budgeting. The second approach has been suggested by Clark (1997). This approach involves the measurement of the effects of country risk on the outcome of investment as the value of an insurance policy that reimburses all losses resulting from an event. The third approach, which has been suggested by Mahajan (1990), is based on the use of option valuation theory to derive the pricing of country risk, particularly the risk of expropriation. Wafo (1998) justifies the use of this approach by the following argument: if the likelihood of expropriation depends on project outcomes, then the only proper valuation technique is contingent claims analysis. Wafo also argues that standard valuation approaches, such as the adjustment of future cash flows, are adequate only when the probability of expropriation is independent of the value of the project.

POLITICAL RISK: THE DEFINITION ONCE MORE

Political risk is the part of country risk that is normally more relevant to FDI. Most of the literature on FDI refers to political risk, and not to country risk, which may be more relevant to international lending by banks (see, for example, Nagy, 1979). Because of the special importance of political risk, the rest of this chapter is devoted to a more elaborate treatment of this kind of risk.

The concept of political risk has been around for some time. Baskin and Miranti (1997) suggest that attempts were made in the seventeenth century to deal with various sorts of risk, including political risk. The concept of political risk started to appear in the literature when it became important in the 1960s as newly independent countries tried to overcome their capital shortage problems by taking over the MNCs. Thus, expropriation and nationalization became critical concerns in the 1960s for companies with foreign operations. After the ousting of the Shah of Iran in 1979, political instability was added to confiscation, nationalization and expropriation as a source of political risk. For example, four months before the removal of the Shah, a country risk assessor for Gulf Oil detected severe political pressure building within Iran. As a result, the company began planning to deal with the subsequent loss of Iranian oil, which at one time amounted to 10 per cent of its crude supplies.

The increasing realization of the importance of political risk led to attempts to quantify it. Rummel and Heenan (1978) conducted the first study that dealt with the assessment of political risk, in which they proposed a method for converting political instability into probabilistic terms, thus providing a scientific definition of political risk. Another attempt to define and assess political risk is represented by the development, by Theodore Haner, of the business environment risk information index (BERI) as a quantitative guide to political risk ratings. In 1979, William Copli and Michael O'Leary began to develop the Political Risk Services (PRS) evaluation system, which was used widely by MNCs in the 1980s. Since then, new approaches to political risk have been developed, with the aim of quantifying political risk and integrating it into the decision-making process of an enterprise.

Wafo (1998) summarizes the historical evolution of the concept of political risk as follows:

1. In the period from antiquity to the 1960s, there was neither an elaborate concept of political risk nor a precise political risk consciousness, although the manifestations of political risk were taken into account.
2. In the 1970s, the birth of the concept of political risk was linked to the spread of collective doctrines (nationalism and Marxism).
3. In the period since the 1980s, the concept of political risk has assumed increasing importance for academics and professionals alike. This period has also witnessed the birth of quantitative risk assessment methods, the probabilistic interpretation of political risk, and the systematic use of these quantitative approaches on the corporate level by the professionals.
4. The period since 1990 has witnessed the scientific refinement of the concept of political risk through the contribution of other fields of research such as political science, sociology, decision theory and psychology.

Let us now turn to the task of finding a precise definition for political risk. Before analysing political risk it must be defined, and it must be defined precisely. However, despite the widespread coverage of the subject, political risk has not received a clear-cut consensus definition. Indeed, Rummel and Heenan (1978) refer to political risk as 'one of the most misunderstood and misinterpreted aspects of multinational operations'. The literature contains various definitions of political risk. It can be defined as 'unpredictable demands raised by foreign state or society on the assets, returns or cash variable of shareholders from international investment' (Wafo, 1998). Robock and Simmonds

Table 5.3 Sources of political risk

Source	Manifestation
Restrictions on entry of foreign investors	Restrictions on entry of foreign investors
	Restrictions on the types of enterprises that foreign investors may undertake
	Restrictions on ownership
Systems for controlling FDI inflows	Outright ban on selected industries
	Vague criteria on official approval of FDI
	High taxes and weak incentives
	Equity limits
	Local content requirement rules
Limits on foreign exchange transfers	Restrictions on capital and profit repatriation
	Long repatriation deals
	Limits on repatriation by net worth
	Limits on repatriation by foreign exchange earnings
Government intervention	Price controls
	Setting prices for natural resource expropriation
	Regulating monopolies
	Large state enterprises sector
Social instability	Fragile political structures
	Weak organizational level in the society
	Corruption
Political violence	Crime
	Civil war
	Civil disobedience
	Riots
Government incapability	Inability to regulate the economy and conduct reforms
	Lack of democratic institutions and spirit
Turbulent relations with international organizations	Turbulent relations with the IMF and the World Bank
	Turbulent relations with the UN
Lack of commitment to international environment and labour rules	
Turbulent relations with foreign investors in the previous five years	Lack of commitment to bilateral investment rules
	Subtle expropriation of gained returns
Hostile attitude of elites and society towards FDI	Hostile declarations of parties
	Hostile programmes
Hostile attitudes towards foreigners	Violence against foreigners
	Intolerance towards foreigners
	Restriction on expatriate labour
Reluctance of host countries to reveal reliable information	Lack of transparency
	Secrecy with respect to most political and economic decisions

Source: Wafo (1998).

(1973) view political risk as existing in international investment when discontinuities occur in the business environment as a result of unanticipated political change. Another definition is presented by Haendel (1979), who defines political risk as the risk or probability of occurrence of some political event(s) that will change the prospects for the profitability of a given investment.

A simple and straightforward definition of political risk is that it is that part of country risk related to political factors. We have already stated a number of political factors that give rise to political risk. Now, we look at a comprehensive list of political risk factors as presented by Wafo (1998). The political risk factors or sources of political risk are classified under thirteen different headings, as shown in Table 5.3. The terms are mostly self-explanatory.

Political risk may be classified according to two criteria: (i) incidence; and (ii) the manner in which political events affect the investing firms. If incidence is used as a criterion for classification, then political risk can be classified into macro risk and micro risk. Macro risk pertains to the situations when FDI is affected by adverse political developments in the host country, irrespective of the nature of the investor or the underlying project. Micro risk, on the other hand, implies that only selected areas of FDI or particular firms are affected. For example, a military take-over of the government in the host country is a macro political risk, but new legislation restricting foreign ownership in the mining sector is a micro risk, affecting only firms involved in the mining industry.

If the manner in which firms are affected is used as a criterion for classification, then political risk can be classified into three kinds:

1. Transfer risk, which arises from uncertainty about cross-border flows of capital, payments, know-how and so on. One example of transfer risk is the unexpected imposition of capital controls, and withholding taxes on dividends and interest payments.
2. Operational risk, which is associated with uncertainty about the host country's policies affecting FDI. One example of operational risk is changes in environmental policies and minimum wage legislation.
3. Control risk, which arises from uncertainty about the host country's policy regarding ownership and control operations. An example is the nationalization of the local operations of MNCs. This happened, for example, when Mao Zedong took power in China in 1994, and when Castro took over in Cuba in 1960. In the

1950s, Gamal Abdul Nasser nationalized the Suez Canal, which was controlled by British and French interests, eventually leading to the invasion of Egypt by Britain, France and Israel in 1956.

POLITICAL RISK INDICATORS

Political risk indicators are designed to give the corporate manager some idea about the political environment in a country. They are designed to forecast the future political evolution of a particular country. Two kinds of political indicators are generally available: general indicators and partial indicators. General political risk indicators are based on all available political variables, designed to describe fully the political situation in a country. Partial political risk indicators are based on one political variable such as democracy, political violence or government stability.

Rummel and Heenan (1978) describe the general political risk indicators as aiming at anticipating changes in government policies and personnel, and at providing qualitative evaluation of the positions

Table 5.4   Political risk elements in the PRI

Category	Factor
Internal causes of political risk	Fractionalization of the political spectrum and the power of these fractions
	Fractionalization by language, ethnic and/or religious groups and the power of these fractions
	Restrictive (coercive) measures required to retain power
	Mentality, including xenophobia, nationalism, corruption, nepotism, willingness to compromise
	Social conditions, including population density and wealth distribution
	Organization and strength of forces for a radical left-wing government
External causes of political risk	Dependence on and/or importance to a hostile major power
	Negative influence of regional political forces
Symptoms of political risk	Social conflict involving demonstrations, strikes and street violence
	Instability as perceived by non-constitutional changes, assassinations, and guerrilla wars

Source: Wafo (1998).

to be taken by opposition parties or pressure groups. One of the most frequently used general political risk indicators is the business risk environment information index (BERI). In constructing this index, socio-political changes are measured by the political risk indicator (PRI) and constitute only one part of the country risk assessment. The PRI is based on ten elements classified under three headings, as shown in Table 5.4.

The PRI takes values ranging between 0 (the lowest rating, and thus the highest risk) and 100 (the highest rating, and hence the lowest risk). A country with a PRI of 70–100 has a low risk in the sense that political changes will not lead to conditions that are seriously adverse to business. A PRI in the range 55–69 indicates moderate risk in the sense that political changes that are seriously adverse to business have occurred but, under the government in power, there is a low probability that such changes will occur in the future. A PRI of 40–54 implies high risk, in the sense that political developments with serious consequences for business, exist or could materialize in the future. Finally, a PRI of 0–39 implies prohibitive risk in the sense that political conditions severely restrict business operations and that a loss of assets is possible. This scaling is represented diagrammatically in Figure 5.5. Another general indicator of political risk is the world political risk forecasts (WPRF). This indicator is heavily based on expert opinion which is used to build up a predictive political view of the underlying country.

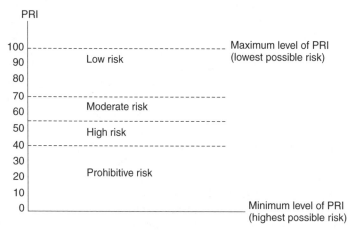

Figure 5.5   Interpretation of the values of PRI

Partial political indicators pertain to, or are based on, one part of the political system. Examples of partial political indicators are the government stability indicators and those measuring democracy, political violence, political volatility, and corruption. There are, for example, two methods for calculating indicators of government stability from published data. The first is based on the average, over a given period of time, of such incidents as coups and government changes. The second approach is based on the probability of a government change, estimated from a probit regression.

Political risk indicators are used to monitor political risk after a project has been taken. The political environment in any country is dynamic in the sense that it changes over time. Changes taking place over time include changes in the laws and regulations affecting FDI in general, or the underlying project in particular, as well as changes in public opinion. This is why the monitoring of political risk after a project has been implemented is crucial. Haendel (1979) suggests that the monitoring of political risk can be accomplished by using Bayesian analysis, which serves to revive (on the basis of new information) the prior probabilities used initially to calculate the NPV. Schweitzer (1976) describes how the CIA used Bayesian analysis to predict political changes in the Middle East.

Monitoring political risk also means explaining the nature of the relationship between the host country and the investor. In this sense, FDI decisions are seen as resulting from negotiations between the host country and the investor. One way to understand the nature of the relationship between the two parties is by resorting to Vernon's (1968) theory of 'obsolescing bargaining'. This theory essentially reflects the concerns of foreign investors in developing countries over the possibility that government policies might easily change *ex post* (that is, after the implementation of the project) in ways that are detrimental to the profitability of the investment. The theory refers to changes in the relative bargaining power of the country and the investor over time. A variety of considerations suggest that the bargaining position of the host country generally strengthens over time relative to that of the investor. One explanation for this proposition is based on informational asymmetry, as the host country has access to all information needed by the investor, to which the investor does not have access. However, given the financial power of MNCs and their full control over technology transfer, any increase in the host country's bargaining power will most probably be marginal.

THE EFFECTS AND MANAGEMENT OF POLITICAL RISK

Research has shown that the main determinants of the decision to invest abroad are market prospects and risk factors. Political risk is obviously part of the risk considerations, and this is particularly the case with investment in less developed countries. Burgmann (1996) concludes that some factors contribute to the increased risk of MNCs compared to domestic firms, and these include foreign exchange risk, political risk and tax uncertainty. Ramcharran (1999) examined the effect of political and economic risk on FDI for twenty-six countries using cross-sectional data for the years 1992, 1993 and 1994. He found a significant relationship between FDI and these risks.

The management of political risk includes the identification and assessment of political risk, its quantification, the anticipation of losses and the prevention or reduction of the incidence of losses. Kelly (1974) identifies the following five steps in the management of the political risk associated with FDI:

1. The identification and analysis of loss exposure.
2. The measurement of exposure associated with these risks.
3. The development of alternative techniques for treating each exposure.
4. The reduction and implementation of the best technique or combination of techniques to forecast each exposure.
5. The evaluation of results in an effort to improve the procedures of identification, measurement and treatment.

There are in general two major ways of dealing with political risk: (i) risk avoidance or transfer; and (ii) risk negotiation. The first approach is based on the utilization of existing financial and non-financial methods as well as legal arrangements to avoid risk or to transfer it to a third party. The second approach is based on negotiating a deal with the host government. The two approaches are not mutually exclusive and can be employed simultaneously.

Political risk can be managed via some operating strategies and with the help of some international institutions. One of the most important operating strategies is carrying out FDI via joint ventures with a partner from the host country that can be a government body. This is the business form that is most used frequently in strategic alliances (Mariti and Smiley, 1983). The setting up of joint ventures with parties from the host countries is particularly useful when a firm wants to enter a country with a hostile government and/or restrictive legislation. Wafo (1998, p. 58) concludes that the literature recognizes a close relationship between the entry mode (a joint venture or otherwise) and political risk. Buckley and Casson (2000b) identify three conditions under which the establishment of joint ventures becomes attractive, the third of which refers to political factors.

The second operating strategy for managing political risk is based on the choice of the capital structure and the source of capital. The objective of this strategy is to transfer risk to a third party. This can be done by financing FDI projects with funds from the host government, other governments, international development agencies, overseas banks, and customers. Debt service in this case will be met out of production, not out of the parent firm's funds. Should a take-over by the host government materialize, the net worth that is lost in the project would be minimal. Other strategies will be discussed later, with special reference to the risk of take-over by the host government.

International organizations, such as the World Bank and the OECD, are instrumental in the management of political risk. They have been active in their attempts to establish an international investment law. These two organizations have been considering four ways to reduce political risk in developing countries. These are:

1. Measures that aim at influencing the host government's investment policy.
2. Measures that deal with the creation, and setting up, of a new multilateral insurance agency for political risk.
3. The creation of an organization for arbitration and conciliation of investment disputes.
4. Attempts to reduce the effect of political risk by extending the rules of the World Trade Organization (WTO) to the international investment domain (such as the transparency of investment rules and the application of the concept of the 'most-favoured nations').

The World Bank has three agencies working in this field. One of these organizations is the International Finance Corporation (IFC), which began operations in 1956. Its objective is to promote economic development in Third World countries by supporting the private sector. The investment promotion activities of the IFC include an advisory service on policies and institutions that can assist members in attracting and regulating foreign investment. There is also the International Centre for Settlement of Investment Disputes (ICSID), created in

1956. Its function is to assist in the conciliation and arbitration of investment disputes between member countries. The third agency is the Multinational Investment Guarantee Agency (MIGA). The proposal to establish the MIGA was launched at the Seoul meetings of the World Bank and the International Monetary Fund in 1985. This agency provides insurance to cover the types of political risk that are beyond the control of the host government. Specifically, the MIGA offers long-term (up to 15 or 20 years) political risk insurance coverage to eligible investors for qualified investments in developing member countries. The particular kinds of risks covered by the MIGA are: (i) transfer restrictions; (ii) expropriation; (iii) breach of contract; and (iv) war and civil disturbances.

There are also multilateral agreements between countries that deal with political risk. Wafo (1998) presents a list of reasons that drive the desire to establish multilateral agreements: (i) an increased number of host countries having a more significant stake in these agreements; (ii) a more positive attitude towards FDI by many host countries since the 1980s; (iii) a body of bilateral treaties on FDI; and (iv) the presence of institutions that could serve as an acceptable forum in which to develop an international investment agreement, such as the World Bank.

The Multilateral Agreement on Investment (MAI), which was negotiated at the OECD, is the most important proposal of this kind. The negotiations ceased in 1999 without reaching any consensus on the form the agreement should take. The objective behind this agreement was to create a strong and comprehensive multilateral legal framework for FDI. It would also reduce barriers to FDI and increase legal security for international investors. The question that arises here concerns the need for an MAI, given that investment flows have been growing rapidly. The answer is that the unevenness of investment regimes causes foreign investment to flow to relatively few countries, particularly developing countries. One objective of the MAI is therefore to encourage FDI to flow to countries typically regarded as being off limits because of a higher level of political risk.

There is, however, another view of the MAI that portrays it as being biased against the host countries in favour of the foreign investors. Specifically, the objectives of the MAI, according to this view, are the following:

1. Opening all sectors of economies to foreign companies.
2. Requiring countries to treat foreign investors in the same way as local companies.

3. Banning performance requirements and measures of accountability.
4. Setting binding dispute settlement rules, allowing investors to challenge laws and seek financial compensation.

This sceptical view of the MAI raises the following concerns:

1. The MAI was negotiated with little public input. The wide range of concerns about international capital mobility, labour rights and financial stability were largely ignored.
2. Developing countries had no role in drafting the MAI.
3. Pre-emption of local state and national laws.
4. Corporate investors would get new rights but there are no mechanisms to hold them accountable to the social and environmental concerns of the source or recipient countries.
5. The MAI would contain weak, non-binding environmental provisions.

In short, the sceptical view of the MAI can be summarized as follows. The MAI would bring about an enormous transfer of power from governments to the boards of directors of the world's largest corporations. It would pose serious challenges to environmental and other social goals, including democratic governance. The MAI would increase the rights and opportunities of MNCs without increasing their responsibilities. And while the MAI would result in an increase in FDI, it would also result in a redistribution of benefits from the host countries to MNCs.

Political risk can also be managed via bilateral agreements. These agreements can take two forms: bilateral government treaties, and bilateral investment treaties. Bilateral government treaties are concluded with the objective of guaranteeing a commitment by the host government with respect to FDI. Bilateral investment treaties, on the other hand, are designed to improve the conditions for investment by firms of each signatory country in the other country. Bilateral investment treaties cover several issues of interest to the investor: treatment of the investor after an investment has been made in the host country, expropriation, compensation, and dispute settlement.

Furthermore, many countries have tried to deal with political risk by setting up government guarantee companies. An example is the US Investment Guarantee Program, managed by the semi-governmental Overseas Private Investment Corporation (OPIC). Typically, OPIC insures American investors against expropriation loss, inconvertibility of currency, war, riots, and insurrection. Commenting on the impact of OPIC's activity, US Senator Frank Church is quoted as having said 'once the government assumes the insurance of the company, the company's interest and that of the government become identical, and the company can threaten to fall back on the U.S. government, whenever it deals with a foreign government' (US Congress Committee on Foreign Relations, 1973).[7] A similar function is performed in Japan by the Ministry of Economy, Trade and Industry (formerly, the Ministry of International Trade and Industry), in the UK by the Export Credits Guarantee Department (ECGD), and in Canada by the Export Development Corporation.

The most severe political risk is a host government take-over, which may take the form of confiscation or expropriation (without and with compensation, respectively). There are several strategies to deal with exposure to host government take-over. To start with, pre-negotiation with the host government is important. Areas of pre-negotiation include the size and form of the initial investment, the amount of local labour employed in the project (local versus imported), tax burden, ease and cost of local financing, remittance amount and composition (dividends, interest and fees), and protection given to the original investment and accumulated profits. One strategy is to use a short-term horizon, in which case the emphasis is placed on recovering cash flows quickly. Should a take-over take place, losses will be minimized. The MNC will also exert a minimum effort to replace worn-out equipment at the subsidiary. Another strategy is to use unique supplies or technology. In this case, the host government will have no incentive to take over the business, since the project will not be operational without the help of the investing firm. Schnitzer (1999) shows how investors can use their control rights to protect their investments from what he calls 'creeping expropriation' once the investment is sunk. The third strategy is to hire local labour. If local employees of the subsidiary are affected by the take-over, they could put pressure on their government to avoid such an action. A similar result would materialize if the project was financed by borrowing local funds. In this case, the local banks would exert pressure on the host government to avoid the take-over. The last protective measure would be to buy insurance from the OPIC and similar agencies.

Several studies have been conducted to measure the effect of political risk on FDI. These studies typically follow two approaches to the empirical quantification of the effect of political risk on FDI. The first is the genuine political-orientated approach, which stresses the importance of political factors as determinants of FDI. The second approach, which is economic-orientated, considers political factors in conjunction with economic factors. In both of these approaches, FDI is viewed as being supply-determined (that is, determined by the decisions of the MNCs), whereas demand in the host countries is considered to be infinitely elastic. We have already come across some of these studies (Chapter 2).

Empirical studies based on surveys consistently found that executives consider host country political instability to be a major determinant of FDI project location decisions (see, for example, Basi, 1963; Aharoni, 1966; Root, 1968; Green, 1972 and Frank, 1980). However, studies based on the statistical analysis of data revealed mixed, if not contradictory, results: some have found significant effects of political risk on FDI flows, whereas others have not. For example, Brewer (1983) found a very weak correlation between government instability and restrictions on international funds associated with FDI projects. The relationship between expropriation and government instability also is not clear, as found by Kobrin (1984). And Levis (1979) found that political variables are of secondary importance as compared with economic factors in determining FDI flows. Finally, Schneider and Frey (1985) used a politico-economic model that incorporates a large number of possible determinants of FDI and concluded that FDI is determined simultaneously by economic and political factors.

A FINAL REMARK

In this chapter we examined the measurement and management of country risk and political risk, as well as the effects they exert on FDI-related decisions. While the empirical evidence on the effects of country risk and political risk is mixed (as is invariably the case with empirical testing), it is intuitively sound to imagine that an MNC will shy away from countries characterized by macroeconomic mismanagement, erratic government decision-making, frequent kidnapping of foreign business executives, and so on. In Chapter 6, another important factor for FDI will be examined: international taxation.

6 International Taxation

International taxation involves the imposition and levying of taxes on cross-border transactions. This action invariably gives rise to problems, since it involves more than one tax system with inherent differences. Countries differ, *inter alia*, with respect to the types of taxes they impose, the tax rates, the tax base to which the tax rates are applied, and whether or not tax is levied on income generated by their citizens if these citizens reside outside their national boundaries. Individual country practices with respect to taxation have evolved over a very long period of time.[1]

International taxation is very important for FDI decisions and international business activity in general. Hines (1999) concludes that taxation has a significant influence on the location of FDI, corporate borrowing, transfer pricing, dividends, and royalty payments. In another study, Altshuler *et al.* (1998) analysed corporate tax return data covering the period 1984–92 and found that a typical US MNC would tend to locate its projects in countries where taxation is lowest. Razin *et al.* (1996) argue that the failure to have a tax scheme in which the rates of return across countries are equated can result in inefficient capital flows across countries. In this study, they emphasize the efficiency of a non-uniform treatment of FDI and other capital flows for them to exist in an efficient manner. The importance of taxation for FDI and international business activity has been established beyond any doubt.

There are at least two aspects to the study of international taxation. The first concerns the relationship between MNCs and the taxing authorities, which are invariably involved in a 'tax game'. As the tax authority sets up a new defence to plug a loophole in the tax system, MNCs adjust their strategies to open up a new hole or to take advantage of existing ones. In its *Guidelines for Multinational Enterprises*, the OECD states specifically that 'it is important that enterprises contribute to the public finances of the host countries by making timely payments of tax liabilities'. It is also stated that enterprises should comply with the tax laws and regulations in all countries in which they operate, and should exert every effort to act in accordance with laws and regulations. The international taxation environment also affects the decision of MNCs in several respects, including location decisions, organizational form decisions, financing decisions, remittance policy, transfer pricing policy, working capital management, and capital structure policy.

The second aspect of international taxation pertains to the relationship between countries with different taxation systems. These relationships could take the form of co-operation, as represented by double taxation treaties and the exchange of information, or tax competition, whereby countries poach economic activity from each other by reducing taxes. A double taxation treaty whereby the home country gives credit for taxes paid in the foreign country may lead to inconsistency between the interests of the MNC and its home country, as shown by Feldstein (1994).

This chapter deals briefly with these and other aspects of international taxation. The starting point is to explain why taxation systems differ from one country to another. Types of taxes imposed in various countries are then described. This is followed by a discussion of the methods used to avoid double taxation, invariably involving tax treaties. After that we move on to a discussion of the role of tax havens and the related issue of tax competition. The important issue of tax planning in the international environment is discussed subsequently, and this is followed by an examination of tax incentives and tax competition. Finally, we deal with the implications of globalization and the Internet for taxation.

THE PHILOSOPHY OF NATIONAL TAX SYSTEMS

Although tax systems vary from one country to another, it is commonly accepted that each country has the right to tax income earned inside its borders. Countries may be willing to make some sort of compromise on national sovereignty – by joining international bodies such as the IMF, EU, WTO and NATO – but the right to set taxes is a no-go area. This is a right that countries want to preserve. Tax nationalism, it seems, is here to stay as indicated by the resistance of most EU countries to tax harmonization within the EU.

There is, however, no agreement on the taxable items or the tax base, how expenses are determined, and what kinds of taxes should be imposed (for example, direct versus indirect taxes). Moreover, there are differences in adherence to tax laws that can be attributed to cultural differences and attitudes towards enforcement. For example, and for unclear reasons, it has been established that tax evasion in

Europe increases the closer the country is to the Mediterranean (tax evasion is definitely greater in Greece and Italy than in Sweden and Norway, for example). This has led some observers to develop a hypothesis (which has not been tested!) on the relationship between climate and the tendency for tax evasion.

Equity and Neutrality

The equity principle stipulates that, under similar circumstances, taxpayers should pay similar amounts of tax. In other words, tax equity means that all similarly-situated taxpayers should participate in the cost of operating the government according to the same rules. There are, however, divergent views on this issue. One view is that income earned in the host country by a subsidiary should be taxed at the rate to which the parent MNC is subject in its home country. The other view is that this income should be taxed at the rate prevalent in the host country.

Tax neutrality, which is a principle of economic efficiency and equity, is determined by three criteria. The first of these criteria is capital export neutrality that, if satisfied, means that the tax system should be effective in raising revenue for the government without having any adverse effect on the economic decision-making process of the taxpayer. In this case, tax should not prevent resources from being allocated to the optimal use (in terms of risk and return) no matter where in the world this use happens to be. The second criterion is national neutrality, whereby income is taxed in the same manner regardless of where in the world it is earned. In practice, it is difficult to apply this concept. The third criterion is capital-import neutrality, which implies that the tax burden imposed by a host country on a foreign subsidiary should be the same regardless of the country of incorporation. It should also be the same as the tax burden placed on domestic firms. This criterion means that if the domestic tax rate is higher than the tax rate in the host country then the home country's government will not require additional tax over and above the amount paid to the host government.

Sources of Income

Foreign sources of income are either the export of goods and services, or the earnings of foreign branches and subsidiaries. Income derived from exports is taxable when it is earned. Tax incentives may be used to encourage exports, in which case foreign income will be taxed at a lower rate than domestic income.

Taxing income earned from the activities of foreign branches or subsidiaries by the home government is more complex. There are two methods of declaring tax jurisdiction: the territorial (or source) method, and the worldwide (or residential) method. According to the territorial method (also called the territorial exemption method) the tax is levied on all income earned within the country irrespective of the nationality of the taxpayer. Hence, foreign income is not taxed by the home government, but rather by the government of the country where it is generated.[2]

According to the worldwide method (also called the worldwide credit method), the government levies tax on the worldwide income of residents, no matter where the income is earned. Hence, the income generated by a subsidiary located in one country is taxed by the government of the host country as well as the government of the home country where the parent MNC is located. This gives rise to double taxation, a problem that can be tackled either via tax credit or tax treaties. In this case, what we have on our hands are two governments seeking to tax the same amount. This method, which applies to repatriated investment income (usually including dividends, interest, rent and royalties), is criticized on the grounds that it encourages the accumulation of earnings in tax havens or low-tax countries.

Determination of Expenses

There are differences in the way countries treat certain expenses for tax purposes. There are three points to consider here:

1. If R&D expenses are capitalized, their impact on the taxable income will be spread over the period in which they are written off. If they are treated as expenses in the period in which they are incurred, the impact will be immediate.
2. There are differences in opinion with respect to the useful life of an asset. For example, the tax burden is affected by whether an asset is written off over a period of five years or ten years.
3. The determination of expenses may create a difference between the statutory and the effective tax rates. The more liberal the determination of expenses, the greater will be the gap between the two rates.

TYPES OF TAXES

The impact of taxation on an MNC depends on whether the tax is considered an income tax, since the tax credit applies to income tax only. In this section, the taxes that an MNC and its subsidiaries face will be discussed briefly.

Corporate Income Tax

Income tax is a direct tax in the sense that it is paid directly by the tax payer on whom it is levied. The tax is levied on active income; that is, income that results directly from the production of goods and services. Corporate income tax rates range between zero per cent in Bahrain, Bermuda and the Cayman Islands to well over 40 per cent in many countries.

There are two approaches to taxing corporate income: the classic approach and the integrated approach. Under the classic approach, income received by each taxable entity is taxed. Thus the earnings of a company could be taxed twice: when they are earned, and when they are received as dividends by shareholders. The integrated approach aims at eliminating this kind of double taxation by considering both the company and its shareholders, and this can be done in two different ways. The first is to tax undistributed earnings at a higher rate than that used to tax distributed earnings. The second is the so-called imputation tax system, whereby the portion of income tax paid by a company is imputed when shareholders are taxed on their dividends.

Withholding Taxes

A withholding tax is a tax levied on passive income earned by a firm within the tax jurisdiction of another country. Passive income includes dividends and interest payments as well as income from royalties, patents and copyrights. A withholding tax is an indirect tax that is borne by a taxpayer who did not generate the income directly that serves as the source of the passive income. Countries levy withholding tax on payments to the non-resident investor.

Indirect Taxes

The most important form of indirect taxes is value added tax (VAT), sometimes known as the goods and services tax (GST). The basic idea behind VAT is that the tax is applied at each stage of the production process for the value added by a firm to the goods purchased from other firms.

Import Duties

Import duties (also called customs duties and tariffs) are imposed on imports. Since goods entering a country are shipped to specific ports where policing can be intensive, import duties are a good source of revenue when income or sales records are poor. This partly explains why the governments of some developing countries depend on tariffs as a source of revenue. Tariffs also explain why a car can cost five times as much in some countries as in others. Finally, tariffs explain why some firms move production facilities abroad. We have already seen that tariffs, and even the threat of imposing tariffs, provide one explanation for FDI.

Taxation of Foreign Exchange Gains

When cross-border transactions are conducted, foreign exchange gains and losses will typically be present. The tax treatment of these gains and losses is very complex and varies from one country to another. In many countries, foreign exchange gains and losses are taken into account in the overall trading profit. If these gains and losses relate to a capital transactions, they are recognized in some countries but not in others.

THE AVOIDANCE OF DOUBLE TAXATION

Many countries have bilateral tax treaties with other countries, mainly to avoid double taxation. In 1921, the League of Nations commissioned a report which concluded that double taxation interfered with 'economic intercourse and ... the free flow of capital'. The report put forward some rules for determining when tax should be paid to the country in which income is generated, and when it should be paid to the taxpayer's home country. The outcome of this exercise was a model treaty that was subsequently adopted and modified by the OECD to become what is known as the OECD Model Tax Convention, which we shall return to later in this section.

Double taxation of the same funds is invariably detrimental to international trade and investment. One way of avoiding double taxation is tax credits. A subsidiary may be required to pay income tax and withholding tax in the host country. If the income received by the MNC is also subject to income tax in the home country, there will be double taxation. A key point to realize here is that a tax must be considered as income tax as a precondition for the underlying tax-payer to become eligible for tax credit. Unlike income tax, VAT is eligible for deduction, not for credit. The problem is that what is considered as income tax in one country may not be so in another. Dickescheid (1999) shows that a country can maximize national wel-fare by taxing foreign subsidiaries and abstaining from taxing domestic firms operating abroad. The latter can be accomplished via double taxation relief.

One problem with tax credit is that it may lead to inconsistency between the interests of the MNC and the interests of its home country. If the MNC pays taxes on the earnings of its foreign sub-sidiaries to the host government, the home country loses revenue to the foreign host country in which the foreign investment is under-taken. If the MNC receives credit for these tax payments, it will be indifferent between taxes paid at home or abroad. Although the firm can maximize the value of shareholders' equity by equating the after-tax return on capital at home and abroad, the loss of revenue to the foreign government means that the interests of the MNC and those of the home country do not coincide. Furthermore, MacDougal (1960) pointed out that the most important welfare effect of FDI (and capital flows in general) arises from the taxation of profits and dividends by the host country when there is a double taxation treaty.

Differences in philosophy on how income should be taxed have given rise to treaties between countries to minimize the effect of double taxation on the taxpayer, protect each country's right to collect taxes, and provide ways to resolve jurisdictional issues. Tax treaties specify the classes of income that would not be subject to tax, can reduce the rate on income and/or withholding taxes, and can deal specifically with the issue of tax credit. They may also deal with specific types of taxes that could be considered creditable. Normally, tax treaties specify such issues as the taxes covered, the persons and organizations covered, relief from double taxation, the exchange of information between the authorities of the contracting countries, and the conditions under which a treaty may be terminated.

In an attempt to achieve uniformity in the treaties concluded by the members of the OECD, model treaties have been adopted. Treaties concluded on a bilateral basis invariably follow the OECD Model Tax

Convention (originating from the League of Nations model discussed earlier). However, since each treaty has to take into account differences in the tax systems and fiscal policies, deviations from the model typically arise. The OECD Model Tax Convention and the worldwide network of tax treaties based upon it help to avoid double taxation by providing clear consensual rules of taxation. For most types of income, particularly business profits and investment income, double taxation is avoided in treaties based on the OECD Model Tax Convention by allocating taxing rights between the resident and source countries, and by requiring the former to eliminate double taxation where there are competing taxing rights. Most bilateral tax treaties follow both the principles and the detailed provisions of the OECD Model. There are close to 350 treaties between OECD member countries, and over 1500 worldwide, based on the Model. The Working Party on Tax Conventions has regular contact with non-OECD members to discuss developments in the Model and problems of application and interpretation of bilateral treaties. Starting in 1997, the Model is now presented in two volumes. Volume I includes the introduction, the text of the articles of the Model, and the commentary thereon. Volume II includes the new section on the positions of non-member countries, reprints of sixteen previous reports dealing with tax conventions that the Committee on Fiscal Affairs has adopted since 1977, the list of tax conventions concluded between member countries, and the text of the *Council Recommendation on the Model Tax Convention*.

Individual bilateral treaties differ with respect to content. A specific article may not appear, or tax relief may vary. In general, treaties have common articles dealing with such issues as personal scope, taxes covered, dividends, interest, royalties, capital gains, avoidance of double taxation, exchange of information, territorial extension, and termination. If a subsidiary is entitled to a reduced rate of withholding tax in accordance with a tax treaty, a claim needs to be submitted by the payer to the tax authorities in advance to be eligible for the reduced rate. Otherwise, the full amount has to be paid and a refund is claimed subsequently.

TAX HAVENS

A tax haven is defined as a 'place where foreigners may receive income or own assets without paying high rates of tax on them'.

According to the OECD's Forum on Harmful Tax Practices, the main features of a tax haven are: (i) no taxes, or only nominal effective tax rates; (ii) lack of effective exchange of information; (iii) lack of transparency; and (iv) absence of a requirement of substantial activity.

Tax havens offer a variety of benefits such as low taxes or zero taxes on certain classes of income. Some tax havens impose tax on income from domestic sources but exempt income from foreign sources. And some of these havens allow special privileges. For example, the Bahamas, Bermuda and the Cayman Islands are free from tax for overseas companies (including corporate income tax, capital gains tax, withholding tax, and securities turnover tax). Others, such as the British Virgin Islands, offer low tax rates. Some tax havens, such as Luxembourg, specialize in facilities for establishing holding companies. Because of these benefits, thousands of so-called mailbox companies have appeared in places such as Liechtenstein, Vanuatu and the Netherlands Antilles. As a result of this variety, tax havens fall into two specific categories: (i) pure tax havens, which impose zero or low tax rates; and (ii) hybrid tax havens, which offer specific tax incentives.

Perhaps some facts and figures on tax havens would help to shed some light on the importance of the role played by tax havens in the world economy. First, the growth of FDI in tax havens has been enormous. Over the period 1985–94, for example, total FDI by the G7 countries in tax havens in the Caribbean and the South Pacific grew more than five times, to about $200 billion. According to Hines and Rice (1994) tax havens accounted for 1.2 per cent of the world population and 3 per cent of GDP, but they accounted for 26 per cent of the assets and 31 per cent of the net profits of American MNCs. An example of the ability of tax havens to attract FDI and to internationalize business can be found in the case of the migration of British bookmakers to Gibraltar to avoid a 9 per cent tax on betting in the UK. This move was started by the bookmaker, Victor Chandler, whose business has now moved entirely to Gibraltar. Other betting firms followed this move, including Coral, Ladbroke's and William Hill. These firms currently operate 24 hours a day, taking tax-free bets by telephone and via the Internet. As a result, Victor Chandler has become Gibraltar's largest private-sector employer, accounting for 7 per cent of its GDP.

In international tax planning, there is obviously a clear theoretical advantage in arranging for profits to accrue to a company located in a tax haven because the tax imposed may be less than what would otherwise accrue to an entity in a high tax country. To take advantage of a tax haven, an MNC would normally set up a subsidiary there through which different forms of income would pass. The subsidiary is then used as an intermediary for the purpose of shifting income from high-tax countries to the tax haven. For example, an MNC could sell its products at cost to a subsidiary located in a tax haven, and when the subsidiary sells these products to a third party, the profit will be concentrated in the tax haven. Of course, the alternative would be to sell the products directly, in which case the profit would be concentrated in the high-tax home country.[3]

In some countries, then, the tax authorities take a tough line towards MNCs that operate within their national borders while taking advantage of tax havens. When filing tax returns in a high-tax country, MNCs typically underestimate as far as possible the profit earned in that country, attributing as much profit as possible to their operations in tax havens. They do so by arranging 'transactions' between their subsidiaries in the two countries and setting transfer prices so that they would maximize the profit made by a subsidiary located in the tax haven. We shall deal with transfer pricing in Chapter 8.

In recent years there has been a significant increase in the number of centres offering tax haven facilities, such as the islands of Malta and Madeira. So what makes a country or a territory a tax haven? The following are the key factors: (i) a high degree of investor protection; (ii) willingness to prevent money laundering; (iii) political and economic stability; (iv) low or zero taxes; (v) existence of tax treaties with other countries; (vi) the absence of exchange controls; (vii) the presence of developed legal, banking and accounting systems; (viii) good transportation and communication facilities; and (ix) the ability to form a company easily and cheaply. Table 6.1 provides a description of some tax havens.

Anti-Abuse Measures and Legislation

Clearly, a widespread use of tax havens results in a major loss of revenue to those countries where taxation is avoided. Some OECD countries have suggested that it may be possible and worthwhile to strike a deal with tax havens to buy their 'good behaviour' (*The Economist*, 'Survey', 29 January 2000, p. 15). This is because the amount of tax revenue that is lost to the world is too large compared with what tax havens receive. It has also been suggested that OECD

Table 6.1 The main features of selected tax havens

Tax haven	Description	Main features
Bahamas	An independent country within the British Commonwealth, with a well-developed legal system based primarily on the UK model	No taxes A long-established tax haven Secrecy of information is guaranteed Excellent communication facilities Well-developed trust business, shipping business and offshore insurance
Cayman Islands	A British dependent territory whose economy depends largely on tourism and tax-haven business, with a legal system based on the UK model	Excellent confidentiality, particularly in banking Zero taxes Absence of exchange controls Political stability Well-developed banking and trust companies, mutual funds, shipping and insurance
Isle of Man	A highly stable offshore centre in a convenient location with excellent legal and other services. It is a crown dependency with considerable political autonomy	Political stability Highly qualified labour force Good financial, regulatory, and supervisory framework Low taxes Fast formation of companies Very attractive for investment, fund management and other financial services Long-established shipping register and life assurance activities
Malta	An independent republic in the Mediterranean that is seeking full membership of the European Union	Good standards of law, accounting and education with significantly lower costs than in mainland Europe Good international communication facilities Encouragement of offshore business through the Malta International Business Activities Act Strict confidentiality laws Strict prevention of criminal activity Double taxation treaties with more than 20 countries Speciality in shipping

governments could, and should, exert co-ordinated pressure on MNCs so that they would not use tax havens. After all, the large majority of MNCs belong to the OECD countries.

Many countries have legislated domestic measures to curb the abuse of tax havens. These measures appear in many forms, the most common of which is legislation that permits the tax authorities to tax certain unremitted income of tax-haven companies, where the company is controlled by residents. In the UK, this is known as the Controlled Foreign Companies (CFC) legislation. A CFC is defined as a company that is resident outside the UK, controlled by persons resident in the UK, and subject to a low level of taxation in the territory in which it is resident. A 'low' level of taxation is defined as being less than three quarters of the prevailing UK rate.

The comparable legislation in the USA is the Subpart F provisions, which provide for the taxation of US shareholders of controlled foreign corporations on their pro rata share of certain categories of undistributed profits from tax haven activities and certain other activities of the foreign corporation. In the US legislation, a CFC is defined as a foreign subsidiary that has more than 50 per cent of its voting equity owned by US shareholders. A US shareholder is any US citizen, resident partnership corporation, trust or estate that owns (or controls directly) 10 per cent or more of the voting equity of the CFC.

The question that arises here is: why does it make a difference for tax purposes whether a foreign corporation is a CFC? If the foreign corporation is not a CFC, its income is deferred automatically until it is remitted as dividends to shareholders. If the foreign corporation is a CFC, the deferral principle may not apply to certain kinds of income. Why? Because US corporations historically did business in tax havens and benefited from low or zero taxes. If a tax-haven corporation was involved in the active production of, and sale of, goods and services, then there was no problem. However, the US government noticed that many firms were setting up tax-haven corporations to avoid paying US tax. Legislation was thus introduced to minimize tax avoidance. The legislation allows the US corporation to apply the deferral principle to its portion of income from the active conduct of a trade or business of a CFC, but it cannot defer its portion of passive income, which is referred to as Subpart F income in the Internal Revenue Code. Subpart F income is divided into seven groups: (i) insurance of US risks; (ii) foreign-base company personal holding company income; (iii) foreign-base company sales income; (iv) foreign-base company service income; (v) foreign-base company shipping income; (vi) boycott-

Table 6.2 Categories of Subpart F income

Category	Description
Insurance of US risk	Income received by insurance companies set in tax havens as insurance premiums to cover US risk
Foreign-base company personal holding company income	Dividends, interest, royalties and similar income items arising from holding rights rather than the production and sale of goods and services
Foreign-base company sales income	Income arising from the sale or purchase of goods produced and consumed outside the country where the CFC is incorporated
Foreign-base company service income	Income arising from contracts utilizing technical, managerial, engineering or other skills
Foreign-base company shipping income	Income arising from using aircraft and ships for transportation outside the country where the CFC is incorporated
Boycott-related income	This item resulted from the Tax Reform Act of 1976, which was intended to penalize companies supporting the Arab boycott of Israel
Foreign bribes	Bribes paid to foreign government officials, as explained in the Foreign Corruption Practices Act of 1976

related income; and (vii) foreign bribes. Table 6.2 gives a description of these categories of Subpart F income accruing to CFCs set up in tax havens.

In summary, there are several implications of the Subpart F concept. For foreign corporations that are not CFCs, income is not taxable until a dividend to the MNC is declared. For CFCs, active income is also deferred, but passive or Subpart F income must be recognized by the MNC when earned, regardless of when a dividend is declared.

TAX PLANNING IN THE INTERNATIONAL ENVIRONMENT

MNCs operate across a number of different national tax environments. Differences include the types of taxes applicable to the MNC's profits, and the level of the tax rates. The tax environment affects several policy areas: these areas will be discussed in turn.

Location Decisions

When an MNC decides to enter another country to expand its markets it may do so in a number of ways: it may establish a representative office to market the products, with all actual sales being conducted in the home country, or it may establish a sales office, a branch or a subsidiary. The way the MNC decides to conduct its operations in a foreign country will affect its tax liability there. The first step in deciding whether or not an MNC has a tax exposure in another country is to consider whether the MNC is 'trading with' or 'trading in' that country. The tax laws of most countries do not regard an MNC as having a taxable presence, nor are its activities regarded as giving rise to taxable income, if the MNC merely sells goods or provides services to local residents without having some presence there.

Once an MNC has decided to invest overseas, it must take a decision as to where (that is, in which country) to locate the project. One factor that determines this decision is the tax burden. The total tax burden is determined by a number of factors, including the tax relief and the relative levels of different tax rates. The decision would normally be to pick the country that offers the lowest tax burden, subject to some operational constraints. An example of these constraints is proximity to markets, sources of raw materials, and ports where transportation costs become crucial.

The location of foreign operations is influenced by three major tax factors: tax incentives, tax rates and tax treaties. Tax incentives can reduce materially the cash outflow required for an investment project, consequently leading to an increase in the NPV of the project. Tax rates determine revenues and expenses for tax purposes. Tax treaties are critical in terms of how they influence the cash flows related to withholding taxes on dividends, interest payments and royalties.

Organizational Form Decisions

An organizational form decision boils down to making a choice from among several alternatives: entering a foreign market via exports, branches or subsidiaries. When exporting goods and services a firm must decide whether to service the products from the home country or a foreign location. When the MNC decides to license technology abroad, it must be aware of the withholding taxes and relevant tax treaties.

The majority of tax treaties make it explicit that the trading profits of an MNC are not subject to taxation in a particular location unless trading is done through a 'permanent establishment'. The term 'permanent establishment' is defined in Article 5 of the OECD Model Tax Convention, and it is reproduced with some modification in bilateral treaties. The term implies a fixed place of business through which trade is partly or wholly carried out. Article 5 specifically mentions several types of business which do not amount to a permanent establishment. For example, there is no permanent establishment if a stock is held in a country solely for the purpose of storage, display or delivery. The same applies to an office that is designed purely for purchasing or gathering information (that is, a representative office). This is also true of a construction site that exists for less than a specific period, normally twelve months. On the other hand, an agent concluding contracts on behalf of an MNC will amount to a permanent establishment unless the agent acts for a number of third parties in the ordinary course of business.

We shall now consider branches as an organizational form. A foreign branch is not an independently incorporated firm that is separate from the parent MNC. Rather, it is an extension of the MNC. As a result, active or passive income earned in the host country is consolidated with the domestic income of the parent MNC for the purpose of determining domestic tax liability, irrespective of whether or not the income has been repatriated.

Operating abroad through a branch has several benefits. Because branch profits and losses are not subject to deferral, it is often beneficial to open a branch when first operating abroad, since the initial years are loss years. The MNC can then use branch losses to offset domestic income for tax purposes. Branch remittances are not subject to withholding tax as dividends from subsidiaries. It is necessary, however, to consider whether the host country taxes the profits of a branch at a higher rate than the normal rate and whether, if it does, treaty protection is available (for example, under the non-discrimination article).

Finally, we come to a consideration of subsidiaries. A foreign subsidiary is an affiliate organization of the MNC that is incorporated independently in the host country, which may be owned partially or totally by the MNC. Active foreign-source income is taxed by the home government only when it is remitted to the MNC, but passive income is taxed as it is earned, even if it has not been repatriated. This is a major advantage of operating through a subsidiary, but the disadvantage is that any losses cannot be recognized by the MNC. Thus, the subsidiary is preferable after the start-up years,

when operations become profitable. Depending on local laws, therefore, a subsidiary will invariably produce higher tax liability on
remitted profits than a branch. This is because, although profits are
taxed at the same rate, branch profits are not normally subject to any
further tax charge on remittance to the MNC, whereas dividends paid
by a subsidiary to the MNC are subject to withholding tax.

There are other considerations for the choice between a branch and
a subsidiary. First, the local audit and accounting requirements for
a branch are generally less tedious than for a subsidiary. Second, a
subsidiary may be able to take advantage of local incentives and grants,
which may not be available to a branch. Third, a subsidiary takes longer
to form, and it is less flexible in its formation and closure than a branch.
Finally, there may be some commercial advantages in trading through
a subsidiary as opposed to a branch (for example, local profile).

Withholding tax could be another disincentive for MNCs considering establishing a subsidiary in another country. If the subsidiary is
located in a country that is not a tax haven, its profits will be subject to
corporate income tax there. On payment of the dividend from net
profits, the subsidiary will be required to deduct withholding tax. The
MNC receiving the dividend will be entitled to relief for this withholding tax against its eventual tax liability on the dividends. However,
there may be no liability in the hands of the MNC, either because the
dividend is not treated as taxable income under the domestic laws of
the MNC's home country, or because the MNC has available deductions that reduce the taxable amount. For this reason, the dividend
article of most tax treaties provides for a reduced rate of withholding
tax from dividends paid to shareholders who satisfy certain conditions.

Assuming that the decision falls on the subsidiary rather than the
branch, it then becomes necessary to consider the ownership of the
subsidiary. There are basically three options: (i) holding the subsidiary
directly or through a subsidiary resident in the home country;
(ii) creating a holding company in the host country; and (iii) creating
an offshore holding company that is resident in a third country. The
second and third options offer potential benefits that the first option
does not provide. For example, if external financing is required to
fund the acquisition of a subsidiary, a local holding company may
allow efficient utilization of interest against the profits of the subsidiary, particularly if the host country pools profits and losses of companies within a group. The use of a local holding company also
provides flexibility in any future sale: a disposal can be made either
of the shares in the local holding company or of the shares in the

trading subsidiary by the local holding company. In the first case, the gain arises in the country where the MNC is resident, but in the second case, the gain transfers to the other country.

On the other hand, an offshore holding company offers three potential benefits: capital gains protection, withholding tax minimization, and double tax credit relief. First, if established in an appropriate jurisdiction, gains realized by the holding company on a sale by the subsidiary can escape tax altogether. Second, in certain cases, the judicious use of an offshore holding company can reduce aggregate withholding tax burden when profits are repatriated from the subsidiary to the MNC. Third, an offshore holding company can increase double tax relief on dividends from high- and low-taxed subsidiaries.

Finally, national tax systems may put a huge price on attempts to reorganize national businesses into single global operations. This could happen, for example, when a firm operating in country A wants to scale back operations in this country to the status of a sales agent, by transferring marketing operations to country B. The tax authorities in country A may well view this move as a transfer of goodwill from country A to country B, in which case this firm will incur a significant tax liability.

Financing Decisions

Financing decisions also have tax consequences. Most countries allow interest, but not dividends, to be treated as a deductible expense. It follows that, when the MNC provides financing for a subsidiary, then debt financing should be preferred to equity financing. The tax advantage from financing the foreign subsidiary with loans from the MNC will be greater if the corporate income tax rate is higher in the host country. Finally, the repayment of loan principal is normally treated as a non-taxable return of capital to the MNC.

Consider the following example that explains the effect of taxation on financing decisions. Suppose that an MNC has two subsidiaries, A and B. Subsidiary A is located in a low-tax country and needs to borrow funds, whereas subsidiary B is located in a high-interest country and has excess funds. The MNC may in this case request B to provide A with a loan at a low interest rate. This operation will invariably lead to a decline in the performance of B, since it could generate a better return on its funds by employing them somewhere else. Given the presence of taxes, the MNC as a whole may indeed benefit from such a strategy, because this operation leads to an increase in the after-tax inflows. Without taxes, it may be better for subsidiary A to borrow from a local bank.

Remittance Policy

Remittance policy refers to the form that the remittances take. This policy and the choice of subsidiaries from which remittances are best obtained are affected by tax consideration. If royalties and interest payments are tax deductible expenses, then these will be preferred over dividend remittances.

Transfer Pricing Policy

Consider the previous example of an MNC with subsidiaries A and B. Assume that both subsidiaries plan to retain all of their earnings for the purpose of expanding operations. In this case, the MNC will benefit most if A generates the majority of the before-tax earnings. If the two subsidiaries trade with each other, then the MNC will request A to charge B abnormally high (transfer) prices for its products, and vice versa. This operation will boost the earnings of A and reduce the earnings of B. The idea is that if more earnings can be transferred from B to A, then the combined after-tax earnings of both subsidiaries will be higher. There is substantial evidence that MNCs use transfer pricing to reduce their taxes, although some countries do not allow this practice. Moreover, this practice affects the distribution of the tax revenue received by various countries. We shall deal with transfer pricing in detail in Chapter 8.

Working Capital Management

One aspect of working capital management that is affected by tax considerations is short-term investment. In our example, subsidiary B would choose an alternative investment avenue to that of lending to A if it were not for tax considerations.

Capital Structure Policy

If a subsidiary that is located in a high-tax country wants to expand operations, it will be beneficial if the subsidiary finances the expansion by borrowing locally rather than by receiving funds from the MNC. This is because interest payments on loans are tax exempt, which reduces total tax liability. We shall deal with the issue of the choice of capital structure in Chapter 7.

TAX INCENTIVES AND COMPETITION

There are two types of tax incentives: those by countries to attract foreign investors, and those by countries to encourage exports. Tax incentives to invest in a particular country usually involve tax holidays of one form or another. Some countries do not offer tax holidays for foreign investors, but rather they provide tax credits for companies that invest outside the metropolitan areas. Haaparanta (1996) analyses the effects of tax competition between two countries on the allocation of an exogenously given amount of FDI by an MNC. Dickescheid (1999) examines tax competition between two countries that indulge in mutual FDI via subsidiaries of the domestic industry. Schnitzer (1999) uses a dynamic model of FDI to present a rationale for tax holidays. Haufler and Wooton (1999) analyse tax competition between two countries of unequal size and conclude that, in equilibrium, the large country receives the investment if the difference in the sizes of the national markets is significant. This is because MNCs prefer to locate in the larger market, where they can charge a higher price. Tax incentives to encourage exports may take the form of not imposing VAT on exports. The most recent example of this practice is the exemption of exports from the GST, which was introduced in Australia in July 2000.

In the USA the Foreign Sales Corporation Act of 1984 was introduced to replace the Domestic International Sales Corporation (DISC) legislation that had been in existence since 1972. The DISC was established to encourage exports by US firms. Although the DISC was not a taxable entity, its income was taxed to its shareholders (generally the MNC that established the DISC) at a reduced tax rate. However, the DISC was just a shell rather than an operating company, so it violated the subsidy rules established by GATT. The Foreign Sales Corporation (FSC) was established in response to the criticism from GATT members.

In order to deal with the concerns of GATT, a qualified FSC must satisfy the following requirements: (i) it must be incorporated and have its main offices in a foreign country or a US possession (apart from Puerto Rico); (ii) it must have economic substance rather than just being a paper corporation; (iii) the export services it performs for the parent MNC must be performed outside the USA; and (iv) up to 25 shareholders may own an FSC, which permits export trading companies to set up FSCs if they so desire. In general, an FSC is defined as a foreign corporation established as a subsidiary of a US company that buys from the US corporation for the purpose of resale. If a company qualifies as an FSC, a portion of its income is exempt from US corporate income tax. Also, the legislation provides for a 100 per cent dividends-received deduction for dividends distributed by the FSC out of earnings from trade income. The difficult part of the legislation is the determination of the FSC. In order for a transaction to qualify as a foreign trading gross receipt under the economic processes, 50 per cent of the total direct costs of the transaction must take place in a foreign location.

Similarly, a US possession corporation is defined as a separate domestic US corporation actively engaged in a US possession (Puerto Rico and the US Virgin Islands). A possessions corporation can be used to limit US tax on active income, certain investment income earned in the possession, and from the sale of all assets used to conduct the business of the possession corporation. The benefit is granted through a tax credit to the parent corporation. To qualify as a possession corporation, at least 80 per cent of gross income of the corporation must be from within the possession, and at least 75 per cent of gross income must come from active trade or business within the possession.

It is arguable that greater mobility of capital has encouraged tax competition between countries, particularly tax havens. Indeed, there is some evidence, albeit circumstantial and anecdotal, suggesting that tax competition should be taken seriously. The regulatory activity that is taking place around the world seems to reflect a belief that tax competition does exist, that it is intensifying, and that it can be harmful. Falling corporate tax rates around the world are indicative of attempts by governments to accommodate the desire of international investors for lower taxes.

But this tax competition is not limited to tax havens. A report to the EU's Helsinki summit of December 1999 identified sixty-six different varieties of tax competition practised by member countries. These practices range from The Netherlands' willingness to negotiate secret advance agreements with foreign firms on how much tax they will pay, to Gibraltar's tax exemptions for branches of non-resident companies operating there. The report made it clear that, with the exception of Sweden, all EU countries indulge in 'harmful tax practices'. Furthermore, the EU has been campaigning against the practice of singling out particular tax payers for preferential tax treatment. For example, Ireland offers a 10 per cent tax on the profits earned by foreign manufacturing companies that move there, and this practice has been extended to financial companies. There are also examples of the motives for indulging in tax competition that involve some non-EU countries. First, Ireland opposes harmonizing corporate tax rates in the EU because its low rates makes it more competitive. Second, Britain once blocked an EU directive on saving tax for fear that it might hurt the City of London. Third, tax authorities in Luxembourg and Switzerland do not wish to share information with tax authorities in other countries for fear they may lose wealthy customers wishing to reduce their tax bills. Fourth, the USA may well seek a worldwide ban on Internet taxes, because it is the biggest net exporter of e-commerce (the Internet Tax Freedom Act of 1998) (*The Economist*, 'Globalisation and Tax', 29 January 2000, pp. 4–5).

The desirability or otherwise of tax competition is a debatable topic. Those who oppose tax competition put forward the following views:

1. Tax competition is harmful because countries may, as a result, experience narrowing of tax bases, be forced to change their tax mixes, or stop taxing the way they would like.
2. Tax competition makes it harder to tax mobile factors of production, such as capital, which means that more taxes should be imposed on the less mobile factors, such labour.
3. Avi-Yonah (1999) argues that while tax competition may force governments to deliver services more efficiently, it may reduce the extent of redistribution. This, in turn, results in a weaker social net, which is needed more than ever under globalization. Thus, Avi-Yonah argues that this cause-and-effect relationship may give rise to a backlash against globalization of the sort that pushed the world into depression in the 1930s.

Proponents of tax competition, on the other hand, argue as follows:

1. If competition between business enterprises is good, then competition between governments should also be good. It forces governments to be more efficient.
2. Tax competition cannot be harmful, because the words 'competition' and 'harmful' are inconsistent.

3. Tax competition is useful because it gives taxpayers more choice (in terms of combinations of tax and government services).
4. Poor countries have the right to strive for a higher standard of living by pursuing tax policies that attract FDI.

It is obvious that this debate has not yet resulted in a consensus view on whether tax competition is good or bad. This issue involves a lot of value judgement, and this probably is why it is difficult to reach a consensus view. It may well be that the truth lies somewhere in between the extreme views.

A related issue is that of the so-called harmful tax practices. According to the OECD, harmful tax practices may exist when regimes are tailored to erode the tax base of other countries. This can occur when tax regimes attract investment or savings originating elsewhere, and when they facilitate the residents legally evading tax due to their home country. To assist governments to respond to this challenge, by eliminating harmful tax practices, in May 1998 the OECD governments issued a report on harmful tax competition. The report created a forum on harmful tax practices, set out guidelines for dealing with 'harmful preferential regimes' in member countries, and adopted a series of recommendations for combating harmful tax practices. The key factors used to identify and assess harmful preferential tax regimes are (i) zero or low effective tax rates; (ii) 'ring fencing' of regimes; (iii) lack of transparency; and (iv) lack of effective exchange of information.

GLOBALIZATION, THE INTERNET AND TAXATION

Globalization entails a diminishing role for national borders and the gradual fusing of separate national markets into a single global market. Although the term 'globalization' was coined in the 1980s, the idea of a unified global market has been around for a long time. By some measures, the world was more globalized a century ago when the gold standard was in operation, and when the philosophy of *laissez-faire* was in fashion. For example, it was then easier for people to emigrate to find work, irrespective of their qualifications (over one million people a year had been drawn to the New World by the start of the twentieth century). The collapse of the gold standard and the outbreak of the First World War brought with it anti-trade policies and isolationist sentiments in the 1920s, and more so in the 1930s. But since the late 1970s and the early 1980s, there has been a trend towards liberalization and the removal of controls on current account and capital account transactions. These measures, as well as innovations in communications and transport, have boosted the trend towards globalization, leading to the emergence of some problems for tax collectors. *The Economist* (29 January 2000) reported that Rupert Murdoch's News Corporation earned profits of around US$2.3 billion in the UK during the period between 1987 and 1999 without paying corporate income tax in that country. After all, tax havens and tax competition are associated firmly with globalization. Another aspect of globalization is that it has been accompanied by the tendency towards internationalism by the taxing authorities that choose to tax their citizens on the basis of their global income.

Globalization and the removal of exchange controls and other barriers to the free movement of capital have promoted economic development. However, they have also increased the scope for tax avoidance and evasion, which cause many problems. Governments lose revenues as a result, and so taxes on those who do not escape the tax net must rise to fill the gap. Countries where tax compliance is highest lose out, as trade flows are diverted elsewhere. The OECD's Committee on Fiscal Affairs has taken a number of steps to combat international tax avoidance and evasion. The main focus of this work is on improving the means for co-operation between governments. The Committee has promoted the exchange of information between tax authorities as the best way of fighting non-compliance in transactions across countries. For this reason, the OECD's Model Tax Convention contains an article on the exchange of information. Current work to improve the exchange of information includes looking not only at barriers to effective exchange of information but also at how to make a better use of the latest information.

The Internet, which symbolizes borderlessness and the irrelevance of physical location, has definitely reinforced the momentum of the move towards globalization. This development is alarming. According to the OECD, the combination of globalization and e-commerce may well damage tax systems so badly that it could 'lead to governments being unable to meet the legitimate demands of their citizens for public services' (*The Economist*, 29 January 2000). The problem is that the Internet comes at a time when tax collectors are already getting worried about what they believe to be a troublesome aspect of globalization – that is, tax competition among countries aiming to attract international capital. The Internet has the potential to increase tax competition by making it easier for MNCs to shift their activities to tax havens.

Consider the following effects and challenges of the Internet (some overlap may be present):

1. The Internet provides a new channel for moving goods and services from producers to consumers, making it even easier to avoid sales taxes. For example, music can be downloaded via the Internet from a retailer located in a small tropical island in the middle of the ocean. Taxing virtual goods and retailers is much more difficult than taxing physical goods. In the USA, Internet buyers rarely pay sales taxes, because mail-order firms do not have to collect taxes on sales in other states. Online buyers located in Germany, for example, buying from a company in the USA will only pay VAT if the customs officers open every parcel that arrives from the USA.

2. Taxpayers may become increasingly hard to identify.

3. The Internet may blur the line between tax avoidance (which is legal) and tax evasion (which is illegal).

4. The Internet is a factor that intensifies tax competition between governments.

5. The Internet makes it hard to pinpoint the identity or location of people carrying out potentially taxable activities. This is because a domain name on the world wide web may give no clue as to the location of its originator.[4]

6. Tax collectors gather information from third parties, such as retailers and bankers. E-commerce may well cut out these middlemen (who currently play an important role in collecting taxes), because customers can buy directly from the producers on the Internet.

7. The Internet may also make it possible to conduct secret transactions that take place through the use of anonymous e-money.[5] Tax authorities fear that this kind of technology will foster tax evasion.

8. Even if they can pinpoint the taxpayers, the tax authorities may find it difficult to collect tax payments.

9. The Internet makes it easier to take advantages of tax havens. Internet banking will offer simple access, low transaction costs, a degree of anonymity, and instant ability to move funds around the world.

10. The tax systems operate on the basis of knowing the location of a particular economic activity. The Internet will make it possible

for an individual to operate in many countries from the same desk.

11. National governments may also suffer from reduced tariffs when goods move freely across national boundaries.
12. The global Internet further complicates the definition and collection of location-dependent income and corporate taxes.

The extent of these problems is often emphasized. The European Commission is worried about losing tax revenue through the Internet. As a result, it has proposed that companies with annual online sales of more than 100 000 euros in the EU should register for VAT in at least one EU country, and then collect tax on all services downloaded from the Internet. In the USA, many state and local officials have become quite agitated about the adverse effect of the Internet on the state and local tax base (since sales taxes are levied by the state). Newman (1995) echoes this view by stating that 'state and local government finances are becoming road kill on the information superhighway'.

The debate over Internet tax effects has raged at the highest level in the USA, particularly since 1998, when the Congress passed the Internet Tax Freedom Act, which has a rather misleading title. Contrary to the popular impression (and perhaps wishful thinking), this act did not place a moratorium on Internet sales taxes, but rather on discriminatory taxes and Internet access taxes. The act also created a commission to study the sales tax issue, but the commission was unable to reach a consensus view. Congress has since proposed extending the Tax Freedom Act temporarily, but the major issues have not yet been resolved.

The question that arises here concerns the sums of money involved; that is, the amount of tax revenue that will be lost as a result of e-commerce. In the USA, for example, sales taxes account for about 33 per cent of state revenues. Some politicians put the figure for lost tax revenue in the near future at US$20 billion. With a figure like this the fear politicians have over e-commerce is understandable. However, Graham (1999) argues that most of these claims are not based on actual data. Goolsbee (2001) argues that any legitimate estimate of future revenue losses must begin with a forecast of Internet sales. Williams *et al.* (1999) predicted that total Internet sales in the USA will rise from US$20.3 billion in 1999 to US$184.5 billion in 2004. The corresponding figures for lost tax revenue are US$612 million and US$6.9 billion, respectively. By extrapolation, Goolsbee (2001, p. 16) expects that it would take more than a decade for lost tax revenue to reach 10 per cent of sales tax revenue. It is noteworthy that the current estimates put the tax revenue loss from out-of-state catalogue sales at around US$6 billion, about ten times as much as the revenue lost because of Internet sales (US General Accounting Office, 2000). Goolsbee concludes that the revenue loss from the Internet is rather small.[6]

But eventually the value of Internet sales will be so huge that the fears of politicians will be vindicated. So, what can be done? To maintain at least the current level of tax revenues, state and local governments need to figure out how to apply the existing rules of taxation to electronic transactions. Initial efforts to tax Internet commercial activities by various governments have resulted in numerous instances where even the basic tax regulations have been found to be inadequate. Even the distinction between sales tax and income tax becomes unclear when business is conducted on the Internet, as many information products can be classified either as products or services (Erickson, 1996). But most of all, the fluidity of online entities makes it difficult to establish at any point in time what is being taxed, who should be taxed and who can impose taxes. Moreover, the European Commission's proposal to impose VAT in at least one EU country on companies that sell online would be impossible to enforce. Goolsbee (2001) argues that this kind of tax is likely to be extraordinarily difficult to enforce, and of extremely little revenue consequence in the medium run even if enforcement is possible.[7] The 'bit tax', to be levied on the volume of electronic transmissions would face significant political opposition.

A largely neglected issue arising from the Internet Tax Freedom Act was the moratorium that forbad states from applying sales taxes to monthly Internet fees. According to Karsel *et al.* (1999), total spending on Internet access was about US$10 billion in 1999. If all states applied sales taxes to these fees, the amount collected would more than compensate for the lost revenue from online sales. However, Goolsbee (2001) argues that taxing Internet access may create considerable deadweight loss. This is because it has been shown that Internet usage is highly price sensitive (Varian, 1999; Goolsbee, 2000). It is a well-known prediction of microeconomic theory that high elasticities invariably mean large distortions, but since Internet service providers typically charge flat monthly fees, applying taxes to access fees is not likely to have much impact on the hours of use. Such taxes may still influence the decision of whether to obtain access in the first place. Moreover, the impact of taxes on the decision to adopt new technology can make these deadweight losses even larger.

The issue of future international taxes on e-commerce has not been resolved. The United Nations has already put forward a proposal to tax e-mail in developed countries to pay for computer access in developing countries. In talks with the World Trade Organization, the USA has been arguing against special taxes on e-commerce. Of course, the motivation for this is quite clear: the USA is the biggest net exporter of e-commerce. No one really knows how things will shape up in the future.

There is a special concern about the activity of global financial firms. Technological change and financial deregulation have globalized financial markets dramatically. Financial firms are now capable of selling financial products round the clock. This phenomenon of global trading challenges taxpayers and tax administrations to come up with a fair way of allocating and taxing the profits in each country where global trading is carried out. In 1998 the OECD published a considerably revised and updated version of the discussion draft *The Taxation of Global Trading of Financial Instruments*. Current related work focuses on four main areas:

1. Providing guidance on how to apply the general principles of the guidelines to complex situations.
2. Monitoring the practical implementation of the guidelines, and amending and updating the existing guidance given in the light of this monitoring.
3. The improvement of administrative procedures.
4. Encouraging non-member countries to associate themselves with the guidelines.

A FINAL REMARK

Taxation is undoubtedly a very important determining factor of FDI, and its effect runs through a number of channels. We have seen that the tax factor affects the decision concerning the location of an FDI project. And once an investor has chosen the location, taxes are perhaps the most significant factor determining whether the project should be run by a branch or a subsidiary. Following this decision, taxes also play a role in the relationship between the parent MNC and its foreign establishment with respect to the remittances, transfer pricing, and other areas. The tax factor also affects the perceived profitability of an FDI project as it plays a role in determining the cost of capital, and hence also the discount rate. In Chapter 7, the effect of the tax factor on the cost of capital and capital structure will be analysed.

7 The International Cost of Capital and Capital Structure

A firm's capital consists of equity (retained earnings and funds obtained by issuing stock) and debt (borrowed funds). The firm's cost of retained earnings reflects an opportunity cost representing what the existing shareholders could have earned if they had received the earnings as dividends and invested the funds themselves. The firm's cost of new equity capital that is obtained by issuing new stock reflects the opportunity cost of what the new shareholders could have earned if they had invested their funds elsewhere. The cost of new equity capital is higher than the cost of retained earnings because it also includes the expenses associated with selling the new stock; that is, the cost of placing the new issue of stock. The firm's cost of debt is easier to measure because interest expenses are incurred by the firm as a result of borrowing funds.

The cost of capital has a major impact on a firm's value. To fund its operations, a firm uses a capital structure (that is, a combination of equity and debt) that minimizes its cost of capital, and therefore maximizes its value. The lower the firm's cost of capital, the lower its required rate of return on a given proposed project. Therefore, estimating the cost of capital is a step that must be taken before indulging in the capital budgeting exercise. This is because the NPV of any project depends, in part, on the discount rate, which is equal, or closely related, to the cost of capital (recall the formula used to calculate NPV in Chapter 4).

The cost of capital has important implications for capital budgeting. MNCs operating in countries where the cost of capital is high will be forced to decline projects that may be feasible for MNCs operating in countries where the cost of capital is low. Moreover, MNCs operating in countries where the cost of capital is high are likely to divest existing projects because of the high cost associated with funding these projects. For example, Lloyds Bank (a major British bank) once decided to sell its commercial banking operations in the USA because the rate of return on these operations was inadequate relative to its cost of capital.

For an MNC, financing can take a much wider range of forms than for a purely domestic firm. In domestic corporate finance, a distinction normally is made between debt and equity financing, and that is the end of the matter. For an MNC, an equally important distinction is made between intra-company fund transfers and financing sources that are external to the MNC. International financing, to which MNCs invariably resort, traverse both currency and national boundaries. For an MNC, internal and external sources of funds may vary over a range of dimensions, including maturity, currency of denomination, geographical sourcing and institutional sourcing.

Generally speaking, an MNC can raise finance from either internal or external sources. Internal sources include retained earnings and funds provided by subsidiaries. External sources include national and international capital markets. National capital markets, for example,

Figure 7.1 Some sources of funds for MNCs

provide short-term and medium-term financing in the form of over-drafts, bridge loans and discountable medium-term loans. They can also provide long-term financing in the form of long-term bank loans, leases, bonds and equity. International capital markets provide funds in the form of Eurobonds, international bonds and international equity. Figure 7.1 provides a schematic representation of these sources of funds. It must be emphasized, however, that this list of the sources of funds is not exhaustive, but rather is representative.[1]

Faced with such a lucrative menu, the MNC's choice depends on several factors, including: (i) the need to maintain or strengthen the extent of control over subsidiaries; (ii) the need to receive regular cash inflow from subsidiaries; (iii) the purpose for which financing is needed; (iv) other aspects of the overall business strategy, such as the objective of minimizing global tax liabilities; (v) expectations concerning the future path of exchange and interest rates; and (vi) the desire to minimize exposure to various types of risk, such as foreign exchange risk and country risk.

THE COST OF CAPITAL AND INVESTMENT DECISIONS

In this section we present a theoretical representation of the cost of capital and investment decision-making. The marginal cost of capital (MCC) is defined as the cost of new financing, which remains constant initially, irrespective of changes in the quantity of new financing. However, as new funds are supplied progressively, the suppliers will require higher returns to provide more funds. Thus, the MCC curve

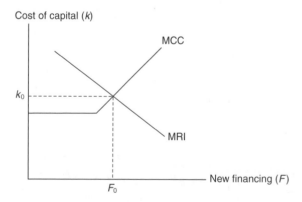

Figure 7.2 The cost of capital and investment decisions

becomes upward-sloping rather than flat once this threshold has been reached, as shown in Figure 7.2.

This is what happens on the supply side, but what about the demand side? Demand is determined by the marginal return on investment (MRI), which is the rate of return on new investments. In Figure 7.2, the MRI curve is shown to be downward sloping, because if the investment projects are arranged in a descending order with respect to their rates of return, this is exactly what we would get. Equilibrium is reached at the point of intersection of the MCC curve and the MRI curve, giving an equilibrium level of the cost of capital, k_0. Some comparative static analysis can be conducted by shifting the MCC and MRI curves. For example, the MCC may shift to the right, implying willingness of creditors to supply more new funds at each level of the cost of capital if it is believed that the economy is heading towards rapid growth and higher profitability. In this case, the cost of capital will drop. On the demand side, the MRI curve could shift to the left if the firm became more risk averse, implying that fewer projects would be accepted at each level of the cost of capital. In this case, the cost of capital would decline.

THE WEIGHTED AVERAGE COST OF CAPITAL

The firm's weighted average cost of capital, k, is calculated as a weighted average of the cost of debt capital, k_d, and equity capital, k_e, with the weights determined by the proportion of debt and equity in the capital structure. Thus, if the capital of a firm consists of D debt and E equity, then the cost of capital is given by:

$$k = \left(\frac{D}{D+E}\right)k_d(1-\tau) + \left(\frac{D}{D+E}\right)k_e \qquad (7.1)$$

where τ is the tax rate. The first term that reflects the weighted cost of debt, $[D/(D+E)]k_d$, is multiplied by the term $(1-\tau)$, which is less than unity. This is because debt financing involves tax saving, given that interest expenses are tax deductible.

The cost of equity capital, k_e, is the equity market's expected rate of return on the firm's stock, based on the equity market's opportunity cost of forgoing investment in other stocks with the same risk. In addition to the business risk of the firm's operations, the cost of equity capital depends on the firm's relative debt level, $D/(D+E)$, since the degree of financial leverage influences the risk of equity.

Because interest payments are tax deductible, it appears that using debt is beneficial in the sense that it reduces the cost of capital, leading to an increase in the value of the firm. This is true to a certain extent, in the sense that increasing the debt–equity ratio, D/E, leads to a decline in the cost of capital, but only to a certain level, at which the cost of capital reaches a minimum. Any further increase in the ratio above this level leads to a rise in the cost of capital. This is because a higher level of debt implies, or may be taken to imply, a higher probability of bankruptcy, which means that new shareholders or creditors will demand a higher required rate of return. This will more than offset the tax saving, leading consequently to a rise in the cost of capital. The relationship between the cost of capital and the debt–equity ratio is illustrated in Figure 7.3.

When an MNC considers a foreign project that has the same risk as the MNC itself, it can use its weighted average cost of capital as the required rate of return (or the discount rate) for the project. If the project has a different degree of risk, the MNC must account for the risk differential in the capital budgeting process. There are various ways of dealing with risk differentials. Risk can be accounted for within the cash flow estimates by using various possible values for the variables used to calculate the NPV. A probability distribution can thus be constructed to assess the probability that the project will generate a rate of return that is at least equal to the firm's weighted

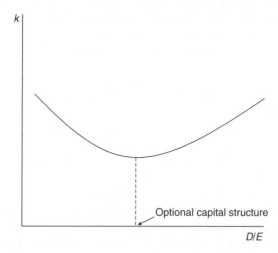

Figure 7.3 The behaviour of the cost of capital in response to changes in the debt–equity ratio

average cost of capital. An alternative method of accounting for risk is to adjust the weighted average cost of capital for the risk differential. Thus, if the project is more risky than the MNC, the required rate of return on the project will be the cost of capital plus a factor that reflects the risk differential.

IMPLICATIONS OF USING THE COST OF CAPITAL AS A DISCOUNT RATE

Using the weighted average cost of capital as a discount rate in capital budgeting analysis has certain implications for calculating the NPV and other project evaluation criteria. First, since the tax deductibility of the interest on debt is accounted for in the definition of the cost of capital, this deductibility should be accounted for again in the definition of the cash flows. For this reason, capital budgeting analysis should be based on after-tax operating cash flows, $O_t(1 - \tau)$, where O_t is the gross operating cash flow arising at time t, and τ is the corporate income tax rate. This expression, however, overstates the amount of tax that is actually paid. The actual amount of tax is paid on the before-tax net cash flow, $O_t - I_t$, where I_t is the interest on the firm's debt, which means that the amount of tax that is actually paid is $\tau(O_t - I_t)$. The overstatement of the actual taxes paid in capital budgeting analysis is because the interest tax shield is ignored in the cash flows. However, the procedure is sound, since the tax shield benefits of the interest deductions are accounted for in the cost of capital. To avoid double counting, tax deductions should be ignored in the definition of the cash flows.

The second implication pertains to the financial leverage of a subsidiary. Assume that an MNC is considering establishing a new subsidiary, using its own funds to finance a portion of the subsidiary's total investment outlay. These funds would be obtained by issuing new debt and equity in amounts that keep its own capital structure unchanged. The remainder of the subsidiary's investment outlay is borrowed by the subsidiary itself. Let us further assume that the subsidiary's debt is not guaranteed by the MNC, and that the subsidiary has the same operating risk as the MNC. After the payments of interest on debt by the subsidiary, the remaining cash flows are paid to the MNC. The question that arises here is the following: which cash flows are employed in capital budgeting analysis, the subsidiary's cash flows before its interest payments or the cash flows received by the MNC?

While it is natural for the MNC to think in terms of the cash flows it receives from the subsidiary (after interest payments) it is generally easier to use cash flows before interest payments. The reason for this procedure is that, since the subsidiary as a whole has the same business risk as the MNC, the MNC's cost of capital is the appropriate discount rate to be used to calculate the present value of the expected total operating cash flows of the subsidiary. Thus, the appropriate discount rate to apply in capital budgeting analysis conveniently is known. By the same token, the MNC's cost of capital is not the appropriate discount rate to be used for finding the present value of the cash flows after the subsidiary's interest payments. This is because the cash flows are levered by the subsidiary's own debt, which makes it more risky than the cash flows generated by the MNC from its operations. In principle, capital budgeting analysis may be performed on the basis of the cash flows received by the parent, but then the parent's cost of capital has to be adjusted to reflect the degree of financial leverage implied by the subsidiary's use of its own debt financing. This adjustment is possible, but it is not intuitive and may lack precision.

The third implication pertains to taxes. A subsidiary must pay taxes to the foreign (host) government, and the MNC has to pay taxes to its (the home country's) government. The subsidiary's after-tax operating cash flows, to which the MNC's cost of capital applies, should be viewed as net of all taxes, domestic and foreign. However, if there is tax credit, then the tax rate used to calculate after-tax operating cash flows is the domestic tax rate. This is the case if the domestic tax rate is higher than the foreign tax rate.

The final implication pertains to the issue of discounting cash flows denominated in two different currencies (the domestic currency and a foreign currency). There is in general no rule for converting the cost of capital in one currency to the cost of capital that is used in conjunction with the same asset's expected cash flows when converted into another currency. In practice, while an MNC knows its own cost of capital that is applied to domestic currency denominated cash flows, it may not have an easy way to know the appropriate foreign currency cost of capital that is used with the same cash flows in foreign currency denomination. Sometimes an *ad hoc* procedure is used, whereby the discount rate that an MNC applies to foreign currency cash flows is taken to be the sum of the domestic currency cost of capital and the difference between the riskless interest rates on the two currencies. This procedure is, however, faulty.

THE COST OF CAPITAL OF MNCs

The cost of capital of an MNC invariably differs from the cost of capital of a domestic firm, because of the differences between domestic firms and MNCs. If the MNC raises capital in more than one country, then its overall cost of capital will be a weighted average of the costs of capital corresponding to individual countries, with the weights being the proportions of capital raised in each country. If the amounts of debt capital and equity capital raised in country i are D_i and E_i respectively, where $i = 1, 2, \ldots, n$ (assuming that the amounts are measured in domestic currency terms) then the total amount of debt and equity capital raised are:

$$D = \sum_{i=1}^{n} D_i \tag{7.2}$$

$$E = \sum_{i=1}^{n} E_i \tag{7.3}$$

The weighted average cost of capital raised in country i is:

$$k_i = \left[\frac{D_i}{D_i + E_i}\right] k_{di}(1 - \tau_i) + \left[\frac{E_i}{D_i + E_i}\right] k_{ei} \tag{7.4}$$

Hence the overall cost of capital is given by:

$$k = \sum_{i=1}^{n} \left(\frac{D_i}{D}\right) \left[\frac{D_i}{D_i + E_i}\right] k_{di}(1 - \tau_i) + \sum_{i=1}^{n} \left(\frac{E_i}{E}\right) \left[\frac{E_i}{D_i + E_i}\right] k_{ei} \tag{7.5}$$

A number of factors can explain the observed differences between the cost of capital of MNCs and that of domestic firms. Some of these factors make the cost of capital of an MNC lower than that of a domestic firm, while others do the reverse. Because of the diversity of these factors, one cannot reach a general conclusion as to whether the cost of capital of a domestic firm is higher or lower than that of an MNC: it all depends on the particular case of each firm. These factors are now discussed in turn.

Size of the Firm

Indulging in multinational operations leads to growth beyond what is available from domestic operations alone. Because of this factor,

MNCs tend (on average) to be larger in size than domestic firms. Large size reduces the cost of both debt and equity capital. Large MNCs borrow substantial amounts of funds, and in the process they receive preferential borrowing rates from creditors such as banks. Moreover, MNCs exploit economies of scale through their relatively large issues of bonds and stocks. Economies of scale lead to lower costs (as a percentage of the amount raised) of new bond or stock issues.

It is also the case that creditors may believe that big firms are financially more powerful than small firms, and they (big firms) are less likely to default on their debt. Therefore, creditors may demand zero or small risk premia from big firms compared with small firms. As we shall see later, the cost of debt capital facing one firm is the basic lending rate of the creditor plus a risk premium. The latter depends on the perceived probability of default, which depends partly on the size of the firm.

Some evidence on the role played by size in this respect can be found in the literature on the characteristics of MNCs, and what distinguishes MNCs from purely domestic firms (see Chapter 1). There is some strong evidence indicating that MNCs are characterized both by having a large size and by being able to obtain a lower cost of capital. For example, Grubaugh (1987) tested three hypotheses to explain why firms would choose to become MNCs, and found support for two hypotheses. The first is that there is a significant difference between MNCs and domestic firms with respect to the cost of capital and capital intensity. This hypothesis reflects the view that MNCs are essentially firms that indulge in capital arbitrage, as suggested by MacDougal (1960). The second is that MNCs are significantly different from domestic firms in terms of size and product diversity. This is a reflection of the view that MNCs are oligopolistic firms that compete by producing in various countries (Hymer, 1976).

Access to International Capital Markets

MNCs source funds from domestic as well as international capital markets. Access to international capital markets allows MNCs to obtain lower borrowing rates. They could also obtain funds at lower costs through their subsidiaries. Or they could indulge in cross-border financing operations, such as parallel loans and swaps.[2] Lall and Streeten (1977) argue that not only do MNCs have access to finance, but also that they have privileged access in the sense that they can obtain funds on better terms than other firms. With the expansion of international banking worldwide, MNCs (which have long-established links with the parent bank) can extend these links and privileges to their subsidiaries. Indeed, it is arguable that one reason for the expansion of international banking has been the desire of banks to open branches in the countries where the subsidiaries of MNCs dealing with them are located, so that they can provide financial services for the subsidiaries.

International financing will not necessarily lead to exposure to foreign exchange risk, because it is likely that the MNC or its subsidiaries have revenues that are denominated in the same currency as the debt. This point can be illustrated formally as follows. Assume that the MNC borrows a foreign currency amount, K, at time t, to be repaid with interest at time $t + 1$. The principal and interest to be repaid by the firm at $t + 1$ is $K(1 + i_t^*)$, where i_t^* is the foreign interest rate prevailing at time t. Because of inevitable changes in the exchange rate, S, between t and $t + 1$, the domestic currency value of the principal and interest at $t + 1$ could be anything, depending on the swing in the exchange rate from S_t to S_{t+1}. This is why exposure to foreign exchange risk arises. If, on the other hand, the firm has foreign currency receivables maturing at $t + 1$ amounting to R_{t+1} foreign currency units, then the net domestic currency position at $t + 1$, E_{t+1}, is given by:

$$E_{t+1} = S_{t+1}\left[K(1 + i_t^*) - R_{t+1}\right] \qquad (7.6)$$

It is obvious that if $K(1 + i_t^*) = R_{t+1}$, then $E_{t+1} = 0$. As long as $R_{t+1} > 0$, the foreign exchange exposure will be lower than if there were no foreign currency receivables.

International Diversification

The cost of capital is affected by the probability of bankruptcy, so the higher this probability, the higher will be the cost of capital, as creditors and shareholders demand higher rates of return on their funds. A basic principle in finance is that diversification reduces risk. In this case, international diversification leads to stability of cash flows and hence to a lower probability of bankruptcy. But why would this be the case? Simply because, for a number of reasons, countries do not go through the same phase of the business cycle at the same time, so one country may be in a slump while another is in a boom. Hence, international diversification smooths out fluctuations in cash flows. By increasing the stability of cash flows and lowering the probability of becoming bankrupt, international diversification leads to a lower cost of capital.

Assume that the firm's total cash flow consists of a domestic currency cash flow, X_t, and a foreign currency cash flow, X_t^*. The domestic currency value of the total cash flow will therefore be $X_t + S_t X_t^*$. The stability of the total cash flow is measured by its standard deviation, which can be calculated as:

$$\sigma(X_t + S_t X_t^*) = \sqrt{\sigma^2(X_t) + \sigma^2(S_t X_t^*) + 2\sigma(X_t)\sigma(S_t X_t^*)\rho(X_t, S_t X_t^*)}$$
(7.7)

where $\sigma^2(.)$ is the variance, $\sigma(.)$ is the standard deviation and $\rho(.)$ is the correlation coefficient. Notice that if $\rho(X_t, S_t X_t^*) = 1$, implying perfect correlation between the domestic currency cash flow and the domestic currency value of the foreign currency cash flow, then there is no reduction in the variability of the total cash flow, because:

$$\sigma(X_t + S_t X_t^*) = \sigma(X_t) + \sigma(S_t X_t^*)$$
(7.8)

However, as long as $\rho(X_t, S_t X_t^*) < 1$, implying less than perfect correlation, the total cash flow will be more stable, in the sense that its standard deviation will be lower than the sum of the standard deviations of the individual cash flows. In the extreme case, when $\rho(X_t, S_t X_t^*) = -1$, we get:

$$\sigma(X_t + S_t X_t^*) = \sigma(X_t) - \sigma(S_t X_t^*)$$
(7.9)

which is the largest possible risk reduction resulting from perfect negative correlation between X_t and $S_t X_t^*$.

Exposure to Foreign Exchange Risk

Funds remitted to an MNC from its subsidiaries are converted into the MNC's functional currency (the domestic currency). Because of the exchange rate factor, the domestic currency value of foreign currency cash flows will be highly volatile. This is because the variability of the exchange rate will augment the variability of the foreign currency cash flow. The variability of the domestic currency value of foreign currency cash flows leads to a higher probability that the firm may go bankrupt, thus raising the cost of capital.

Remember that the domestic currency value of a foreign currency tax flow is $S_t X_t^*$. If we measure the variability of this cash flow in terms of the standard deviation of its rate of change (implied by a dot), it follows that:

$$\sigma^2(\dot{X}_t^* + \dot{S}_t) = \sigma^2(\dot{X}_t^*) + \sigma^2(\dot{S}_t) + 2Cov(\dot{X}_t^*, \dot{S}_t) \qquad (7.10)$$

where $Cov(\dot{X}_t^*, \dot{S}_t)$ is the covariance between $\dot{X}_t^*$ and $\dot{S}_t$. This means that the variability of the domestic currency value of a foreign currency cash flow (measured by its variance) consists of the variability of the cash flow in foreign currency terms, $\sigma^2(\dot{X}_t^*)$, the variability of the exchange rate, $\sigma^2(\dot{S}_t)$, and the covariance between changes in these two variables, $Cov(\dot{X}_t^*, \dot{S}_t)$.[3] Notice that $\sigma^2(\dot{X}_t^* + \dot{S}_t) > \sigma^2(\dot{X}_t^*)$ as long as $\sigma^2(\dot{S}_t) > 0$, which is invariably the case. In fact, there is ample empirical evidence indicating that the variability of the exchange rate contributes significantly to the variability of the domestic currency value of foreign currency cash flows. One should not forget, however, that combining cash flows denominated in various currencies reduces the variability of the total cash flow, as we saw previously (see, for example, Moosa, 1998, p. 554).

Exposure to Country Risk

While international operations imply international diversification, which in turn implies stability of cash flows, they also lead to exposure to country risk. Extreme exposure to country risk (particularly political risk) may lead to an outright confiscation of the project, and hence big losses for the MNC. By following the same argument concerning the probability of bankruptcy, it is easy to conclude that exposure to country risk, as with exposure to foreign exchange risk, leads to a higher cost of capital.

DOMESTIC CURRENCY VERSUS FOREIGN CURRENCY FINANCING

If foreign currency financing creates exposure to foreign exchange risk, why do business firms find it attractive – at least sometimes – to borrow in foreign currency? There are at least two reasons why this is the case.

The first reason is that foreign currency financing introduces foreign exchange risk if the business firm does not already have such an exposure, as we saw in an earlier section. If, on the other hand, the firm already has this kind of exposure, then foreign currency exposure may in fact be reduced by resorting to foreign currency financing. Suppose that a British firm has receivables in yen and Australian dollars due in three months' time. This firm is obviously subject to foreign exchange risk, because the pound values of these receivables are not known until they are realized (unless, of course, the positions are hedged). This firm can eliminate the exposure completely by borrowing amounts in the same currencies and with the same maturity date as when the receivables are due, such that the amounts borrowed and the interest payments are equal to the receivables (that is, the borrowed amounts should be equal to the present value of the receivables). The firm can then utilize the receivables to pay off the loans. No matter what happens to the exchange rates, the firm will not be affected as far as these transactions are concerned.

The second reason is that foreign currency financing may be cheaper. Interest rates on loans in various currencies are different, and in many cases foreign currencies can offer lower interest rates than the domestic currency. However, the cost of capital in a foreign currency has an exchange rate element. Thus, to compare the cost of capital in the domestic currency with the cost of capital in a foreign currency, we need to take into account changes in exchange rates.

Foreign Currency Debt Financing

The effective cost of debt financing in foreign currency (measured in domestic currency terms) depends on the foreign cost of debt capital and the percentage change in the exchange rate. It can be calculated as follows by considering a two-period model. Suppose that an amount, X, of the foreign currency is borrowed at time 0 at the foreign cost of debt capital, k_d^*. The domestic currency value of the amount borrowed, D_0, is given by:

$$D_0 = XS_0 \qquad (7.11)$$

where S_0 is the spot exchange rate prevailing at time 0 (measured in direct quotation as domestic per foreign). When the loan matures at time 1, the domestic currency amount to be repaid (the principal plus interest), D_1, is given by:

$$D_1 = XS_1(1 + k_d^*) \tag{7.12}$$

where S_1 is the spot exchange rate prevailing at time 1. The effective cost of debt capital, κ, is therefore given by:

$$1 + \kappa = \frac{D_1}{D_0} \tag{7.13}$$

or:

$$1 + \kappa = \frac{XS_1(1 + k_d^*)}{XS_0} \tag{7.14}$$

which reduces to:

$$1 + \kappa = (1 + k_d^*)(1 + \dot{S}) \tag{7.15}$$

where $\dot{S}$ is the percentage change in the exchange rate between 0 and 1. Thus:

$$\kappa = (1 + k_d^*)(1 + \dot{S}) - 1 \tag{7.16}$$

By ignoring the term $k_d^* \dot{S}$, an approximate formula for the effective cost of debt capital would be:

$$\kappa \approx k_d^* + \dot{S} \tag{7.17}$$

which tells us that the effective cost of debt capital is approximately equal to the foreign cost of debt capital plus the rate of change of the exchange rate over the borrowing period. So, if $\kappa < k_d$, foreign currency debt financing would be cheaper than domestic currency debt financing, and vice versa. The effective cost of debt capital may be negative, implying that the borrower pays back fewer units of the domestic currency than the amount actually borrowed.

It can be demonstrated that if covered interest parity (CIP) holds, then domestic currency financing and foreign currency financing will lead to the same results if the foreign currency position resulting from foreign currency financing is covered in the forward market. In this case, the foreign currency is bought forward at time 0, which means that the amount to be repaid is converted at the forward rate prevailing at time 0, F_0. Thus:

$$D_1 = XF_0(1 + k_d^*) \tag{7.18}$$

The effective cost of debt capital is, therefore, given by:

$$1 + \kappa = \frac{XF_0(1 + k_d^*)}{XS_0} \tag{7.19}$$

which reduces to:

$$1 + \kappa = (1 + k_d^*)(1 + f) \tag{7.20}$$

where f is the forward spread. Thus:

$$\kappa = (1 + k_d^*)(1 + f) - 1 \tag{7.21}$$

If CIP holds, then:

$$1 + f = \frac{1 + k_d}{1 + k_d^*} \tag{7.22}$$

By substituting Equation (7.22) into Equation (7.21) we obtain:

$$\kappa = k_d \tag{7.23}$$

Thus, if CIP holds, then the effective cost of debt capital will be equal to the domestic cost of debt capital. Hence, foreign currency financing will be useless in the sense that it will not be cheaper than domestic currency financing. If, however, CIP is violated, such that:

$$1 + f > \frac{1 + k_d}{1 + k_d^*} \tag{7.24}$$

which means that the forward spread is larger than the differential cost of debt capital. It follows that:

$$\kappa > k_d \tag{7.25}$$

which means that foreign currency financing is not desirable, since it is more expensive than domestic currency financing. The argument is valid the other way round.

Consider now the choice of the currency of debt financing when the underlying instrument is a long-term bond. For simplicity, let us assume that the instrument is a zero coupon bond, so that all the payments are made on maturity, which we shall assume to be n years. If a domestic currency bond is chosen, then the amount to be paid by the borrowing firm will be:

$$D_n = X(1 + k_d)^n \qquad (7.26)$$

If a foreign currency denomination is used, the foreign currency amount raised is X/S_0. On maturity, the domestic currency equivalent of the foreign currency amount due is:

$$D_n^* = \frac{XS_n}{S_0}(1 + k_d^*)^n \qquad (7.27)$$

where S_n is the exchange rate prevailing on maturity. Equation (7.27) can be rewritten as:

$$D_n^* = X(1 + \dot{S})^n(1 + k_d^*)^n \qquad (7.28)$$

where $\dot{S}$ is the annual percentage rate of change of the exchange rate between 0 and n. Assuming risk neutrality, foreign currency financing will be preferred if:

$$D_n^* < D_n \qquad (7.29)$$

or if:

$$X(1 + \dot{S})^n(1 + k_d^*)^n < X(1 + k_d)^n \qquad (7.30)$$

which can be simplified to give the condition:

$$k_d^* + \dot{S} < k_d \qquad (7.31)$$

If this condition is satisfied, the bond issue should be denominated in foreign rather than domestic currency. On the other hand, if:

$$k_d^* + \dot{S} > k_d \qquad (7.32)$$

the firm should use domestic currency financing.

Remember that debt can be raised in more than one foreign currency at the same time. If two foreign currencies, i and j, are used, then the effective cost of debt financing in the two currencies will be given by:

$$k_{di} = (1 + k_{di}^*)(1 + \dot{S}_i) \tag{7.33}$$

$$k_{dj} = (1 + k_{dj}^*)(1 + \dot{S}_j) \tag{7.34}$$

Assume now that the amounts of debt capital denominated in the two foreign currencies and the domestic currency are X_i, X_j and X, respectively, all of which are measured in domestic currency terms, then the total pre-tax cost of debt capital, $\bar{k}_d$, is:

$$\bar{k}_d = \left(\frac{X}{X + X_i + X_j}\right) k_d + \left(\frac{X_i}{X + X_i + X_j}\right) \kappa_i + \left(\frac{X_j}{X + X_i + X_j}\right) \kappa_j \tag{7.35}$$

or:

$$\bar{k}_d = \left(\frac{X}{X + X_i + X_j}\right) k_d + \left(\frac{X_i}{X + X_i + X_j}\right)(1 + k_{di}^*)(1 + \dot{S}_i)$$
$$+ \left(\frac{X_j}{X + X_i + X_j}\right)(1 + k_{dj}^*)(1 + \dot{S}_j) \tag{7.36}$$

Notice that:

$$\frac{\partial \bar{k}_d}{\partial \dot{S}_i} = \left(\frac{X_i}{X + X_i + X_j}\right)(1 + k_{di}^*) > 0 \tag{7.37}$$

$$\frac{\partial \bar{k}_d}{\partial \dot{S}_j} = \left(\frac{X_j}{X + X_i + X_j}\right)(1 + k_{dj}^*) > 0 \tag{7.38}$$

implying that the total cost of debt capital increases with the appreciation of the foreign currencies against the domestic currency.

International Equity Financing

Unlike loans and bonds whose markets became internationalized a relatively long time ago, the internationalization of equities did not take off until about 1983. International equity markets encompass primary market functions (underwriting of new equity issues) and secondary market functions (trading) of equities outside the issuer's home country. The London International Stock Exchange is the best example of an international secondary equity market, accounting for a large portion of international equity trading. MNCs operate in international equity markets by listing their shares on foreign stock exchanges (the secondary market function) and by selling new shares to foreigners (the primary market function). We shall deal with these functions in turn, starting with listing on foreign stock exchanges.

One of the objectives of listing on foreign stock exchanges is to improve the liquidity of existing shares by enabling foreign shareholders to trade them in their home markets and currencies. Another objective is to boost the listing firm's commercial and political visibility in foreign countries. A third objective is to support a new equity issue. Finally, a fourth objective of foreign listing is to broaden ownership outside the national frontiers, which may help to reduce price fluctuations.

The benefits of listing on foreign stock exchanges must be balanced against the cost of the implied commitment to full disclosure. Because the disclosure guidelines of the US Securities and Exchange Commission (SEC) are more stringent than in other countries, US firms find it easier to list on foreign stock exchanges than do non-US firms wishing to list on US stock exchanges. But having decided to list on a foreign stock exchange, the question arises as to where to list. The choice depends on the motive behind foreign listing. If the motive is to support a new equity issue, the target market should be the listing market. If the aim is to increase the firm's commercial and political visibility, the market should be the one in which the firm has significant physical operations. If the motive is to improve the liquidity of existing shares, then the market should be a major liquid market such as London, New York, Tokyo, Frankfurt or Paris. These markets account for more than half of the total capitalization of stock markets around the world.

Now we turn to the selling of new shares in international markets. A firm may sell its newly-issued shares to foreign investors in one of the following ways:

1. Selling shares in a particular foreign stock market underwritten in whole or in part by institutions from the host country. It may take the form of a private placement.[4]
2. Selling Euro-equity issues to foreign investors in more than one country simultaneously. The integration of the world capital markets has led to the emergence of a Euro-equity market.

3. Selling a foreign subsidiary's shares to investors in the host coun-
    try. This can lower a firm's cost of capital if investors in the host
    country award a higher capitalization rate on the subsidiary's
    earnings than on the firm's earnings.
4. Selling shares to a foreign firm as part of a strategic alliance. This
    may involve the sharing of the cost of developing new technology
    or pursuing complementary marketing activities.

Putting Things Together

Let us now try to determine the cost of capital of a firm that issues
equity capital solely in domestic currency, and debt capital in domestic
and foreign currencies. Assume that the firm services all of its debt
from a domestic currency base. In this framework, fluctuations in the
exchange rate will affect the cost of debt capital, and therefore the
overall cost of capital. The pre-tax cost of debt capital is:

$$\bar{k}_d = \left(\frac{D^*}{D^* + D}\right)\kappa + \left(\frac{D}{D^* + D}\right)k_d \qquad (7.39)$$

The overall cost of capital is:

$$k = (1 - \tau)\left[\left(\frac{D^*}{D^* + D + E}\right)((1 + k_d^*)(1 + \dot{S}) - 1)\right.$$
$$\left. + \left(\frac{D}{D^* + D + E}\right)k_d\right] + \left(\frac{E}{D^* + D + E}\right)k_e \qquad (7.40)$$

where it is assumed that D^* is measured in domestic currency terms.
Notice that:

$$\frac{\partial k}{\partial \dot{S}} = \left[\frac{D^*}{D^* + D + E}\right](1 + k_d^*) > 0 \qquad (7.41)$$

which implies that an appreciation of the foreign currency leads to a
rise in the overall cost of capital.

CAPM AND THE COST OF CAPITAL

The capital asset pricing model (CAPM) can be used to show why the
cost of capital of an MNC differs from that of a purely domestic firm.

The CAPM is used to determine the required rate of return on a stock, k_j, as follows:

$$k_j = i + \beta(k_m - i) \qquad (7.42)$$

where i is the risk-free interest rate, k_m is the market rate of return where the market is represented by a stock price index, and β is the beta of the stock, measuring the degree of correlation between the stock price and the market. The market is represented by a stock price index, which could be a national stock price index if the markets are segmented, and a world index if markets are integrated.[5] Thus, three factors determine k_j: the risk-free interest rate, the market rate of return, and the beta of the stock. An MNC cannot control the risk-free rate or the rate of return on the market, but it can influence its beta. By reducing its beta, an MNC can reduce its cost of capital.

For a well-diversified MNC with cash flows generated by several projects, each project contains two types of risk: (i) unsystematic risk that is unique to the project; and (ii) systematic risk. CAPM suggests that unsystematic risk can be ignored, since it can be diversified away. However, systematic risk cannot be diversified away. In general, the lower the beta, the lower the project's systematic risk and the lower would be the required rate of return on the project. The relationship between (expected) return and systematic risk is represented by Figure 7.4. It shows that when $\beta = 1$, then $k_j = k_m$. Hence, CAPM

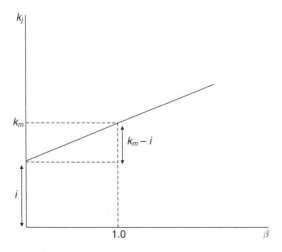

Figure 7.4 The relationship between return and systematic risk

seems to suggest that the cost of capital of an MNC is lower than the cost of capital of a domestic firm.

To apply the CAPM in a global setting, several issues arise. The first issue concerns the definition of the market portfolio: should it be the market portfolio of the home country, the market portfolio of the foreign country, a combination of the two portfolios or a global market portfolio? The second issue concerns changes in currency values: should these changes be included in the market portfolio's rate of return? Then there is the choice of the appropriate risk-free rate, which differs from one country to another. Finally, there is the issue of exposure to foreign exchange risk: should currency exposure be taken into account as a risk factor that requires an adjustment in the expected rate of return?

These issues have been addressed by the global asset pricing model (GAPM) (see, for example, Dumas, 1993). This model is based on the idea of international diversification of portfolios, which is what is practised in reality. Given relatively thorough international diversification, the model is used to determine the risk-adjusted required rate of return from the perspective of a certain currency. The model may be written as:

$$k_j = i + \beta_g(k_g - i) + \beta_q(k_q - i) \tag{7.43}$$

where β_g is a measure of the sensitivity of the asset's rate of return relative to the rate of return on the global market portfolio, β_q is the sensitivity to the rate of change in wealth-weighted index of exchange rates, k_g is the expected rate of return on the global market portfolio measured in domestic currency terms, and k_q is the expected rate of change in the domestic currency value of the wealth-weighted portfolio of other currencies.

Equation (7.43) is applicable to any particular currency regardless of the currency denomination of the asset. This is because k_j in this case is the expected rate of return expressed in domestic currency terms. The risk-free rate is the rate of return on domestic currency risk-free assets. There are two differences between Equations (7.42) and (7.43). The first difference is that the market portfolio in Equation (7.42) becomes the global market portfolio in Equation (7.43). The second and more important difference is that Equation (7.43) embodies two risk factors: one for market risk, and the other for currency exposure risk. Thus, the GAPM shows that an asset has two betas, one measuring market risk, and the other measuring currency risk. These two betas must be measured simultaneously by using multiple regression analysis.

The rate of return on a single asset in terms of a particular currency that is different from the currency of denomination of the asset consists of two components: the rate of return in terms of the currency of denomination and the rate of appreciation (or depreciation) of this currency against the base currency (the currency in which k_j is measured). The global market portfolio is some sort of a weighted average of these returns. In practice, the global rate of return is calculated from the value of a world stock price index measured in a particular currency. Similarly, the rate of change in the base currency can be calculated from the effective exchange rate of the base currency. The GAPM can be used to calculate the expected rate of return on a foreign project.

The GAPM can also be used to forecast the expected change in the exchange rate of the foreign currency in terms of the domestic currency, which is an important input in capital budgeting analysis. For two currencies, the domestic currency and a foreign currency, we have:

$$\dot{S}^e = (i - i^*) + \beta_g(k_g - i) + \beta_q(k_q - i) \tag{7.44}$$

where $\dot{S}^e$ is the expected change in the exchange rate measured as the domestic currency price of one unit of the foreign currency, i is the domestic (risk-free) interest rate, i^* is the foreign interest rate, β_g is the sensitivity of the percentage change in the exchange rate to the rate of return on the global market portfolio, and β_q is the sensitivity to the rate of change in a wealth-weighted index of exchange rates (the effective exchange rate of the domestic currency).

In general, if we are dealing with currencies x and y, such that the base currency is x, then:

$$\dot{S}^e(x/y) = i_x - i_y + \beta_g(k_g - i_x) + \beta_q(k_q - i_x) \tag{7.45}$$

Equation (7.45) says the following. The expected change in the exchange rate, measured as x/y, depends on three factors: (i) the interest rate differential, $i_x - i_y$; (ii) the difference between the rate of return on the global market portfolio and the interest rate on currency x, $k_g - i_x$; and (iii) the difference between the rate of change in the index of the exchange rate (the effective exchange rate of currency x) and the interest rate on currency x, $k_q - i_x$.[6] If $\beta_g = \beta_q = 0$, then:

$$\dot{S}^e(x/y) = i_x - i_y \tag{7.46}$$

which is uncovered interest parity (UIP). Hence, Equation (7.46) solves the risk premium problem associated with uncovered interest parity.[7] Furthermore, if $i_x = i_y$, then:

$$\dot{S}^e(x/y) = 0 \tag{7.47}$$

Obviously, Equation (7.47) cannot hold unless certain stringent conditions are satisfied.

THE COST OF CAPITAL ACROSS COUNTRIES

Understanding cross-country differences in the cost of capital can explain why MNCs based in some countries may have a competitive advantage over others. Furthermore, understanding the differences between the cost of debt capital and the cost of equity capital can explain why MNCs based in certain countries have more debt-intensive capital structures.

Differences in the Cost of Debt Capital

The cost of debt capital is determined by the risk-free rate and the risk premium. The cost of debt capital is higher in some countries than in others, because the risk-free rate and/or the risk premium is higher. Differences in the risk-free rate are due to several factors that affect the supply of, and demand for, loanable funds, and hence the level of the interest rate. For example, the interest rate varies with the state of the economy, tending to rise when the economy is booming, and to decline when the economy is in a slump. There is also a direct relationship between the level of the nominal interest rate and expected inflation, as represented by the Fisher equation.[8] This is the reason why interest rates could reach triple figures in countries experiencing hyperinflation. In general, the level of interest rate is higher in countries with extremely high inflation rates (Turkey, for example). Other factors that affect the level of interest rate are the stance of monetary policy (tight or expansionary), tax laws (whether or not these laws encourage saving), and demographical factors (younger households tend to save less).

The risk premium is meant to compensate creditors for the risk of default by the borrower. This risk varies across countries because of differences in economic conditions, relationships between companies and creditors, government intervention, and the degree of financial leverage. The risk premium tends to be lower in countries where economic conditions are more stable. The risk of default increases as the economy moves into recession, and so we should expect the risk premium to increase as economic activity slows down. The risk premium will also be lower in countries where the relationship between creditors and companies is so close that creditors stand ready to extend credit in the event of financial distress (in Japan, for example, or, at least, this is what used to be the case). Government intervention implies its willingness to rescue failing firms. The risk premium will be higher in countries where the government is not prepared to be called to the rescue. Finally, the risk premium should be higher in countries where companies are allowed high degrees of financial leverage (for example, Japan and Germany).

The following is a brief diagrammatic exposition of the determination of the risk-free rate and the risk premium. We shall utilize the basic premise that the cost of debt capital is determined by its supply and demand. Let us assume that there are two types of borrowers: those who are free, and those who are not free, of the risk of default. Let us assume initially that these two types of borrowers have identical demand schedules, implying that they demand the same amount of debt capital at the same cost (this assumption is not necessary for this analysis, but it is convenient). However, they are faced with two

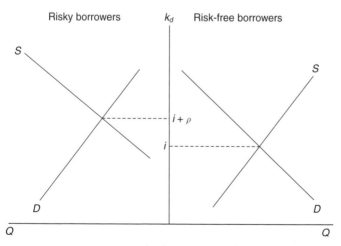

Figure 7.5 The determination of the cost of debt capital

different supply schedules, because the creditor is willing to supply more at the same level of the cost of debt to the risk-free borrowers. This situation is illustrated in Figure 7.5, in which the quantity of debt, Q, is measured on the horizontal axis, and the cost of debt capital, k_d, is measured on the vertical axis. The supply and demand schedules facing risk-free borrowers are shown on the right-hand side of the diagram, whereas the left-hand side shows the supply and demand schedules facing risky borrowers. It is shown that the cost of debt capital facing risk-free borrowers is i, whereas the cost for risky borrowers is $i + \rho$, where ρ is the risk premium.

The supply and demand model described by Figure 7.5 can be used to explain the effect of all of the variables stated earlier, as shown in Figure 7.6. Suppose, first of all, that the creditor started to feel, because of the expectation of a forthcoming recession, that risky borrowers would become even more risky, while the risk-free borrowers would remain unchanged (perhaps because they indulge in non-cyclical activities). The creditor would reduce the supply of debt capital to risky borrowers, leading to an increase in the risk premium from ρ_0 to ρ_1. Thus, the cost of debt capital will be higher for risky borrowers, as illustrated in Figure 7.6. If, on the other hand, demand for debt capital by both risk-free borrowers and risky borrowers declines, then the cost of debt capital for both will decline. This

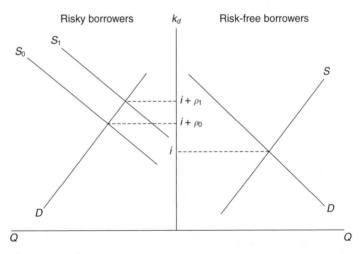

Figure 7.6 The result of a reduction in the supply of debt capital for risky borrowers

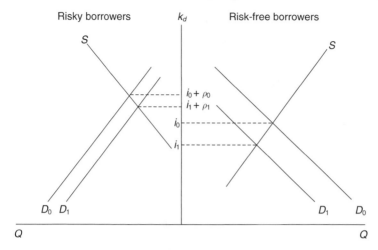

Figure 7.7 The result of a reduction in the demand for debt capital by risk-free and risky borrowers

situation is shown in Figure 7.7. Notice that the decline in the risk-free rate is greater than the decline in the risk premium, because the reduction in the demand by the risk-free borrowers is, in this case, greater than the reduction in the demand by risky borrowers.

This supply and demand model can also explain cross-country differences in the cost of debt capital and its components (the risk-free rate and the risk premium). The differences would be caused by different positions of, and shifts in, the supply and demand curves resulting from differences in the factors stated earlier. Table 7.1 gives an example of cross-country differences in the cost of debt capital, as represented by the yield on corporate bonds for developed countries and a representative interest rate for developing countries and countries in transition. The inflation rates are also given to indicate the extent of the effect of inflation on the (nominal) cost of debt capital. Figure 7.8 is a scatter diagram showing the relationship between the cost of debt capital and the inflation rate for developing and transition countries (all the countries in Table 7.1 except Turkey).

Differences in the Cost of Equity Capital

We now turn to cross-country differences in the cost of equity capital. Recall that the cost of equity capital is an opportunity cost: what

Table 7.1   The cost of debt capital and inflation rates in selected countries*

Developed countries			Developing/transition countries		
Country	Cost of debt	Inflation rate	Country	Cost of debt	Inflation rate
Australia	7.34	6.0	Hong Kong	3.78	1.3
UK	6.69	1.8	India	7.37	2.3
Canada	7.36	3.6	Indonesia	16.53	10.8
Denmark	7.20	2.7	Malaysia	3.30	1.6
Japan	1.36	−0.4	Philippines	10.25	6.5
Sweden	5.30	2.8	Singapore	2.25	2.0
Switzerland	4.09	1.8	South Korea	5.78	5.4
USA	7.03	3.3	Taiwan	4.10	0.4
Euro area	5.59	2.9	Thailand	3.50	2.8
			Argentina	9.38	1.0
			Brazil	16.81	7.1
			Chile	3.64	3.7
			Colombia	12.73	1.9
			Mexico	10.39	7.1
			Peru	12.88	2.6
			Venezuela	14.96	12.6
			Egypt	9.08	2.4
			South Africa	10.59	6.5
			Turkey	59.00	52.4
			Czech Republic	5.07	4.6
			Hungary	11.13	10.3
			Poland	17.08	6.6
			Russia	25.00	25.0

Source: *The Economist*, various issues
Note: *Figures prevailing in the first half of 2001.

shareholders could earn on investment with similar risk if the equity funds were distributed to them. This return consists of the risk-free interest rate and a risk premium. Differences in the risk-free rates lead to differences in the cost of equity capital, which also depends on investment opportunities in the underlying country. Countries with abundant investment opportunities will have higher cost of equity capital than countries with limited investment opportunities.

The cost of equity capital can be estimated by applying the price/earnings (P/E) ratio to a given stream of income (see, for example, McCauley and Zimmer, 1989). The P/E ratio is related to the cost of capital because it reflects the stock prices of the firm relative to its

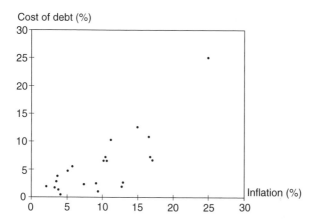

Figure 7.8 The relationship between the cost of debt and inflation in developing and transition countries

performance (as measured by earnings). A high P/E ratio implies that the firm receives a high price when it sells new stock for a given level of earnings, which means that the cost of equity capital is low.

Once the cost of debt and equity are known, and given the capital structure, Equation (7.1) can be used to estimate the overall cost of capital in a particular country. It is normally the case that countries that have low interest rates (such as Japan) produce a low cost of capital. This is because the risk-free interest rate affects not only the cost of debt but also the cost of equity. MNCs can attempt to access capital from countries with low cost of capital, but when this capital is used to support operations in another country, foreign exchange risk arises, as we saw earlier.

CHOOSING THE CAPITAL STRUCTURE

Choosing the capital structure implies the choice of the debt–equity ratio. Recall that there is a trade-off between using debt and equity for financing operations. Debt is useful because interest payments are tax deductible, but too much debt gives the impression that the company is financially vulnerable, which raises the cost of equity. The firm should aim at a level of the debt–equity ratio that minimizes the cost of capital and hence maximizes the value of the firm (Figure 7.3). The advantages of using debt as opposed to equity vary from one company to another, because of two sets of factors. The first set pertain to the specific characteristics of the company, whereas the second set pertain to the characteristics of the countries where the subsidiaries and the underlying projects are located.

There are three corporate characteristics that affect the capital structure: the stability of the firm's cash flows, its credit risk, and access to earnings. Firms with more stable cash flows can handle more debt because these cash flows can be used to cover periodic interest payments. One way to achieve stability of cash flows is to diversify across countries, as we saw earlier. Hence, firms that are more diversified geographically tend to have more stable cash flows and more debt-intensive capital structure (that is, a higher debt–equity ratio). Similarly, firms with lower credit risk (lower probability of default on loans) can handle a more debt-intensive capital structure. Lower credit risk would be the case if the firm has a strong and competent management, and if it has marketable assets that can serve as collateral. Finally, firms that are more profitable can use retained earnings to finance their operations, in which case they would use equity-intensive capital structures. This is why growth-orientated MNCs have a higher debt–equity ratio than MNCs with less growth.

There are factors that pertain to the host country, and this is why we can observe country differences in the capital structure. For example, firms in Japan and Germany traditionally have used a higher debt–equity ratio than those in the USA or the UK. This is because the probability of bankruptcy in Japan and Germany is lower, given that the governments in these countries are more willing to step in and rescue troubled firms. It is also a tradition that banks in these countries are not only creditors but also shareholders, in which case they have a vested interest in rescuing troubled firms.

The factors influencing the capital structure that pertain to the host country include the following. The first of these factors arises when there are restrictions on stock ownership in the host country. If, for one reason or another, investors in the host country are not allowed, or are unwilling, to invest in foreign shares, an MNC operating in that country will find it easier to raise equity capital there. In this case, the MNC will have a more capital-intensive structure. Conversely, the MNC will have a more debt-intensive capital structure if it operates in a low-interest-rate country. The MNC will also opt for debt-intensive capital structure if it operates in a country with a weak currency. In this case, most of the cash flows arising from the project are used to meet interest payments. A similar situation arises when country risk is high. An MNC that operates in a country where the risk of confiscation or blocked funds is high tends to borrow intensively in that country, and hence it will have a debt-intensive capital structure. Local debt financing will also be used when there is a withholding tax on remittances.

In general, therefore, MNCs prefer to have a debt-intensive capital structure when their subsidiaries are subject to low local interest rates, weak currencies, a high degree of country risk, and high taxes. An MNC may deviate from its target capital structure in each country where financing is obtained, while achieving its target capital structure on a consolidated basis. This policy of ignoring the local target capital structure in favour of a global capital structure can be justified under certain circumstances. For example, an MNC operating in a country that does not allow the listing of its shares on the local stock exchange will have a higher debt–equity ratio than otherwise desired. This high debt–equity ratio can be counter-balanced by using lower ratios in other countries.

Some MNCs may allow a specific foreign subsidiary to issue stock to local investors or employees as a means of infusing equity into the subsidiary. In this case, the subsidiary is referred to as 'partially-owned' rather than 'wholly-owned' by the MNC. This strategy can affect the MNC's capital structure. Partially-owned subsidiaries have the possible advantage that they may open up additional opportunities within the host countries, but they have the disadvantage that they may lead to a conflict of interest. We have already seen that this kind of conflict may arise when a project that is not feasible from the MNC's perspective is feasible from the subsidiary's perspective.

MORE ABOUT THE CHOICE OF CAPITAL STRUCTURE

The 'capital structure puzzle' is a term coined by Myers (1984) to explain why firms within a single industry have different capital structures. Myers (1984) argues that firms seem to follow a 'pecking order' whereby they prefer to use internal financing in order to avoid issue costs (the term 'pecking order' was first introduced by Donaldson, 1961). If internal financing is insufficient, firms use debt financing first, then equity financing. This is because the issue costs are higher for equity financing. International conditions can cause an MNC either to accelerate the shift from one financing method to another, or to rearrange the pecking order, which can be disrupted by several factors.

Country risk is one of these factors. If country risk is high, then the subsidiary may consider a financing strategy that would strengthen its political position. External debt and equity financing in the host country will give potential creditors and shareholders a vested interest in the company. This would be the case even if internal funds were available. These funds will then be remitted to the MNC. This is an obvious case in which external funds are used before internal funds.

The second factor is interest rate differentials. If interest rates are lower in the host country, the subsidiary is likely to prefer external debt. Any internal funds would be transferred to the MNC. This mode of financing has the additional advantage that it would not lead to an increase in exposure to foreign exchange risk, since part of the revenues will be used to meet debt repayments. If, on the other hand, interest rates are high in the host country, then the MNC will use its internal funds to finance the subsidiary.

The third factor is exchange rate expectations. If the foreign currency is expected to strengthen over time, it may provide an immediate cash infusion to finance growth in the subsidiary. As a result, there would be a transfer of internal funds from the MNC to the subsidiary. This implies more external financing by the MNC, and less by the subsidiary. If, on the other hand, the MNC expects the foreign currency to depreciate, then it will require the subsidiary to obtain funds in the host country.

Blocked funds and withholding taxes also play a role. If the subsidiary is prevented from remitting funds, it would be forced to use more internal financing and less external financing. Thus, the MNC will have fewer internal funds available for financing. The rank order of financing will not be disturbed, but the MNC will be forced to use more external financing. Moreover, if withholding taxes imposed by the host country on remitted earnings are high, the MNC may attempt to transfer explicit or implicit costs to the subsidiary. Thus, the subsidiary will generate less earnings, reducing the amount of internal funds available to it. The same would happen if the host country's corporate income tax rate was higher than that in the home country. In that case, the subsidiary would resort to using debt financing. Finally, if the MNC backs the debt of the subsidiary, then the subsidiary's borrowing capacity will increase, in which case it will need less equity financing.

Thus, some global conditions that lead to higher external financing by the subsidiary will also result in a higher debt–equity ratio for the MNC as a whole. These conditions are: (i) a high level of country risk in the host country; (ii) low interest rates in the host country; (iii) expected weakness of the foreign currency; (iv) high withholding taxes in the host country; and (v) high corporate income tax in the host country. Conversely, some global factors that cause lower external financing for the subsidiary will also lead to a lower debt–equity ratio for the MNC as a whole. These conditions are: (i) high interest rates in the host country; (ii) expected strengthening of the foreign currency; and (iii) blocked funds imposed by the host government.

There are at least two reasons why an MNC may use external equity financing ahead of debt. The first is agency costs. If a foreign subsidiary cannot easily be monitored by investors from the home country, the MNC may induce the subsidiary to issue stock rather than debt. Monitoring via movements in stock prices is easier. The second reason is that an MNC may be more capable of developing a global image if its stock is listed on a foreign exchange than if it uses debt financing. External equity financing comes before debt financing under these conditions.

Some recent research casts doubt on the validity of the traditional corporate finance model, suggesting that firms select optimal capital structures by trading off various tax and incentive benefits of debt financing against financial distress costs. Hovakimian *et al.* (2001) argue that while there is support for the trade-off models in the empirical literature, recent evidence suggests that a firm's history may play a more important role in determining its capital structure. Titman and Wessels (1988), for example, show that highly profitable firms often use their earnings to pay back debt, which makes them less levered than less profitable firms. Moreover, Masulis and Korwar (1986) and Asquith and Mullins (1986) show that firms tend to issue equity following an increase in stock prices. The implication of this observation is that firms that perform well tend subsequently to reduce their debt–equity ratio.

Some researchers argue that the negative correlation between profits and leverage is consistent with Donaldson's (1961) pecking order that is used to describe how firms make their financing decisions. Donaldson argued that firms prefer to fund new investment with retained earnings (as opposed to borrowed funds), but they prefer debt to equity financing. If this is the case, then firms accumulate retained earnings, becoming less levered when they are profitable and accumulate debt, and becoming more levered when they are unprofitable. If firms are indifferent about their capital structures, as suggested by Miller (1977), then they will not make future capital structure choices that offset their earnings history. Shyam-Sunder and Myers (1999) argue that the pecking order story provides a better empirical description of capital structure than do traditional trade-off models.

There are also dynamic models of capital structure, such as those of Fischer *et al.* (1989) and Leland (1994). In these models, transaction costs are introduced to generate short-run pecking order behaviour. These models suggest that firms will readjust their capital structures periodically, towards a target ratio that reflects the costs and benefits of debt financing that are found in static trade-off models. The models also suggest that firms repurchase equity after an increase in share prices to adjust towards an optimal capital structure. However, this prediction is inconsistent with the observation that firms tend to issue equity following stock price increases.

Hovakimian *et al.* (2001) test the hypothesis that firms tend to move towards a target debt–equity ratio when they either raise new capital or repurchase existing capital. Their results suggest that, although past profits are an important predictor of observed capital structures, firms often make financing and repurchase decisions that offset these earnings-driven changes in their capital structures. The results also suggest that stock prices play an important role in determining a firm's financing choice. Firms experiencing large stock price increases are more likely to issue equity and retire debt than are firms experiencing stock price decline.

A FINAL REMARK

The cost of capital is an important variable that determines the profitability of FDI projects, because it is used as a discount rate to calculate the NPV or APV of a project. The capital structure frequently is chosen in such a way as to minimize the cost of capital. Both the cost of capital and capital structure are determined by firm-specific and country-specific factors.

We have by the end of this chapter covered three interrelated topics that affect the decision to indulge in FDI: country risk, taxation, and the cost of capital. This is the stage at which we move to the last two topics, which are closely related: transfer pricing, and the control and performance evaluation functions in MNCs. The following chapter deals with the critical issue of transfer pricing, which we have come across on several occasions in earlier chapters.

8 Transfer Pricing

Transfer pricing, also known as internal pricing or intracorporate transfer pricing, refers to the pricing of goods and services that are bought and sold (transferred) between members of a corporate family. In other words, transfer pricing is the process of determining the prices of (intermediate and finished) goods and services sold by the parent MNC to a subsidiary, by the subsidiary to the parent MNC, and by one subsidiary to another. There are several reasons why MNCs set arbitrary high or low prices on cross-border transfers, making this issue very sensitive politically. This practice often becomes a source of hostility between MNCs and host governments, not least because it may be used for the purpose of tax evasion.

THE DEFINITION AND DETERMINANTS OF TRANSFER PRICING

The term 'transfer pricing' often carries a derogatory meaning in today's business world because it gives the impression that there is a systematic manipulation of the transfer pricing policy for tax avoidance or evasion.[1] Transfer prices arise in intra-firm trade, which encompasses transactions involving international shipments of products between branches or subsidiaries operating under the control of the parent MNC. Transfer pricing is not only used for tax purposes but also for other purposes such as risk reduction, control and evaluation. Normally regarded as being highly secretive, transfer pricing has become an essential and crucial part in the operations of MNCs. Moreover, it is difficult to determine a consistent transfer pricing policy because of the lack of an appropriate theoretical model and empirical evidence on the optimality of transfer pricing. This is partly because of the reluctance of managers to provide information on the procedures used by their companies. The diversity of transfer pricing policies can be attributed to the fact that the choice of a particular policy is influenced by the internal management control process. Indeed, one of the objectives of the internal management control process is to determine the transfer pricing policy.

In setting transfer pricing policies, many factors are considered. Some of these factors are discussed below.

Tax Considerations

MNCs use transfer pricing to move profit out of countries with high taxes to countries with low taxes. Suppose that there two subsidiaries, one in a high-tax country and the other in a low-tax country. To reduce the combined tax liability of the two subsidiaries (that is, to increase the combined after-tax profit), the subsidiary located in the high-tax country will sell goods to the other subsidiary at lower than normal prices, and buy from it at higher than normal prices.

This proposition can be formalized as follows. The two subsidiaries under discussion are designated A and B. The after-tax profits of the two subsidiaries are expressed simply as the difference between their revenues and costs according to the following equations:

$$\pi_{A,t} = (1 - \tau_A)(R_{A,t} - C_{A,t}) \tag{8.1}$$

$$\pi_{B,t} = (1 - \tau_B)(R_{B,t} - C_{B,t}) \tag{8.2}$$

where π is profit, R is revenue, C is cost, τ is the corporate income tax rate, and the subscripts A, B and t indicate the underlying subsidiary and the time period. Thus, the combined after-tax profit in period t is:

$$\pi_t = (1 - \tau_A)(R_{A,t} - C_{A,t}) + (1 - \tau_B)(R_{B,t} - C_{B,t}) \tag{8.3}$$

Let us assume that because $\tau_A > \tau_B$, the structure of transfer pricing is changed at $t + 1$ such that Subsidiary A sells products to Subsidiary B at lower prices, while Subsidiary B sells its products to Subsidiary A at higher prices, than previously. As a result, the costs of Subsidiary A will increase, while those of B will decline by the same amount. The reverse is true for revenue. Thus:

$$\Delta R_{A,t+1} = \Delta C_{B,t+1} \tag{8.4}$$

$$\Delta R_{B,t+1} = \Delta C_{A,t+1} \tag{8.5}$$

and:

$$\pi_{t+1} = (1 - \tau_A)(R_{A,t+1} - C_{A,t+1}) + (1 - \tau_B)(R_{B,t+1} - C_{B,t+1}) \tag{8.6}$$

or:

$$\pi_{t+1} = (1 - \tau_A)(R_{A,t} + \Delta R_{A,t+1} - C_{A,t} - \Delta C_{A,t+1})$$
$$+ (1 - \tau_B)(R_{B,t} + \Delta R_{B,t+1} - C_{B,t} - \Delta C_{B,t+1}) \tag{8.7}$$

Hence:

$$\Delta\pi_{t+1} = (1 - \tau_A)(\Delta R_{A,t+1} - \Delta C_{A,t+1}) + (1 - \tau_B)(\Delta R_{B,t+1} - \Delta C_{B,t+1}) \tag{8.8}$$

By substitution, we obtain:

$$\Delta\pi_{t+1} = (\tau_A - \tau_B)(\Delta C_{A,t+1} - \Delta C_{B,t+1}) \tag{8.9}$$

since $\Delta C_{A,t+1} > \Delta C_{B,t+1}$ and $\tau_A > \tau_B$, it follows that $\Delta\pi_{t+1} > 0$. Notice that the increase in the combined after-tax profit will be zero either if there is no change in costs and revenues resulting from changes in transfer prices ($\Delta C_{A,t+1} = \Delta C_{B,t+1}$), and/or the tax rates are equal ($\tau_A = \tau_B$).

Global Regulation

Burns and Ross (1981) argue that no single group has the authority to establish international transfer pricing standards of taxation, because each country establishes rules for companies operating within its boundaries. However, many factors are now causing greater interest in the establishment of international standards for taxing inter-company transactions. For example, the USA, Canada, Germany and the UK, require transfer prices to be 'arm's length'; that is, the price that would be used if the two companies were unrelated. In the USA, the taxation authorities have been putting the squeeze on companies that responded by allocating more of their taxable profit to arise there in an attempt to keep the authorities happy. Growth in international transactions between related companies has led to a need for international standards.[2] There is still no agreement on what constitutes an 'arm's length' price.

Management Incentives and Performance Evaluation

If the transfer price set by the parent company management is not acceptable to the management of the subsidiary, managerial disincentives may arise. Transfer pricing policies that are designed to minimize global taxes often produce aberrations in the multinational performance evaluation and control systems. The overall results could be achieved only at the cost of what seems to be a poor performance of some subsidiaries resulting from tax-reduction transfer pricing policies. The subsidiaries that will be affected in this case are those whose net profit is reduced artificially because they are located in high-tax countries. Unless performance evaluation measures used by the parent MNC's management can eliminate the adverse effects of the transfer pricing policy on the operating performance of the subsidiary, the results could lead to suboptimal behaviour by the managers evaluated against the overall corporate objectives.

Halpern and Srinidhi (1991) reached the conclusion that the MNC's degree of negotiating power with a subsidiary has an influence on the final outcome of the transfer pricing policy. They found out that when the negotiating power of a subsidiary is low, after-tax profits are maximized. When the negotiating power of the subsidiary increases beyond a certain level, total after-tax profit will not be maximized.

Fund Positioning

Transfer pricing is one of the techniques used by MNCs to transfer funds from one part of the total business to another. This procedure is used particularly in conjunction with short-term investment and financing decisions, where it is normally the case that a business firm checks the availability of internal funds before resorting to external financing. An MNC with foreign subsidiaries can utilize internal financing by resorting to funds available at its subsidiaries. Moreover, decentralized cash management involves the determination of where and in which currency cash balances are held. Therefore, the process involves the transfer of funds (which may be executed either by direct instructions or via transfer pricing) from one location to another according to the following guidelines:

1. If it is anticipated that the received funds in a particular currency will be needed in the future, then transaction costs make it essential to keep these funds in the same currency.
2. The same reasoning applies if there is no forward market in the underlying currency.
3. If political risk in one country is high, then funds should be kept in the home country rather than in the country in whose currency the funds are denominated.

4. Liquidity considerations make it sensible to keep the funds in the currency in which they are most likely to be needed in the future.
5. Taxes are also important. In the presence of withholding taxes, funds should not be kept in countries with high tax rates.

If the MNC wants to remove funds from one of its foreign subsidiaries, it can charge that subsidiary a higher price for the products it provides to the subsidiary as part of intra-firm trade. If a subsidiary is short of funds it will be charged a lower transfer price. Transfer pricing can also be used to channel profit into a particular subsidiary to raise its credit rating and boost its ability to borrow funds.

Marketing Considerations and Competition

There are a number of reasons why an MNC may depend on its foreign subsidiaries for the sale of finished goods. One reason is the desire to control the distribution facilities when there is a lucrative market. Another reason is the desire to provide a specialized after-sales services. There is also the need to convey information to and from customers, and there may also be a need to retain direct representation in order to maintain contacts with foreign governments. All these marketing considerations can be built into the transfer pricing policies of MNCs. If this is the case, then the marketing objective will influence transfer pricing. For example, initial transfer prices should be lower if the subsidiary is expected to pursue the objective of market penetration than if the underlying marketing objective is market skimming.[3]

The competitive position of a foreign subsidiary can also be affected by the level of transfer prices. Reducing transfer prices is an action that may be taken to shield the operations of a subsidiary from increased pressure from competitors. The exchange rate should also play a role in this process, because it affects the competitive position of a subsidiary operating in a foreign market. Remember that demand in the foreign market depends on the foreign currency price of the product, which depends on the exchange rate. If the foreign currency depreciates against the domestic currency, the foreign currency price will rise and this may affect the competitive position of the subsidiary adversely, particularly if the demand for the product is elastic. In this case, the transfer price measured in domestic currency terms must be lowered.

These relationships can be explained formally, as follows. Let us assume for simplicity that the parent MNC sends its products to the subsidiary, which in turn sells them in the foreign market at a price equal to the transfer price plus a mark-up. Hence:

$$\bar{P} = (1 + \lambda)\frac{P}{S} \qquad (8.10)$$

where $\bar{P}$ is the price at which the subsidiary sells the product in the foreign market, P is the domestic currency transfer price set by the parent MNC, S is the exchange rate expressed as the price of one unit of the foreign currency, and λ is the percentage mark-up. The market share of the subsidiary, which is equivalent to the value of its sales, depends on the price, $\bar{P}$, and the quantity sold, Q, the latter in turn depends on $\bar{P}$. Hence, sales revenue is R, given by:

$$R = Q\bar{P} = f(\bar{P})(1 + \lambda)\frac{P}{S} \qquad (8.11)$$

where $f'(\bar{P}) < 0$. These relationships can be represented diagrammatically. Consider first Figure 8.1, which explains the effect of a change in the transfer price without a change in the exchange rate under elastic and inelastic demand. If the transfer price rises, then it follows from Equation (8.11) that the foreign currency price will also rise, and the effect would be a decline in the volume of sales (the quantity demanded). Notice that the value of sales is represented diagrammatically by the area under the demand curve corresponding to a combination of $\bar{P}$ and Q. So, as P rises, $\bar{P}$ also rises, leading to a reduction in Q, which follows

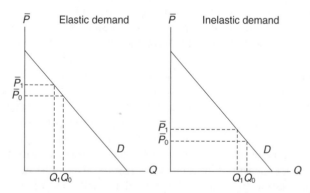

Figure 8.1   The effect of a rise in the domestic currency transfer price

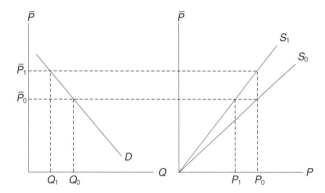

Figure 8.2 Manipulating transfer prices in response to a change in the exchange rate

from Equation (8.11). What happens to R then depends on the elasticity of demand. If demand is elastic, as it would be at a higher price level, then sales will decline. If, on the other hand, demand is inelastic, as it would be at a low price, then total sales will increase.

Now consider Figure 8.2, which represents the effect of a change in the exchange rate. When the exchange rate is S_0 and the domestic currency transfer price is P_0, the foreign currency price is $\bar{P}_0$ and sales revenue is $\bar{P}_0 Q_0$. Suppose that S falls to S_1, implying a depreciation of the foreign currency against the domestic currency.[4] It follows from Equation (8.10) that $\bar{P}$ will rise to $\bar{P}_1$, leading to a decline in the total sales of the subsidiary (under elastic demand) to $\bar{P}_1 Q_1$. In order to preserve these sales and maintain the sales revenue at the original level, the parent MNC must reduce the domestic currency transfer price from P_0 to P_1. At P_1 and S_1, the foreign currency price is back to $\bar{P}_0$, which restores sales revenue to $\bar{P}_0 Q_0$.

Risk and Uncertainty

Foreign operations are subject to several kinds of risk, including foreign exchange risk, purchasing power risk, and political risk.[5] Transfer pricing may be used to reduce exposure to these kinds of risk. A response to the risk of blocked funds could, for example, take the form of increasing transfer prices. By changing transfer prices, funds can be moved effectively from high inflation countries to low inflation countries, and from countries with weak currencies to countries with strong currencies.

Government Policies

There is often some conflict, pertaining to intra-firm trade, between the wishes of the home country's government that deals with the MNC and those of the host country's government that deals with the subsidiary. The home country's government likes the MNC to use the domestic facilities to supply foreign subsidiaries. The host country's government, on the contrary, wants to see an increase in the use of local inputs by the subsidiary at the expense of imports from the parent MNC (in the form of intra-firm trade). This conflict leads to a restriction of the ability to indulge in intra-firm trade, with some consequences for transfer pricing.

Sometimes, anti-trust legislation aimed at preventing companies from colluding on prices also affects transfer pricing policies. In this case, if the transfer prices are too low it may be taken as creating unfair advantage for the subsidiary relative to its competitors.

The Interest of Joint Venture Partners

Transfer pricing can be used to preserve the MNC's share in the profit generated by a joint venture. To accomplish this objective, the MNC charges the joint venture high transfer prices. Of course, this kind of practice would create conflict between the MNC and the foreign partner in the joint venture, because the foreign partner prefers low transfer prices. This is why the transfer pricing policy should be agreed upon prior to the establishment of a joint venture.

Negotiating Power of the Subsidiary

A subsidiary's foreign currency profit is boosted by low transfer prices on its input, and high transfer prices on its output. If this is the case, then the subsidiary will be considered to be a good risk by foreign financial institutions, and thus the negotiating power of the subsidiary with these financial institutions will be greater. On the other hand, high transfer prices on input and low transfer prices on output will reduce the reported profit of the subsidiary, and this may improve its ability to negotiate wages with the trade unions.

Summing Up

There are conditions pertaining to the host country that make it more desirable to set low transfer prices on flows from the MNC and higher transfer prices on the flows to it. These conditions, which are identified by Arpan (1972), include the following: (i) high *ad valorem* tariffs; (ii) lower corporate income tax rate than in the home country; (iii) significant competition; (iv) local loans based on the financial appearance of the subsidiary; (v) export subsidy or tax credit on the value of exports; (vi) lower inflation rate than in the home country; and (vii) restrictions on the value of products that can be imported.

On the other hand, there are conditions that induce high transfer prices on flows from the MNC and low transfer prices on flows to it. These conditions include: (i) local partners; (ii) pressure from workers to obtain greater share of company profits; (iii) political pressure to rationalize or expropriate high-profit foreign firms; (iv) restrictions on remittances; (v) political instability; (vi) substantial tie-in sales agreements; (vii) price of final product controlled by government but based on production cost; and (viii) a desire to mask the profitability of subsidiaries' operations to keep competitors out.

THE TECHNIQUES OF SETTING TRANSFER PRICES

In theory, the transfer price is supposed to be equal to the market price used in transactions involving two independent firms. But often there is no market, so the market price is not known. This is particularly valid for firms supplying services or intangible goods (such as consultancy). This is why MNCs spend a fortune on economists and accountants to justify prices that suit their tax and other needs.

Transfer pricing techniques that are employed by a firm can be classified into: (i) market-based techniques; (ii) non-market based techniques; and (iii) cost centre techniques. The full classification is presented in Figure 8.3. Table 8.1 presents a description of these techniques.

Which of these techniques is used by a particular MNC depends on their relative advantages and disadvantages, and these vary from case to case. In general, the following points are worthy of consideration:

1. The market-based technique is suitable for measuring the profitability of subsidiaries because the resource allocation decisions are based on existing market conditions. Market prices are useful

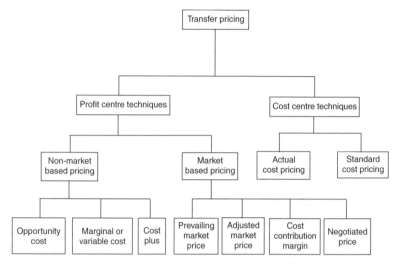

Figure 8.3 Classification of transfer pricing techniques

because they cannot be manipulated by the person whose interest is in conflict with that of the overall organization.

2. There are some problems with market-based techniques. If the underlying product cannot be compared with anything available in the market, then a market price cannot be obtained. Moreover, it could distort the investment decision under certain conditions.

3. The opportunity cost approach could distort investment decisions, because the buying division would be more profitable than the selling division.

4. Under the marginal cost approach there is a tendency for managers to falsify their estimates of marginal cost, which would reduce the profitability of the firm as a whole.

5. The use of cost plus pricing could show an unprofitable division to be profitable, which would distort the information used for performance evaluation.

6. The cost-based techniques are simple and based on readily available data. The standard cost is used to avoid passing on cost inefficiencies to other divisions.

7. Some difficulties arise with the actual full cost transfer pricing. Because the price is set at the level of the actual cost involved, a change in internal or external demand will cause fluctuations in the transfer price.

Table 8.1 Description of transfer pricing techniques

Technique	Description
Market-based techniques	
Prevailing market price	The transfer price is set at the same level as the external market price
Adjusted market price	The transfer price takes into account the higher administrative costs involved in external selling
Contribution margin	The selling and buying units negotiate either a share of the profit margin earned from sales or a share of the profit margin based on the standard full cost
Negotiated price	The selling and buying units determine the transfer price by negotiation
Non-market based techniques	
Opportunity cost	The transfer price is set to be equal to the sacrifice suffered by the supplier for not selling to external customers
Marginal or variable cost	The transfer price is equal to the direct production costs incurred by the selling unit, and these may include or exclude overheads
Cost plus	An arbitrary mark-up is added either to the standard full cost or the actual cost of the product
Cost centre techniques	
Actual cost	The transfer price is set either to be equal to the actual full cost or to the actual variable cost
Standard cost	The transfer price is set either to be equal to the standard full cost or to the standard variable cost

There is ample empirical evidence on the practices of MNCs with respect to transfer pricing. Al-Eryani *et al.* (1990) surveyed 164 MNCs and found that larger ones operating in restrictive legislative environments were more likely to use market-based transfer pricing. This is attributed to the fact that these MNCs are exposed to public scrutiny. It was also found that restrictions (such as exchange controls, price controls, and restrictions on imports) were not a significant determinant of market-based transfer pricing. The major hypotheses tested in this study are shown in Table 8.2; only two of these hypotheses were in fact supported by the results of testing.

In an earlier study, Burns (1980) carried out a similar survey of 62 US MNCs. This survey resulted in a ranking, in order of importance, of the following fourteen factors: market conditions in the foreign country; competition in the foreign country; reasonable profit for foreign subsidiaries; US federal income tax; economic conditions in the foreign country; import restrictions; customs duties; price controls; taxes in the foreign country; exchange controls; domestic export incentives; floating exchange rates; management of cash flows; and finally, other domestic taxes. Hoshower and Mandel (1986) examined the transfer pricing of twenty-five large divisionalized US-based MNCs, and found that the majority of these located their transfer pricing decisions at the divisional rather than the central corporate level.

There is also some evidence indicating that the nationality of the MNC affects the transfer pricing system, and the relative importance given to the various factors considered in setting transfer prices.

Table 8.2   Results of Al-Eryani *et al.* (1990) survey of transfer pricing

Hypothesis	Results
The more important the legal variables to MNCs, the greater the market-based transfer pricing. Legal restrictions refer to issues such as taxation, anti-trust laws and financial reporting requirements	Supported
The larger the MNC, the more likely it is that it will use market-based transfer pricing	Supported
The more unstable the political and social environment, the less likely it is that MNCs will use market-based transfer pricing	Not supported
The more severe the external economic restrictions, the less likely it is that MNCs will use market-based transfer pricing	Not supported
MNCs are less likely to use market-based pricing when internal economic conditions require underpricing (for example, the competitive position)	Not supported
The larger the number of subsidiaries operating in developing countries the less likely it is that market-based transfer pricing will be used	Not supported

Arpan (1972) surveyed the transfer pricing system used by sixty MNCs, and reached the following conclusions. First, American, French, British and Japanese MNCs prefer cost-orientated transfer prices, whereas Canadian, Italian and Scandinavian MNCs prefer market-based transfer pricing. Second, there are distinguishable national differences in the relative importance attached to factors determining the transfer process (income tax, customs duties, inflation, exchange rates, exchange controls, financial appearance of subsidiaries, expropriation threat, export subsidies, tax credit, and competition). Third, non-US MNCs considered only about half as many internal parameters as their US counterparts. For example, non-US MNCs view transfer pricing more as a means of controlling subsidiary operations than as a technique for motivating and evaluating the performance of subsidiaries. We shall deal with performance evaluation in Chapter 9.

A FORMAL EXPOSITION OF THE EFFECTS OF TRANSFER PRICING

We shall now illustrate formally the effect of transfer pricing on the tax revenues of the foreign and home governments. Assume that the MNC sells its subsidiary an amount, X, of a product at a domestic-currency transfer price, P. Thus, the MNC receives XP domestic currency units in sales revenue, while the subsidiary pays XP/S foreign currency units as the cost of obtaining the shipment. Assuming, for simplicity, that there are no customs duties in the foreign country, and that there are no other costs associated with the transaction. If the subsidiary then sells the goods at a foreign currency selling price of $\bar{P}$, then the profit generated by the subsidiary will be:

$$\pi_s = X\left(\bar{P} - \frac{P}{S}\right) \tag{8.12}$$

The revenue collected by the foreign government as a result of taxing the profit of the subsidiary at the foreign income tax rate, τ^*, is:

$$T^* = \tau^* X\left(\bar{P} - \frac{P}{S}\right) \tag{8.13}$$

By partially differentiating Equation (8.13) with respect to P, we obtain:

$$\frac{\partial T^*}{\partial P} = -\frac{\tau^* X}{S} < 0 \tag{8.14}$$

which means that a higher transfer price leads to a lower tax revenue for the foreign government.

The tax revenue collected by the home government is calculated by applying the domestic income tax rate, τ, to the MNC's profit from this operation. The MNC's profit consists of two components: (i) the difference between the amount received from the subsidiary for the goods, XP, and the cost of production, XC; and (ii) the amount remitted by the subsidiary converted into domestic currency. If we assume that the subsidiary remits its full after-tax profit, then the profit of the MNC will be:

$$\pi_m = X(P - C) + SX(1 - \tau^*)\left(\bar{P} - \frac{P}{S}\right) \tag{8.15}$$

Assuming further that no tax credit is granted by the home government, its tax revenue will be:

$$T = \tau X\left[(P - C) + S(1 - \tau^*)\left(\bar{P} - \frac{P}{S}\right)\right] \tag{8.16}$$

By partially differentiating Equation (8.16) with respect to P, we obtain:

$$\frac{\partial T}{\partial P} = \tau\tau^* X > 0 \tag{8.17}$$

which means that a high transfer price leads to a higher tax revenue for the home government.

If, on the other hand, full tax credit is granted by the home government, then:

$$T = \tau X\left[(P - C) + S(1 - \tau^*)\left(\bar{P} - \frac{P}{S}\right)\right] - S\tau^* X\left(\bar{P} - \frac{P}{S}\right) \tag{8.18}$$

which gives:

$$\frac{\partial T}{\partial P} = \tau^* X (\tau + 1) > 0 \tag{8.19}$$

which does not change the result. Now let us go back to the assumption of zero tax credit. From Equations (8.13) and (8.16) we can calculate the ratio of the home government's tax revenue to the foreign government's tax revenue. We get:

$$\frac{T}{T^*} = \frac{\tau\left[(P - C) + S(1 - \tau^*)(\bar{P} - \frac{P}{S})\right]}{\tau^*(\bar{P} - \frac{P}{S})} \tag{8.20}$$

which can be simplified to:

$$\frac{T}{T^*} = \frac{\tau}{\tau^*}\left[\frac{P - C}{\bar{P} - \frac{P}{S}}\right] + \frac{S(1 - \tau^*)}{\tau^*} \tag{8.21}$$

By partially differentiating equation (8.21) with respect to P, we obtain:

$$\frac{\partial(\frac{T}{T^*})}{\partial P} = \frac{\tau}{\tau^*}\left[\frac{(\bar{P} - \frac{P}{S}) + (\frac{P-C}{S})}{(\bar{P} - \frac{P}{S})^2}\right] > 0 \tag{8.22}$$

which implies that a higher transfer price will increase the ratio of tax revenue of the home government to that of the foreign government. This result will not change if we allow for tax credit, because in this case we have:

$$\frac{T}{T^*} = \frac{\tau X\left[(P - C) + S(1 - \tau^*)(\bar{P} - \frac{P}{S})\right] - S\tau^* X(\bar{P} - \frac{P}{S})}{\tau^*(\bar{P} - \frac{P}{S})} \tag{8.23}$$

or:

$$\frac{T}{T^*} = \frac{\tau X}{\tau^*}\left[\frac{P - C}{\bar{P} - \frac{P}{S}} + S(1 - \tau^*)\right] - SX \tag{8.24}$$

in which case:

$$\frac{\partial\left(\frac{T}{T^*}\right)}{\partial P} = \frac{\tau X}{\tau^*}\left[\frac{\left(\bar{P}-\frac{P}{S}\right)+\left(\frac{P-C}{S}\right)}{\left(\bar{P}-\frac{P}{S}\right)^2}\right] > 0 \qquad (8.25)$$

Let us now introduce customs duties by assuming that a subsidiary buys X units of a product at a domestic currency transfer price of P, paying the MNC the foreign currency amount XP/S. If customs duties are charged on imports at the rate of θ per cent, then the full cost to the subsidiary will be $(XP/S)(1+\theta)$. The amount received by the customs authorities will therefore be:

$$D = \theta\left(\frac{XP}{S}\right) \qquad (8.26)$$

It is obvious from Equation (8.26) that $\partial D/\partial P > 0$, implying that the higher the transfer price, the greater will be the amount received by the foreign government in the form of customs duties. If the subsidiary sells the goods at the foreign currency price $\bar{P}$, then the profit realized by the subsidiary from the sale of these goods is:

$$\pi_s = X\left[\bar{P}-\frac{P}{S}(1+\theta)\right] \qquad (8.27)$$

Now, the amount received by the host government in the form of income tax is:

$$T^* = \tau^*X\left[\bar{P}-\frac{P}{S}(1+\theta)\right] \qquad (8.28)$$

By partially differentiating Equation (8.28) with respect to P and θ, we obtain:

$$\frac{\partial T^*}{\partial P} = -\frac{\tau^*X(1+\theta)}{S} < 0 \qquad (8.29)$$

and:

$$\frac{\partial T^*}{\partial\theta} = -\frac{\tau^*XP}{S} < 0 \qquad (8.30)$$

respectively, which means that the tax revenue received by the host government falls in response to a rise in the transfer price or a rise in the rate of customs duties.

Let us now consider the effect on the home government's tax revenue. The profit made by the MNC is:

$$\pi_m = X(P - C) + SX(1 - \tau^*)\left[\bar{P} - \frac{P}{S}(1 + \theta)\right] \quad (8.31)$$

By partially differentiating Equation (8.31) with respect to θ and P, we get the following:

$$\frac{\partial \pi_m}{\partial \theta} = -XP(1 - \tau^*) \quad (8.32)$$

and:

$$\frac{\partial \pi_m}{\partial P} = X[1 - (1 - \tau^*)(1 + \theta)] \quad (8.33)$$

which means that the profit of the MNC will be affected adversely by a higher rate of customs duties. It also means that, in the presence of customs duties, the effect of a higher transfer price on the profit of the MNC will be ambiguous. The tax revenue received by the home government (assuming no credit is granted) will in this case be:

$$T = \tau X(P - C) + \tau SX(1 - \tau^*)\left[\bar{P} - \frac{P}{S}(1 + \theta)\right] \quad (8.34)$$

Therefore:

$$\frac{\partial T}{\partial \theta} = -\tau XP(1 - \tau^*) \quad (8.35)$$

and:

$$\frac{\partial T}{\partial P} = \tau X[1 - (1 - \tau^*)(1 + \theta)] \quad (8.36)$$

Finally, we shall consider the case where there are no customs duties but there are blocked funds amounting to a fraction, ϕ, of the after-tax profit of the subsidiary. In this case:

$$\pi_m = X(P - C) + (1 - \phi)SX(1 - \tau^*)\left[\bar{P} - \frac{P}{S}(1 + \theta)\right] \quad (8.37)$$

where $\phi < 1$. It follows that:

$$\frac{\partial \pi_m}{\partial P} = X[1 - (1 - \phi)(1 - \tau^*)(1 + \theta)] > 0 \qquad (8.38)$$

and:

$$\frac{\partial \pi_m}{\partial \phi} = -SX(1 - \tau^*)\left[\bar{P} - \frac{P}{S}(1 + \theta)\right] < 0 \qquad (8.39)$$

which means that a higher transfer price raises the MNC's profit in the presence of blocked funds and, naturally, that the profit is affected adversely by the fraction of blocked funds.

REGULATION AND THE MANIPULATION OF TRANSFER PRICES

The practice of MNCs with respect to transfer prices may not be compatible with the requirements of the regulatory authorities of the countries concerned. If the MNC charged its subsidiary high transfer prices, the host country would lose. This loss would take the form of: (i) the loss of tax revenue net of customs duties; (ii) the loss of profit to local shareholders of the subsidiary; (iii) the loss of workers in the form of static wages; and (iv) the loss of customers, who have to pay higher prices for the final products.

Normally, the regulatory authorities require that prices charged by a parent MNC to a foreign subsidiary are arm's-length or competitive prices. Arm's-length prices are defined as comparable uncontrolled prices in the sense that uncontrolled sales are considered comparable to controlled sales if the physical property and circumstances involved in the uncontrolled sales are identical to the physical property and circumstances involved in controlled sales. This kind of regulation suggests the following criteria for setting up fair market-based transfer prices:

1. The price of the underlying product must be comparable to those of the same or similar products in terms of size, quality and other attributes.
2. Under certain circumstances, a difference may be necessary. These circumstances pertain to location, tradition, trade regulations and government policies.

3. The transfer price must be equal to or reflect the current market price, without a time lag.
4. The transaction should not be of a size that is big enough to affect the open market price.

Do MNCs use arm's-length prices? An answer to this question can be found in the survey of 164 US multinationals conducted by Al-Eryani *et al.* (1990). The results of the survey showed that only 35 per cent of the companies surveyed use arm's-length transfer prices. The remaining majority use either cost-based prices or negotiated prices. The problem here is that if MNCs try to manipulate transfer prices to a significant extent, then the governments of the home and the foreign country will lose tax revenue, and there will be some undesirable effects on the joint venture partners (profit), consumers (prices) and trade unions (implications for wage negotiations).

MNCs may be tempted to manipulate transfer prices to their advantage, for a variety of reasons. The first of these reasons is the desire to minimize global tax on profits, as we showed earlier. The second reason is customs duties: the lower the declared transfer price, the lower will be the customs duty imposed on the product. In this case, there would be a conflict between the interests of the customs and the tax authorities. The customs authorities would want to see a high declared transfer price, because it means higher revenue. The tax authorities, on the other hand, prefer to see lower transfer prices, because this would result in a higher taxable corporate income. Of course, the MNC will also have to choose between higher and lower after-tax profit for the subsidiary.

Another reason for manipulating transfer prices is exposure to foreign exchange risk. Changing transfer prices in itself does not lead to changes in exposure to foreign exchange risk. However, if the change in transfer prices is accompanied by a change in the timing of foreign currency payments, then the exposure would change. Changes in the timing of payments can be done either via leading (by paying in advance because of expectation of foreign currency appreciation) or lagging (by paying after the due date because of the expectation of further depreciation of the foreign currency).

We can illustrate the relationship between transfer pricing and exposure to foreign exchange risk formally. For this purpose, let us assume that the MNC buys products from the subsidiary at a foreign currency transfer price of P^*. If the amount sold by the subsidiary to the MNC is X, then the total foreign currency value of the shipment is XP^*. In domestic currency terms, what the MNC has to pay is $C = XSP^*$, which means that this amount goes up and down as the exchange rate changes.

Now, since C also depends on P^*, it follows that, to keep C constant, the MNC can manipulate the transfer prices to offset the effect of changes in the exchange rate. This is illustrated in Figure 8.4. The relationship $C = XSP^*$ can be represented either in the $C - P^*$ space, as in Figure 8.4(a), or in the $C - S$ space, as in Figure 8.4(b). In both cases, the relationship is represented by a straight line that passes through the origin with a slope of XS in (a) and XP^* in (b). Consider Figure 8.4(a) first. Initially, the MNC pays C_0, because the exchange rate and the foreign currency transfer price are S_0 and P_0^*, respectively. If the exchange rate rises to S_1 (the foreign currency appreciates) the cost to the MNC will rise to C_1 as the $C = XSP^*$ line shifts to the left. In order to keep the cost at the same level, C_0, the foreign currency transfer price must be reduced from P_0^* to P_1^*. Now consider Figure 8.4(b), which gives exactly the same result. As the exchange rate rises from S_0 to S_1, the cost to the MNC will rise to C_1. In order to maintain the cost at the initial level, the foreign currency transfer price must be reduced, and this is represented by a shift in the $C = XSP^*$ to the right.[6]

Instead of manipulating the transfer price, the MNC could use leading and lagging to offset changes in the exchange rate. Assume that the transaction between the MNC and the subsidiary is concluded

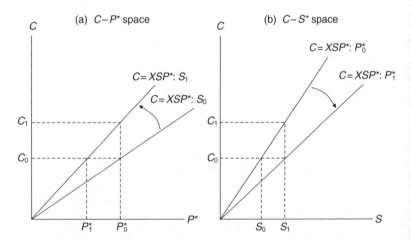

Figure 8.4　Manipulating transfer prices to offset changes in the exchange rate

at time t, such that the payment is to be made at time $t+1$. This means that $C = XS_{t+1}P^*$. If the foreign currency is expected to appreciate such that $S_{t+1} > S_t$, then the MNC may prefer to pay at t the amount $C = XS_tP^*$. This is leading. If, on the other hand, it is expected that the exchange rate will fall continuously, such that $S_{t+2} < S_{t+1} < S_t$, then the MNC will prefer to pay at $t+2$ the amount $C = XS_{t+2}P^*$. Notice that, in all cases, the subsidiary will receive the amount XP^*.

Yet another motive is profit repatriation. If there are restrictions on remittances from a subsidiary to the MNC, then the latter may resort to high transfer prices to circumvent these restrictions. This will induce higher import duties, which creates some sort of conflict.

Thus, transfer prices may diverge from market prices for reasons of marketing or financial policy, or to minimize tax payments. To ensure that the tax base of an MNC is divided fairly, it is important that transfers within a group should approximate those that would be negotiated between independent firms. The arm's-length principle is set out in Article 9 of the OECD Model Tax convention. The OECD has released the last of eight core chapters to be added to its 1995 publication *Transfer Pricing Guidelines for Multinational Enterprises and Tax Administrations*. The new chapter covers the subject of cost contribution arrangements under the arm's-length principle, which is the agreed international standard governing related party cross-border transactions. The February 1998 update contains details of procedures for monitoring the application of the guidelines and the role of the business community in this process. In October 1999, the OECD published an update in the form of a new annex to the guidelines, providing guidance on conducting advance pricing arrangements under the mutual agreement procedure.

It remains the case, however, that the official action taken to regulate transfer pricing has occurred in developed countries despite the publicity that the action has received. Developing countries are invariably victims of improper transfer pricing policies because they are ill-equipped to deal with the complex tasks involved in the monitoring of transfer pricing policies.

A FINAL REMARK

Although transfer pricing is used by MNCs for many purposes, they do not really like it in practice. Transfer pricing forces MNCs to spend time and resources doing things that are pointless from a business point of view. Phillip Gillett, a group tax controller at ICI, a British MNC, is quoted by *The Economist* as having said, 'trying to price unfinished goods sold by one plant to another within the same company is a waste of time'. He likens this practice to 'asking Ford to value a camshaft half-way along the production line: a nonsense' (*The Economist*, 'Survey', 29 January 2000, p. 14).

In the same article, Mr Gillett proposes to replace transfer pricing with a system better suited to the needs of MNCs. He suggests a 'unitary tax', which involves taking a firm's total profits and allocating different slices of that total to individual countries on the basis of a formula that reflects the firm's relative economic presence in that country. The country in question can then tax this slice of profit at their going rate.

Thus, transfer pricing can make the difference between positive and adverse effects of FDI on both home and host countries. It has happened that an MNC operating through its subsidiary in a particular country failed to pay taxes to the host government for a very long time, simply because the subsidiary did not report any profit throughout this period. One wonders why this MNC continued to operate in that country, given that it is not a charitable institution. The answer is very simple: the MNC was making a profit, but showing that the subsidiary was making a loss by manipulating transfer prices. On paper, therefore, the performance of the subsidiary was rather poor, when in fact it was not. This is why the effect of transfer pricing has to be taken into account in the control and evaluation process. This is the subject matter of Chapter 9.

9 Control and Performance Evaluation in MNCs

This chapter examines the control and performance evaluation functions in MNCs, with particular emphasis on the effects of various forms of control upon the performance evaluation of divisions, subsidiaries and managers. Therefore, we shall also discuss the design of performance evaluation and control systems. Another issue that falls within this topic pertains to the advantages and disadvantages of various measures of performance. As we shall discover, this topic is closely related to the topic dealt with in Chapter 9 – that is, transfer pricing. This is because transfer pricing affects the control and evaluation systems used by MNCs.

ORGANIZATIONAL ASPECTS OF MNC BEHAVIOUR

Lall and Streeten (1977) consider the organizational aspects of the expansion of MNCs in four parts: (i) the internal structure of management and control; (ii) the strategies of financing and transfers; (iii) the attitudes to joint ventures; and (iv) the implications of the evolving structure for the distribution of power.

To start, the international expansion of business firms makes it necessary to co-ordinate various functions between the parent MNC and subsidiaries in such a way as to promote the overall objective of the firm. Obviously, this kind of co-ordination requires different organizational structures because of such factors as size, diversification of activities and geographical spread. Specifically, a rearrangement of hierarchy is needed to cope with the diffusion of power, and the complexity of international and internal communication implicit in growing size. According to Lall and Streeten (1977), the tendency has been to knit the structure of organizational power into tighter hierarchies, with the most important decisions taken at the centre and the more routine ones left to the subsidiaries.

The second issue is that of financial strategies that include capital financing, financial transfers and asset/liability management. As far as capital financing is concerned, it has been observed that MNCs prefer to commit a small amount of their own capital for the initial investment and to raise the bulk of their capital requirements locally. There are a variety of channels through which funds can be transferred between different parts of the MNC. These include transfer pricing, royalties, fees and interest payments. Lall and Streeten (1977) also refer to some 'more devious means'. As regards asset/liability management, Lall and Streeten note that MNCs use a variety of strategies to deal with exposure to foreign exchange risk. These include the leading and lagging of payments, and speculating actively against weak currencies.

The third issue is that of attitude towards joint ventures. In general, MNCs prefer to retain control over their foreign operations and to expand via wholly-owned subsidiaries. The explanation of this tendency is straightforward: the very reason for becoming an MNC indulging in international operations is to exploit monopolistic or oligopolistic advantages.

The final issue is that of the distribution of power within MNCs and in the society as a whole. Lall and Streeten (1977) make the following observations on this issue. First, the rearrangement of the hierarchy implied by organizational changes has led to an increasing concentration of power at the head office of the MNC. Second, the growth of MNCs has posed an increasing challenge to the traditional power of national governments. Indeed, they argue that new forms of political and economic control are needed to cope with it in the future.

DEFINITION OF CONTROL IN MNCs

Daniels *et al.* (1979) define control as 'the planning, implementation, evaluation and correction of performance in order to achieve organizational objectives'. Shapiro (1992) recognizes three elements of the control process: setting objectives, measuring results, and comparing results with objectives. He also recognizes the objectives of control as 'communication, evaluation and motivation'. Martinez and Jarillo (1989) point out that the managerial challenge facing MNCs is how to co-ordinate the increasing number of dispersed and yet inter-dependent international activities.

The control process is more difficult in an MNC than in a purely domestic firm. One has to bear in mind that an MNC and its sub-sidiaries form a complex system in which each pair of units can have numerous transaction-type linkages with one another. Figure 9.1 shows the financial linkages in a system consisting of the parent

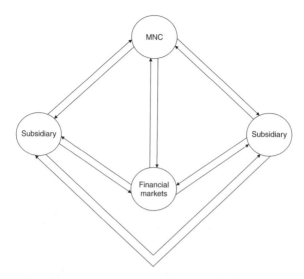

Figure 9.1   Financial linkages in an MNC–subsidiaries system

MNC and two subsidiaries. Within each financial linkage there are several types of transactions. For example, a financial linkage between the parent MNC and a subsidiary may involve: (i) parent equity investment; (ii) parent loans; (iii) purchase–sale on open account; (iv) sale–purchase of fixed assets; (v) transfer prices; (vi) dividend remittances; (vii) loan repayments; (viii) interest payments; and (ix) payment of fees. Daniels *et al.* (1979) identify four factors that make the control function more difficult in the case of an MNC. First, the geographical and cultural distances separating the parent company from its subsidiaries, and the subsidiaries from each other, make the control process more costly in terms of the time and expenses involved and make errors in communications more likely. Second, the setting of standards, performance evaluation systems and inter-subsidiary comparisons is extremely complicated because of the diversity of subsidiaries with respect to market size, products, labour costs and currencies. Third, factors such as host government regulations and the objectives of foreign shareholders, which are beyond the MNC's control, can impede the functioning of the control system. Finally, uncertainty concerning the economic and political conditions in the host country makes long-term planning difficult. Hence, the final results may differ significantly from those expected at the time of implementation if conditions alter in the meantime.

Bursk (1971) asserts that there are difficulties stemming from the peculiar nature of the international environment that must be recognized in the design of control systems. They also argue that those in charge of designing financial control systems within MNCs encounter problems because they do not fully appreciate the relevance to their task of the peculiar characteristics of the diverse international environment. Moreover, they do not have a clear concept of what a control system is intended to accomplish.

One aspect of the control function gives rise to the concepts of centralization, decentralization and divisionalization. In MNCs, decisions made at the subsidiary level are decentralized, whereas those made above the subsidiary level are said to be centralized. Generally speaking, MNCs tend to decentralize responsibility for decision-making as much as possible. According to Solomons (1965), the main device used by MNCs to implement decentralization is the profit centre. Divisionalization adds to decentralization the concept of delegated profit responsibility. A profit centre is an operating subdivision that encompasses a sufficient scope of operations to permit the measurement of profit. This clearly presupposes that the manager of the subdivision has either complete autonomy of decision-making or complete control over operating revenues and expenses. The theory behind divisionalization and the concept of the profit centre is that, if each profit centre maximizes its profit, then the organization's total profit will also be maximized.

Complete decentralization or divisionalization demand independence of subsidiaries. This may turn out to be suboptimal, because if subsidiaries are forced to act as virtually independent companies they would be unable to take advantage of the opportunities existing in the international environment. It is also likely that the experience of individual managers is limited to only one or two countries. This means that they are unlikely to appreciate the effect upon the MNC as a whole resulting from decisions taken in the best interests of their own subsidiary. Moreover, not all subsidiaries of MNCs have individual profit maximization as their basic objective. In this case, the application of the concept of profit centre may be inappropriate.

But just as complete decentralization has certain drawbacks, full centralization has its own disadvantages. Full centralization means that all decisions are referred to top management. If this is the case, then top management would be faced with too great a volume of day-to-day decisions to be able to devote the necessary time and attention to major corporate level decisions. The removal of all decision-making responsibility from the subsidiary can also reduce motivation and inhibit the use of initiative by subsidiary managers.

MNCs tend to be more centralized than do domestic firms. One explanation for this difference is suggested by Bodinat (1974), who argues that only a centralized and integrated organization with a global outlook is in a position to take advantage of the opportunities created by the differences between countries. Yet Scott (1972) believes that MNCs tend to use a form of management known as 'co-ordinative management', which comprises a mixture of co-operative, centralized and independent management in which corporate headquarters and subsidiary managers work together. Although the headquarters retains the right to final approval of major decisions, a great deal of co-operation takes place between headquarters and the subsidiaries.

Goold and Campbell (1987) distinguish between financial control, strategic planning and strategic control. With financial control, the headquarters is slim, supported only by a strong finance function. Underneath, there are layers of general management, but the prime profit responsibility is pushed down to the lowest level. Companies using this arrangement focus on annual profit targets. In strategic planning, while divisionalization is consistent up to a point, the centre participates in, and influences the development of, divisional strategies. In this case, less emphasis is placed on corporate control. Performance targets are flexible and are reviewed within the context of long-term strategic progress. Finally, under strategic control, the centre focuses more on establishing demanding planning processes and on reviewing divisional proposals. Bartlett and Goshal (1989) identify three global imperatives that influence the organizational structure, the degree of centralization of decision-making, and the organizational culture of the firm. The first of these factors is the force of global integration, as firms need to achieve economies of scale in areas such as product lines and manufacturing operations. The second is the force for local differentiation, as different market structures and consumer preferences, and government interference require attention to local differences. The third factor is the force of worldwide innovations.

CENTRALIZED VERSUS DECENTRALIZED CASH MANAGEMENT

In this section we consider one example of centralization versus decentralization: the choice between centralized and decentralized cash management, a choice that often faces MNCs with subsidiaries in various countries. Centralized cash management implies that receipts and payments in various currencies are managed by a central body, normally in the MNC's head office. Decentralized cash management implies that these receipts and payments are managed locally by the subsidiaries.

Most of the advantages of centralized cash management are associated with economies of scale. The first of these perceived advantages is netting, which involves the calculation of the overall corporate position in each currency by adding up the short and long positions of various subsidiaries. Netting provides a natural hedge when there is a short position in one currency and an equivalent long position in the same currency. For example, suppose that a subsidiary of a British MNC has a long position in the Australian dollar, and that another subsidiary has an equivalent short position in the same currency. If cash management was decentralized, the first subsidiary would hedge the long position – by selling the Australian dollar forward for example – while the second subsidiary would hedge its position by buying the dollar forward. Under a system of centralized cash management, the combined position will be a net zero, and so there would be no need to hedge any of the individual positions. This obviously involves a reduction in transaction costs.

Another advantage of centralized cash management is currency diversification. Even if the combined position is not zero, centralized cash management may result in a combined position that is so diversified that the foreign exchange risk is sufficiently reduced, again removing the need to hedge individual positions. Specifically, if the combined exposure is well diversified, in terms of currency, and if the exchange rates of these currencies against the domestic currency are not highly correlated, this will effectively provide a natural hedge.

Finally, pooling is another advantage. By pooling cash balances in a centralized location, cash requirements by any subsidiary anywhere can be met without having to keep balances denominated in various currencies in every locality. The requirements of a subsidiary that is short of cash in a certain currency can be met from the central 'pool of resources'.

There are at least two reasons why decentralized cash management may be preferable. The first is when delays are expected in transferring funds to countries where the banking system is inefficient. Having the funds ready may be required to settle a transaction exposure with unknown timing. The second is when it is felt that local representation is necessary in order to maintain on-the-spot links with clients and banks. This is why this issue is not as much about the choice between centralized and decentralized cash management systems, but about the determination of the extent of centralization and decentralization.

EMPIRICAL STUDIES OF THE CONTROL FUNCTION

There are some important empirical studies of the control function of MNCs. Meister (1970) surveyed 252 US MNCs and concluded that MNCs can be classified into the following types: (i) centralized at corporate headquarters; (ii) centralized at the headquarters of an international management unit; and (iii) split between corporate headquarters and some subordinate headquarters (for example, regional headquarters or central international unit). In another study, Robbins and Stobaugh (1973a) surveyed 187 US MNCs and found that the financial system of an MNC develops in a predictable pattern as the company's business grows. Three phases can be identified in the development of such a system. The first is ignoring the system's potential, a phase that occurs in small MNCs that have just started foreign operations. At this stage little is known at the corporate level about the unique problems of multinational business, and therefore little attention is paid to the international finance function. The second phase involves the exploitation of the system's potential, the progress into which occurs when corporate management becomes aware that international financial decisions demand different skills from those required to make domestic financial decisions. The third phase entails compromising with complexity. By this stage, the MNC finds itself facing a dilemma over control. The choice normally falls on a large central international financial staff that delegates responsibility to subsidiaries in the form of guidelines. In another study, Goold (1991) studied a small sample of European MNCs, in which he identified the following stages in a formal strategic control system: (i) periodic strategy revisions for each business; (ii) annual operating plans; (iii) formal monitoring of strategic results; and (iv) personal rewards and central intervention.

The issue of centralization versus decentralization is one aspect of the classification of mechanisms used to co-ordinate activities in MNCs. There are two broad categories: (i) structural and formal mechanisms; and (ii) informal and subtle mechanisms. These mechanisms are described in Table 9.1. Martinez and Jarillo (1989)

Table 9.1   Control mechanisms

Mechanism	Description
Structural and formal mechanisms	
Departmentalization of organizational units	Grouping activities within organizational units to find the right organizational structure
Centralization versus decentralization	Deciding who controls decision-making: MNCs or subsidiaries
Formalization	The extent to which policies and rules are written down in manuals and expected to be adhered to
Planning	Issues as diverse but important as planning and budgeting
Output and behaviour control	Reporting mechanisms, performance evaluation, and personal or behavioural evaluation
Informal and subtle mechanisms	
Lateral relations	A variety of task forces and meetings held across the formal structure to accomplish corporate objectives
Informal communication	The network of personal contacts developed over time in the organization
Organizational culture	The outcome of the process of socialization of individuals that allows things to be done by different people in similar or consistent ways

conclude that control is shifting from the formal to the informal mechanisms.

PERFORMANCE EVALUATION IN MNCs

It is generally accepted that performance evaluation is an essential part of the control system. Performance evaluation entails the comparison of results with predetermined objectives. Evaluation of the performance of foreign subsidiaries and managers is essential, not only to judge how existing subsidiaries are performing, but also to indicate the direction in which they seem to be moving, how corporate strategies and policies should be modified to improve future performance, and the likelihood of corporate objectives being realised.

Borkowiski (1999) argues that if the objective of MNCs is to maximize profits and returns to shareholders, as suggested by Keating (1997), then performance evaluation criteria should be compatible with this objective. Hence, Keating addresses the following objectives in her study:

1. Do performance evaluation criteria vary, depending on the home country of the MNC?
2. Are home and host country subsidiary managers evaluated according to different criteria?
3. Are managers stationed in a particular country evaluated according to similar criteria, regardless of their home/host status?
4. Does the transfer pricing method used by the MNC prescribe evaluation criteria, or are the criteria independent of transfer pricing?

These questions and others are indicative of the fact that measuring the performance of an individual, a division or even a company as a whole is never easy. Robbins and Stobaugh (1973b) point out that one main reason for the difficulty of evaluation is that different bases of measurement result in different measures of performance. In addition, many events affecting performance are not controllable by the individual or unit under evaluation. There is also the strategic differences in subsidiaries that may result in different performance evaluation measures. Gupta and Govindarajan (1991) identify several issues surrounding performance evaluation that are complex in a global environment.

It is important to separate the evaluation of the subsidiary from the evaluation of the manager's performance. Demirag (1987) argues that the evaluation of the manager's performance separately from that of the subsidiary helps to indicate the extent to which managers are accomplishing the objectives of the MNC as a whole. This distinction is particularly important in MNCs, since the use of centralized decision-making means that many factors that affect the subsidiary's performance are outside the control of the manager, and also because actions taken by one subsidiary manager may have an adverse effect on the performance of other operating subsidiaries. For this reason, Hopwood (1972) argues that financial data available for performance evaluation may be inadequate for evaluating the performance of the manager. There are at least two reasons for this. First, financial reports represent the outcome of the subsidiary's operations, whereas managerial performance is concerned with the efficiency of the process that produces this outcome. Second, financial data may also prove to be inappropriate for managerial performance evaluation, since their emphasis is on short-term performance, whereas managerial evaluation is concerned with long-term considerations. For these reasons, MNCs tend to use non-financial criteria for the separate evaluation of the performance of managers. Moreover, Gupta and Govindarajan (1991) point out that some subsidiary managers are in a better position to cope with the uncertainty inherent in the foreign environment than are others.

In a survey of 105 British MNCs, Demirag (1987) found that non-financial criteria in common use include market share as measured by sales, personnel development, employee morale measured through internal surveys, productivity, and the relationship between local management and the host government. Eiteman and Stonehill (1989) suggest that managerial performance evaluation can also be used to motivate managers by relating compensation to the results of evaluation.

EVALUATION OF DOMESTIC AND FOREIGN OPERATIONS

The evaluation of the performance of foreign operations is more difficult than that of domestic operations, because of such factors as fluctuations in exchange rates and foreign inflation, all of which affect the financial data used for evaluation. But according to Miller (1979), when MNCs first began to evolve, foreign operations were virtually controlled and managed from the corporate headquarters, and domestic methods of performance evaluation were used to evaluate the performance of foreign operations. Demirag (1987) found that a significant majority of British MNCs applied the same performance evaluation measures to foreign operations and domestic operations alike.

There are five factors that affect the evaluation of foreign subsidiaries and their managers: (i) exchange rate fluctuations; (ii) inflation; (iii) transfer pricing; (iv) cost allocation; and (v) translation. The first two factors are beyond corporate control, whereas the last three are within corporate control. These factors will be discussed in turn.

Exchange Rates

Foreign exchange risk arises because of uncertainty about the future spot exchange rate. It refers to the variability of the domestic currency value of certain items resulting from the variability of the exchange rate. These items include assets, liabilities, operating income, profit, rates of return and expected cash flows, whether they are certain (contractual) or uncertain. While risk measures the probability and magnitude of deviations from some expected out-come, exposure is a measure of what is at risk. Risk refers to the probability of an adverse outcome, while exposure is the size of a potential loss. In international finance, foreign exchange exposure is the amount exposed to foreign exchange risk. Exposure arises because the domestic currency value of assets, liabilities, operating income and other cash flows is sensitive to changes in nominal and real exchange rates.

The effects of fluctuations in exchange rates appear in three kinds of exposure to foreign exchange risk. The first is transaction exposure, which arises if payables and receivables (cash inflows and outflows) are denominated in foreign currencies. Risk is present because the domestic currency values of these items when they are due varies according to changes in the nominal exchange rate. Transaction expo-sure is clearly a cash flow exposure, which may be associated with trade flows (resulting from exports and imports), and capital flows (for example, dividends and interest payments). It involves an actual conversion of foreign currency payables and receivables into the domestic currency. This kind of exposure arises, for example, from (i) a foreign currency asset or liability that is already recorded on the balance sheet; and (ii) a contract or an agreement involving a future foreign currency cash flow.

The second kind of foreign exchange exposure is economic expo-sure, which arises because changes in (real) exchange rates affect the firm's domestic and foreign cash flows. This may sound like transac-tion exposure, but the difference lies in the fact that we are in this case concerned with non-contractual or unplanned future cash flows. These cash flows pertain to sales in foreign markets and sales in domestic markets, as well as input costs, whether the inputs are domestic or foreign.

The third kind of exposure is translation exposure (also called accounting exposure), which arises from the consolidation of foreign currency assets, liabilities, net income and other items in the process of preparing domestic currency-based consolidated financial state-ments (balance sheet and income statement). Translation exposure gives rise to the possibility that the conversion of foreign currency-denominated items into the domestic currency for the purpose of consolidation may show a loss or gain. It is therefore a function of the accounting system and may have little to do with the true value in an economic sense. Firms with identical balance sheet and income statement items may show different consolidated results depending on the translation method used.

Exchange rate fluctuations arise from many factors including interest rates, inflation rates, growth rates, the current account position and other economic fundamentals. But fluctuations in exchange rates are typically more volatile than these economic fundamentals. In the short run, exchange rates are affected less by changes in fundamentals and more by microstructural factors and expectation. Indeed, some economists go as far as to argue that fundamentals are irrelevant to exchange rate determination, a view with which the present author does not agree.[1] It is arguable that, in order for evaluation to be carried out adequately, the effects of fluctuating exchange rates on financial information must be taken into account. In other words, this view stipulates that managers should not be held responsible for the effects of unexpected changes in exchange rates.[2] This view is, however, not necessarily valid. There is no doubt that forecasting exchange rates is a rather difficult and hazardous endeavour, but it is essential because almost all international financial decisions (on investment, financing, hedging and speculation) require exchange rate forecasting as an input.[3] The evaluation process must include an evaluation of the manager's effort to forecast exchange rates, making sure that the forecast has not been arrived at simply on the toss of a coin.

Inflation Rates

Inflation rates are important not least because they do affect exchange rates, although this tends to be a long-run effect. Exchange rates and inflation rates are linked by purchasing power parity (PPP), but it has been observed that there are significant and persistent deviations from PPP in the short run. Even if there were no deviations from PPP, forecasting exchange rates still requires forecasting inflation in the years to come, and this invariably proves to be difficult in long-term FDI projects.

Moreover, inflation affects the financial position and performance of firms in ways that can result in some inefficient decisions by managers who do not understand its impact. In terms of financial position, financial assets (such as cash) lose value during inflation because it erodes their purchasing power. Conversely, holding financial liabilities is beneficial, because the business will be paying its obligations in the future with cash that has lost some of its purchasing power.

The effect of inflation on non-monetary assets is reflected in both the income statement and the balance sheet. During a period of rising prices, revenues from current sales are matched against inventory that may have been purchased several months earlier, and against depreciation that is calculated on the historical cost of plant and equipment despite the fact that the replacement cost has risen significantly.[4] The effects of inflation on financial statements could lead to liquidity problems as the cash generated from revenues is consumed by the ever-increasing replacement cost. The overstatement of income that results from matching old costs with new revenues could lead to demands from shareholders for increased dividends, and employees for higher wages, even though the cash flow is dwindling. The concern is that one cannot make informed decisions without understanding the impact of inflation. For MNCs in particular, these concerns are even greater because of different accounting practices in different countries.

Transfer Pricing

The third factor is transfer pricing, which is a controllable factor that can lead to gross distortions when evaluating foreign subsidiaries and their managers. The accuracy of evaluating a foreign subsidiary and its managers also depends on the degree of responsibility that a subsidiary manager has with respect to the effects of transfer pricing on the performance of the subsidiary. It is important that this degree of responsibility is taken into account, because most MNCs determine transfer pricing at the MNC's headquarters. When profits are used for performance evaluation, transfer pricing policy should be taken into account and the figures should be adjusted for the effect of transfer prices. Top management should ensure that no subsidiary receives undue profits or losses resulting from transfer pricing. Brickley *et al.* (1997) point out that transfer pricing strategies often lead to conflicts and hence to managerial dissonance rather than congruence. Borkowski (1999) examines the effect of transfer pricing on the performance evaluation of domestic and foreign operations. Bushman *et al.* (1995) argue that the transfer pricing effect on subsidiary profits should render MNC-wide performance measures less useful than individual subsidiary measures. MNCs are aware of the adverse effects of transfer pricing on performance evaluation and they try to deal with it by, for example, keeping two sets of books.

Cost Allocation

The allocation of company costs or headquarters cost is another controllable factor that affects evaluation in a similar way to that of transfer pricing, simply because the procedure used for this purpose is bound to affect the profits of a subsidiary. Kollaritsch (1984) has suggested that the best thing to do in this case would be to forget about these costs and only include the costs that are directly under the control of the subsidiary.

Translation of Financial Statements

Finally, the method of translation is also a controllable factor that affects profit. Translation means the conversion of figures in financial statements from one currency to another, more specifically from the currency of the subsidiary (the foreign currency) to the currency of the MNC (the domestic currency). There are two points to discuss here. The first is whether performance evaluation is based on financial information in domestic currency terms (that is, by using translated financial statements) or on financial statements in foreign currency terms. The second point is that if the first option is used, then a decision must be made as to the method of translation.

By evaluating performance without translation, the effect of translation is ignored. McInnes (1971) argues that the effectiveness of the subsidiary and its manager is more meaningful if measured in foreign currency terms. This would be the case particularly if the subsidiaries were not held responsible for changes in exchange rates. In a survey conducted by Robbins and Stobaugh (1973b) MNCs that do not hold subsidiaries responsible for the effect of exchange rates use evaluation without translation. However, translation is sometimes felt to be necessary because it enables top management to understand it more easily than if it were in foreign currency. Ijiri (1983) argues that if MNCs consider their subsidiaries as investments, then the results of these investments should be measured in domestic currency terms, implying that translation should be used in performance evaluation.

A number of surveys have been conducted on the use of translation in performance evaluation, a summary of which can be found in Demirag (1992). The results of these surveys show that, throughout the 1960s, the domestic currency was used for evaluation, but in the 1970s both domestic and foreign currencies were used. A survey of UK multinationals by Demirag (1988) confirmed that both currencies are used. This may be because the MNCs were unable to determine the usefulness of each measure of performance.

Translation methods refer to the choice of the exchange rate used for converting (translating) the values of foreign currency items into domestic currency. The balance sheet contains the values of assets and liabilities as at the end of the accounting period, which may be a year, a quarter or a month. The income statement reports items such as revenues, costs and net income realized over the accounting period. The following three rates can be used for conversion:

1. The closing (or current) rate, which is the rate prevailing at the end of the accounting period (coinciding with the balance sheet date).
2. The average rate, which reflects the average value of the exchange rate over the accounting period. The easiest procedure is to take a simple average of the closing rate and the rate prevailing at the beginning of the period. Otherwise, a time-weighted average may be used.
3. The historical rate, which is the rate prevailing at the date when an asset is acquired or a liability is incurred. The historical rate may therefore fall outside the current accounting period. In fact, this is invariably the case for long-term assets and liabilities.

In translating the income statement items, either the closing or the average rates are used, which means that the amount exposed is net income. The possibility of using historical rates in translating balance sheet items makes the matter more complicated. For the purpose of translating balance sheet items, the following methods are used.

First is the *current/non-current method*, which is based on the traditional accounting distinction between current items (for example, short-term deposits and inventory) and long-term items (for example, real estate, long-term debt). According to this method, the current items are translated at the closing rate, while long-term items are translated at the historical rate. Obviously, the use of the historical rate precludes foreign exchange risk, while the use of the closing rate does not. Hence, if this method is used, the amount exposed to foreign exchange risk is net current assets. There is an obvious problem with this method: the items such as long-term loans are portrayed as being immune to foreign exchange risk, which does not make sense. This is why there has been a move away from this method.

The second method is the *closing (current) rate method*, the most widely used method worldwide. All items are translated at the closing exchange rate prevailing at the end of the accounting period. When this method is used, the amount exposed is shareholders' equity.

Third, there is the *monetary/non-monetary method*. According to this method, the monetary items are those items whose values are fixed in terms of the number of units of the currency of denomination. For example, a bond is a monetary item since its par (or face) value (the value received by the bondholder on maturity) is fixed by contract and displayed on the face of the bond. Real estate, on the other hand, is a non-monetary item, since its value in the currency of denomination may rise or fall. According to this method, monetary items are translated at the closing rate, while non-monetary items are translated at the historical rate. The amount exposed in this case is the value of net monetary items.

Finally, there is the *temporal method*. According to this method, the use of the closing rate or the historical rate is determined by the valuation of the underlying item. The closing rate is used for items stated at replacement cost, realizable value, market value, or expected future value. The historical rate is used for all items stated at historical cost. The rationale for this method is that the translation rate should preserve the accounting principles used to value assets and liabilities in the original (foreign currency) financial statements.

MEASURES OF PERFORMANCE

More than one measure of performance is used for evaluating subsidiaries. These measures include actual profit relative to budgeted profit, return on investments, budgeted sales compared with actual sales, and absolute amount of profit in monetary units. Other measures include comparison with historical data, comparison with similar units in other countries, and comparison with similar units at the home country. Non-financial measures may also be used to evaluate the performance of managers.

Horngren (1977) states that the ultimate test of profitability is the relationship between profit and invested capital. The most popular way of expressing this relationship is by means of a rate of return on investment. The problem is that this measure may not be valid if the objective of the subsidiary is not to make profit by itself but to contribute to the profitability of the organization as a whole.

Other studies, including McInnes (1971), Robbins and Stobaugh (1973b), Morsicato (1978), Persen and Lessig (1979), Choi and Cze-chowicz (1983) and Demirag (1988) have shown that, although the rate of return on investment is one of the most popular performance evaluation criteria used by MNCs, other profit-related measures are used as well. The rate of return on investment has the following advantages. First, it is a single comprehensive figure influenced by everything that is likely to affect the financial position. Second, it measures how well a manager uses the assets to generate profits. Third, it provides a common denominator that can be used directly for comparison. However, it also has disadvantages, which are iden-tified by Horngren (1977) as follows. First, it emphasizes short-term results and over-emphasizes profit while under-emphasizing quality, employee relations and discovery of new products. Second, it may lead to incongruent decisions because of accounting policies with respect to measures of investment and other policies. Third, comparisons among divisional results can be unjustifiable because of economic and accounting differences. Rate of return and other profit-related meas-ures raise more difficulties. First, the information received from profit-related measures may lead to incorrect decisions and motivate managers in ways that are not in the best interests of the MNC as a whole. In addition, top management may use the measures to pro-duce false pictures of a subsidiary's performance (Henderson and Dearden, 1966). Table 9.2 provides a summary of the findings of selected studies of performance evaluation in MNCs. Each of these studies is based on a survey of the practices of a number of MNCs.

It may be worthwhile at this stage to have a more detailed look at the results obtained from one or two of these studies.

Borkowski (1999) extended prior research by comparing perfor-mance evaluation criteria within and across countries. Unlike Bor-kowski (1993), Kopp (1994) and Keating (1997), this study compares host and home country subsidiary managers with their counterparts by specific country location. Given the divergence between theory and

260

Table 9.2 Findings of selected studies of performance evaluation

Study	No. of MNCs	Findings
National Association of Accountants (1960)	51	Responsibility for earning adequate profit in foreign currency. Managements held responsible for protecting investment against exchange rate fluctuations
McInnes (1971)	30	17 per cent used foreign currency evaluation, 30 per cent used domestic currency, 50 per cent used both, and 3 per cent used different methods depending on the operating environment
Bursk (1971)	34	Some awareness of the impact of changes in exchange rates on performance evaluation. Equal use of domestic currency and foreign currency for performance evaluation. No distinction between the performance of the subsidiary and that of the manager
Robbins and Stobaugh (1973b)	189	44 per cent used untranslated data, 44 per cent used translated data, and 12 per cent used both. Those using foreign currency performance evaluation place the responsibility for protection against exchange rate fluctuations on corporate headquarters
Morsicato (1978)	70	Translated data are preferable, except for budgeted and actual sales
Reece and Cool (1978)	459	65 per cent used rate of return on investment
Business International Money Report (1979)	12	58 per cent measured performance in both currencies, and 42 per cent in domestic currency only
Persen and Lessig (1979)	125	4 per cent used foreign currency, 38 per cent used domestic currency, and 58 per cent used both
Czechowicz *et al.* (1982)	108	44 per cent employed domestic, 9 per cent used foreign, and 28 per cent employed both

Abdallah and Keller (1985)	64	Companies use return on investment, profits, budgeted rate of return on investment compared with the actual rate, and budgeted profit compared with actual profit
Appleyard *et al.* (1990)	11	MNCs prefer to use budgeted/actual comparisons followed by some form of rate of return on investment
Bailes and Assada (1991)	336	Japanese firms focus on sales volume, whereas US firms emphasize rate of return on investment
Kirsch and Johnson (1991)	15	The majority of the firms surveyed used both domestic and foreign currencies
Keating (1997)	78	Divisional accounting criteria are the most important evaluation measures, followed by overall corporate accounting measures, including the rate of return on investment

current MNC performance evaluation practices, Borkowski examined the following hypotheses:

1. MNCs tend to use different criteria for evaluating domestic and foreign operations.
2. Performance evaluation criteria used by US-based MNCs do not differ from the criteria used by non-US-based MNCs.
3. Short-term (optimistic) and long-term (pessimistic) country orientation do not influence performance evaluation criteria.
4. Performance evaluation criteria are not affected by an MNC's transfer pricing method.

The results of this study did not support the generally acceptable proposition that MNCs use different criteria to evaluate managers based on the location (host or home country). Borkowski argues that if the MNC's objective is profit maximization, then performance evaluation criteria should be compatible with this objective. There is also some evidence that special performance evaluation criteria vary in importance by country. Finally, the findings reveal that the differing importance of performance evaluation criteria among countries has implications for MNCs with both native-born and foreign-born managers in a subsidiary.

BUDGETING FOR GLOBAL OPERATIONS

Although MNCs are believed to use return on investment for performance evaluation, some studies have shown that operating budget
comparisons are more frequently used by MNCs for this purpose
(see, for example, Morsicato, 1978; Persen and Lessig, 1979; Demirag,
1988). A budget may be defined as a quantitative expression of a plan
of action, and an aid to co-ordination and implementation. The
comparison between actual and budgeted figures produces variances
that can be analysed for the purpose of evaluating operating and
management performance. This analysis is then followed by corrective
actions.

Budgets are used for purposes other than performance evaluation.
They are used for planning because they identify objectives to be
achieved and the means of achieving them. Budgets are also used
for motivation in the sense that they provide a commitment to pre-
determined plans. Co-ordination is another purpose for which budgets can be used. For example, managers prepare budgets for their
units and these progress to higher levels where they are used to
harmonize the entire company. Finally, budgets can be used to edu-
cate managers on the positions and roles of other divisions.

Several problems are associated with budgeting, some of which
stem from conflict between the various objectives of budgeting. For
example, the conflict between evaluation and motivation creates one
of these problems. This conflict can be reduced by using adjustable
budgets whose objectives can be changed under predetermined conditions. Conflict also arises between evaluation and planning. When
a budget is set it does not provide an accurate forecast for planning,
because uncontrollable and unpredictable events may occur.

There are several aspects of the international environment and
global strategy of MNCs that influence the budgetary process. First,
there is the aspect of culture and differences in perceptions of the
values of budgets. A second issue pertains to transfer pricing. If
transfer prices are arbitrarily set high in order to minimize tax payments, profit will also be low. The third issue is that of unstable
economic environment, particularly with respect to inflation. When
inflation is relatively low or stable it is much easier to establish
a budget that will approximate actual performance. In general, the
budget processes should be different in foreign subsidiaries from
those at home because of the differences in the environment, strategic
emphasis, distance, language and culture (for example, Egelhoff,

1988; Bartlett and Goshal, 1989). Empirical studies such as Hassel (1991), and Hassel and Cunningham (1993), found that the effectiveness of budget controls and budgetary participation varied between domestic and foreign subsidiaries.

Hassel and Cunningham (1996) consider three aspects of the budgeting process. The first is the reliance on budget controls – that is, the extent to which the budget is viewed as a major tool for organizational control (see, for example, Parker, 1977). The second is budget communications and influence – that is, the extent to which information is communicated back and forth between headquarters and units (see, for example, Bartlett and Goshal, 1989). The third is the 'environmental dynamism' – that is, conditions in the environment that have been suggested as major factors influencing budget effectiveness and management performance (see, for example, Otley, 1980; Hassel and Cunningham, 1993; Gul and Chia, 1994). They test the following hypotheses:

1. In domestic units of MNCs, the interaction of reliance on budget controls, budget communication and environmental dynamism has a significant effect on performance.
2. In foreign units of MNCs there is no effect on performance from the interaction of reliance on budget control budget communications and environmental dynamism.
3. In domestic units of MNCs there is no effect on performance of the interaction of reliance on budget control, budget communications and environmental dynamism.
4. In foreign units of MNCs, the interaction of reliance on budget controls, budget influence and environmental dynamism has a significant effect on unit performance.

The key findings of the Hassel–Cunningham study is that unit performance is enhanced by budget communication in domestic units when reliance on budget control and environmental dynamism are high. The second finding is that foreign units differ from domestic units, but not in the manner hypothesized. This is to say that budget effectiveness for foreign units is more complete than previous research designs have addressed.

One problem with budgeting concerns the choice of the exchange rate. Two rates must be identified: the rate used for determining the budget, and the rate used to track performance relative to the budget. Lessard and Lorange (1977) suggest three possible rates for this purpose. When a budget is drawn up, two possible exchange rates may be used, either the spot rate or a rate that can be predicted for the end of the period. The budget can be updated by the exchange rate prevailing at the end of the period. For example, the easiest thing to do would be to set and track the budget on the initial spot rate.

Subsequently, Lessard and Sharp (1983) developed a method called 'contingent budgeting', which is a refinement of flexible budgeting whereby the effects of exchange rate fluctuations are the responsibility of those who are thought to be the best in managing exchange rate risks, leaving performance measures to incite incentives to increase the value of the company. Managers should not be held responsible for the effects of exchange rate fluctuations, but should have some responsibility for the effect of exchange rates on real operating items. A contingent budget process consists of the following three stages. In the first stage the budget is prepared in foreign currency terms. Then an audit is undertaken to demonstrate the effects of a change in exchange rates on costs and prices. Finally, when exchange rates are available at the end of the period, the audit can be used to prepare a set of standards based on the actual rates. The actual results can then be compared with the standards for a more adequate evaluation of performance.

A FINAL REMARK

In this chapter we have considered some accounting and management issues that are essential for the performance of MNCs, the initiators and generators of FDI. By analysing these issues, this book has dealt with the economic, financial, accounting and management aspects of FDI. In fact, even the political and social aspects of FDI were referred to briefly (particularly in Chapter 2). All that remains now is to sum up in an attempt to reach a conclusion. This rather difficult task will be taken on in Chapter 10.

10 Summary and Conclusions

RECAPITULATION

This book has taken us on a grand tour of the economic, financial, accounting and management aspects of FDI. We have explored the characteristics, determinants and effects of FDI. We have also gone through the procedures used to determine the financial feasibility of FDI projects and investigated the effects on this feasibility of country risk, taxation and the cost of capital. Then we dealt with the critical issue of transfer pricing, and finally we examined the control and performance evaluation functions in MNCs. It is rather difficult to write a short but a comprehensive summary of what has been discussed, but it is possible to state the following points as some sort of a recapitulation:

1. FDI is the process whereby residents of one country acquire ownership of assets for the purpose of controlling the activities of a firm in another country. Interest in FDI results from (i) its rapid growth; (ii) the concern it raises over the causes and consequences of foreign ownership; and (iii) the fact that FDI has become an important source of funds for developing countries.
2. FDI can be horizontal, vertical or conglomerate. It can also be classified into import-substituting, export-increasing and government-initiated. Another classification is that of expansionary versus defensive FDI.
3. A common sequence that firms use to develop foreign markets for their products consists of (i) exports; (ii) licensing; (iii) foreign distribution; and (iv) foreign production. Steps (iii) and (iv) involve FDI.
4. Theories explaining FDI determination comprise (i) theories assuming perfect markets; (ii) theories assuming imperfect markets; (iii) other theories; and (iv) theories based on other variables. The empirical evidence on these theories is mixed, but the effect of certain individual variables has been established without any doubt (for example, the size of the host economy).

5. There are also theories designed to explain entry modes; that is, the choice among exports, licensing, franchising, subcontracting, M&As, greenfield FDI and joint ventures.

6. FDI gives rise to costs and benefits for the source and host countries. But there is a fundamental disagreement on what constitutes costs and benefits. The division of welfare gains between the two countries is influenced by the bargaining power over the terms of the agreement governing a particular FDI project.

7. The effects of FDI on the host country can be classified into economic, political and social effects. Whether these effects are favourable or adverse is a controversial matter, as they are conditions-specific.

8. International capital budgeting is the process used to evaluate the financial feasibility of FDI projects. Several criteria are used for this purpose, including the NPV, APV, IRR, accounting rate of return, the payback period, and the profitability index.

9. Country risk is exposure to loss in cross-country transactions. It consists of economic risk and political risk, the latter being more relevant to FDI.

10. Taxation significantly affects the location of FDI, the organizational form of the foreign establishment, financing decisions, remittance policy, transfer pricing policy, working capital management, and the capital structure policy.

11. The cost of capital is crucial for capital budgeting, since it determines the discount rate used in project evaluation. MNCs tend to have different cost of capital and capital structures from those of purely domestic firms.

12. Transfer pricing is the pricing of goods and services that are bought and sold between members of a corporate family. The transfer pricing policy followed by an MNC depends on tax considerations, global regulation, performance evaluation, fund positioning, market considerations, risk, government policy, interest in joint ventures and the negotiating power of the subsidiary. Transfer prices can be set on the basis of market prices or costs.

13. Control in MNCs consists of planning, implementation, evaluation and correction of performance in order to achieve organizational objectives. It involves several issues, including centralization versus decentralization. Performance evaluation is an essential part of the control system, comprising the comparison of results with pre-determined objectives.

This brief itemization of the subject matter covered in this book is inevitably superficial, but it serves the purpose of reminding ourselves what was dealt with in the previous nine chapters. Now, we turn to a brief summary of the reasons behind the initiation of FDI.

WHAT MOTIVATES FDI?

From one perspective, FDI can be viewed as an activity that satisfies basic business needs. Hence, there are firm-specific motivations for indulging in FDI. The following is a general outline of the reasons why FDI is undertaken. We came across these motivations when we studied the theories of FDI in Chapter 2.

The Need for Markets

When the growth of sales is limited in the domestic market, a firm considers expanding overseas. Under special circumstances, expansion takes place by establishing production facilities abroad, which allows the firm to exploit the economies of scale. If markets are segmented and there are markets that offer higher profit margins, then firms will move into these markets. Many MNCs give primacy in their business strategies to seeking markets, and a large number of cross-border investments are prompted by the need to expand and diversify markets on a global basis. This is particularly valid for the MNCs engaged in the production of consumer non-durable goods such as food processing, beverages, tobacco, and soap and toiletries. These MNCs tend to spend a relatively high percentage of sales revenue on advertising, and rely on a strong and distinct marketing effort to maintain or increase market position (for example, Coca-Cola sells its products in more than 160 countries).

The Need for Production Efficiency

The need for production efficiency motivates companies to produce in countries where resource inputs are relatively cheap. This is why American companies invest in Mexico and South East Asia for labour-intensive production. Nike, for example, carries out the bulk of its production of training shoes in Asia, paying workers very low wages.

The Need for Raw Materials

To avoid the transportation costs associated with importing raw materials that are unavailable in the home country, a firm will set up a production facility close to the source of raw materials in the foreign country. This is particularly the case if the foreign country is a market for the finished products. This factor underlies FDI in many industrial sectors such as petroleum, metals mining, forest products, and plantation activities. Countries that have served as hosts for this kind of FDI are Canada, Australia, Malaysia and Chile.

The Need for Information and Technology

The need for information and technology has motivated FDI in US companies manufacturing computer software and hardware, as well as pharmaceutical companies.

The Need to Minimize or Diversify Risk

The risk factor has led to FDI in countries being considered more stable and offering low political risk. This explains why some Hong Kong-based MNCs sought to diversify their operations because of uncertainties regarding the return of Hong Kong to China in 1997. Market risk can be reduced by investing in several countries.

Integrating Operations

Vertical integration is achieved when a firm indulges in various stages of the production process. For example, vertical integration is achieved in the oil industry when a firm engages in operations ranging from exploration and extraction to retailing. It is beneficial because it results in assured delivery between various stages of production. If different stages can be carried out better in different locations, then expansion in foreign countries will take place.

Non-transferable Knowledge

If a firm develops expertise in the production of a certain commodity, and if it is difficult to transfer this knowledge, the firm will be better off expanding overseas.

Protecting Knowledge

A firm may have transferable expertise that it does not wish to transfer. In this case the firm itself will take production overseas. An example is the desire by Kentucky Fried Chicken to protect the secrecy of its recipe.

Protecting Reputation

To protect a brand name or product quality, a firm may decide to carry out production abroad. For example, McDonalds expanded overseas to protect its reputation of producing 'tasty' burgers.

Capitalizing on Reputation

Firms with an international (good) reputation may capitalize on it by expanding overseas. International well-known banks, for example, can attract deposits when they set up branches in foreign countries.

Avoiding Tariffs and Quotas

A good example is when Japanese car manufacturers establish production facilities in the USA. When production takes place in the foreign country it will be a substitute for exports that may be subject to tariffs and quotas.

Exchange Rate Considerations

Firms move into countries with weak currencies because the initial set-up cost is low. In general, firms choose to establish production facilities in countries whose currencies are weak or undervalued, and sell their products in countries whose currencies are strong or overvalued. The extent of overvaluation and undervaluation may be measured by deviations from purchasing power parity (see, for example, Moosa, 1998, Chapter 9).

Relationships with other MNCs

Some MNCs expand overseas because they follow others. This is particularly valid for banks and other financial institutions. If an MNC decides to establish a subsidiary in a particular foreign country, the bank or financial institution serving the parent company at home may open a branch in the same foreign country to service the banking and financial needs of the subsidiary. This, in fact, was one of the reasons for the growth of international banking.

An Example

Some of these motives have been used to explain certain cases of FDI. Eng *et al.* (1995, p. 451) give the following explanation for the growth of British FDI in the USA since the 1980s:

1. Recognition of the size of the US market, and that the US is a safe haven in a turbulent world.
2. Emergence of non-US MNCs with the ability to compete successfully in the US market.
3. Depreciation of the US dollar against major currencies in the second half of the 1980s.
4. Narrowing of the gap in production costs between the USA and foreign locations.
5. Concern regarding possible US protectionist measures.
6. Relatively non-restrictive US policy towards inward FDI, together with the active promotion of FDI by individual state governments.

FDI AND MNCs: THE ARGUMENTS FOR AND AGAINST

We have by now realized that the effects of FDI and MNCs operating in foreign countries constitute a highly controversial issue. In an attempt to reach a verdict on whether they are good or bad, let us sum up the arguments for and against FDI and MNCs, starting with the arguments *for* them:

- FDI flows continue to expand even when world trade slows down, or when portfolio investment dries up. These flows are less volatile than portfolio investment flows, because FDI represents a long-term commitment to the underlying project.
- FDI is an important source of funds for developing and transition countries.
- It involves the transfer of financial capital, technology and other skills desperately needed by developing countries.
- FDI raises income and social welfare in the host country unless there are distortions caused by protection, monopoly and externalities.

- It contributes to filling the saving and foreign exchange gaps by providing financial capital.
- It provides a vehicle for reviving the domestic capital market through which domestic savings can be channelled to finance domestic investment.
- FDI boosts growth in the host countries through technology diffusion and the transfer of capital.
- FDI can lead to an increase in employment in the host country by setting up new production facilities and by stimulating employment in distribution. It can preserve employment by acquiring and restructuring ailing firms.
- FDI initially leads to an improvement in the capital account of the host country.
- FDI is likely to boost productivity if (i) it is export-promoting; and (ii) the underlying conditions allow the installation of plants designed to achieve economies of scale.
- FDI boosts the skills of local workers through training.
- FDI helps to provide local firms with increased opportunities by establishing links with local suppliers for locally-produced goods.
- FDI boosts competition in the host country's markets.

This list looks very impressive, but the list of arguments *against* FDI and MNCs is equally, if not more, impressive. Let us examine this list:

- FDI symbolizes new colonialism.
- It results in a loss of sovereignty and in compromising national security. There are several examples of MNCs interfering with the politics of the host country.
- MNCs are often in a position to obtain incentives (from the host country) in excess of their needs and perhaps in excess of the benefits they bring to the host country.
- MNCs exist and operate primarily because of market imperfections, which precludes the conditions under which FDI supposedly boosts welfare.
- Even if FDI leads to a gain in world output, it results in some distributional changes between labour and capital.
- The sheer size of MNCs may jeopardize the national independence of the host country.
- FDI creates enclaves and a foreign elite in the host country.
- It introduces adverse cultural changes.

- FDI does not perform the function of providing capital, for three reasons: (i) it is a relatively expensive source of financial capital; (ii) actual capital flows provided by MNCs may not be large, as they may choose to obtain funds from the local capital market; and (iii) the capital contribution of MNCs may take a non-financial form (for example, goodwill). By raising capital locally, MNCs crowd out domestic investment, which is perhaps more suitable than foreign investment.

- The domination of a developing country by an MNC may economically be detrimental to growth through a lower rate of capital accumulation, greater incidence of undesirable practices and adverse effects on competition.

- It is invariably the case that subsidiaries operating in host countries are wholly-owned by the parent MNCs. The host country has no control over the operations of these subsidiaries.

- FDI can reduce employment through divestment and closure of production facilities. The empirical evidence shows that the overall employment effects of the activities of MNCs on the host country are small.

- Outward FDI destroys jobs at the source country because output of foreign subsidiaries becomes a substitute for exports from the home country.

- FDI leads to an increase in wage inequality in the host country.

- FDI is often blamed for its balance of payments effects. The source country faces a sudden deficit when the FDI occurs, whereas the host country faces a perpetual deficit because of profit repatriation.

- MNCs indulge in the production of luxury goods rather than the basic consumer goods needed in developing countries.

- FDI does not play an important role in technology diffusion because (i) inappropriateness of the technology they provide, as it is too capital-intensive; and (ii) the availability of cheaper sources of technology. Moreover, the R&D activities are concentrated in the MNCs' home countries.

- MNCs are very powerful negotiators, likely to strike favourable terms in bilateral negotiations with the government of a poor country.

- The costs of training labour are not large enough to make a significant contribution to the improvement of the skills of local workers. The practices of MNCs may be irrelevant to the host country, in which case training will not be useful and may even be harmful. Moreover, it is often the case that MNCs reserve key managerial and technical positions for expatriates.

- MNCs worsen income distribution in the host countries.
- They also worsen income distribution worldwide by paying foreign workers low wages, charging ordinary consumers high (sometimes extortionate) prices, and paying 'celebrities' obscene amounts of money to sponsor their products. For example, it is reported that sportsmen Michael Schumacher and Tiger Woods earned more than US$100 million each in the year 2000 alone, most of which was sponsorship money.
- They abuse transfer pricing, depriving host countries of tax revenue. Reportedly, a subsidiary of an MNC operating in a particular country has not made any profit for over thirty years, which makes one wonder why this subsidiary is still operating in the same country.
- They form alliances with corrupt elites in developing countries. There are several examples of billionaires who migrate to developed countries after accumulating massive wealth in extremely poor countries. It is no wonder that the OECD has encouraged MNCs not to indulge in any activity involving corruption and bribes.
- Most MNCs are sufficiently vertically integrated or have incentives to engage in inter-subsidiary transactions that limit the scope for developing strong ties with local suppliers.
- FDI leads to a worsening of market concentration and the possibility of monopolistic or oligopolistic practices.
- Because MNCs have significant financial, political and negotiating power, they avoid blame for a lot of damage to the environment in developing countries.

Obviously, most of the items in this list pertain to developing host countries. Let us now sum up by making an attempt to reach a verdict on FDI and MNCs.

THE VERDICT

It is rather difficult to reach a clear-cut verdict on such a controversial issue. On the one hand, MNCs do not operate in host countries just to help these countries to overcome their economic problems. On the other hand, there is no reason why MNCs operating in host countries with the objective of profit maximization do not produce any positive externalities (self-interest may lead to public good, according to Adam Smith's *Wealth of Nations*). It is, of course, unthinkable that a country should isolate itself from FDI flows just because of the list of arguments against FDI and MNCs that we have just been through. The truth must be somewhere in between the extreme views on this contentious and politically-sensitive issue.

Whether MNCs are good or bad is a normative question that cannot be value-free and objective. One may present views, on either side of the debate, that may be consistent, lack consistency, or be somewhere in between. One may also produce arguments with varying degrees of power of persuasion. However, it may be rather difficult to prove what is right and what is wrong. Empirical evidence may be called upon in this case, but the problem is that this is Economics and not Physics. Empirical evidence in Economics is invariably mixed and often unreliable. The results of empirical testing in economics are typically too fragile and too sensitive to subjective factors to be reasonably reliable.

One can only say at this stage that there is a role for FDI and MNCs to play in the development process. Perhaps the starting point is for MNCs to follow the extensive set of recommendations proposed by the OECD on how they should deal with the host countries. These recommendations provide a highly useful and positive code of conduct. But, it is undoubtedly the case that anti-MNC and anti-globalization protests will continue in the future as long as the activities of MNCs lead to widening the gap between rich and poor, and to massive environmental damage. This topic will most certainly remain as controversial as ever.

Notes

1 Introduction and Overview

1. In general, the source country is considered as the 'home country' (where the investing firm is located), whereas the host country is considered as the 'foreign country' (where the investing firm's foreign establishment is located). Hence, the convention used in this book is to consider matters from the perspective of the investing firm (and hence the investing country). It follows, therefore, that the domestic currency (the base currency of the investing firm) is the currency of the home country, whereas the foreign currency (the base currency of the investing firm's foreign establishment) is the currency of the host country. The word 'local' will be used occasionally to refer to the host country. This may sound confusing, and it *is* confusing, because being 'foreign' and 'domestic' is relative. The convention described here will be used throughout this book.
2. In this book, the word 'subsidiary' is used in general terms to refer to the investing firm's 'foreign establishment' or 'foreign arm'. The difference between subsidiaries and affiliates will be pointed out later in this chapter.
3. This does not mean that portfolio investment does not involve long-term securities. Rather, 'short'-term here pertains to the characteristic of high turnover, meaning that there is a tendency not to keep holding the securities for a long period of time. In other words, there is a lack of long-term commitment on the part of the investor.
4. FDI flows and stocks will be defined later.
5. In particular, two issues are dealt with in the literature and in this book. The first issue is explaining the dramatic expansion of FDI, whereas the second pertains to the effects of FDI on the home and host countries.
6. In this book, the term 'subsidiary' is used as a generic term for the 'foreign establishment' or 'foreign arm' of an MNC.
7. A more recent report puts the number at 690 000 affiliates and 63 000 parent firms.
8. UNCTAD (2000) contains a detailed listing of the largest non-financial MNCs in the world according to total assets in 1998. The ranking ranges between General Electric and Toshiba Corporation.
9. UNCTAD (2000) contains a detailed examination of the effect of mergers and acquisitions on development.
10. In 1999, there were 140 regulatory changes, 131 of which were favourable to FDI. This compares with 145 and 136, respectively, for 1998.
11. This is probably why M&As may appear to be greater than FDI flows.

2   Theories of Foreign Direct Investment

1. Market imperfections are departures from the assumption of perfect competition (that is, large numbers of buyers and sellers, homogeneous products, free access to information, and so on). Market imperfections also take the form of barriers to trade, transaction costs, transportation costs and taxes.

2. The macro factors include such factors as the size of the host economy, interest rates, wages and profitability. The micro factors pertain to the characteristics of firms and industry that confer certain advantages on MNCs compared with other firms. These include product differentiation, technological and advertising effects, the product life cycle and the size of the firm. The strategic factors include various factors that indirectly affect the decision to invest abroad.

3. In this book we deal with mainstream theories of FDI only. The Marxist approach to FDI is dealt with, *inter alia*, in Amin (1974) and in Owen and Sutcliffe (1972). However, the exposition will be based on a wide spectrum of views.

4. Risk neutrality implies that investors do not require a risk premium to be persuaded to take on a foreign investment project. In other words, investors who are risk neutral are indifferent between domestic and foreign projects if they produce the same return. On the other hand, risk aversion implies that investors require a risk premium to choose a foreign project such that the rate of return on the foreign project is higher than the rate of return on the domestic project by an amount that is equal to the risk premium.

5. Risk in this context includes, *inter alia*, foreign exchange risk and country risk.

6. Agarwal (1980) distinguishes between the market size hypothesis and the output hypothesis, depending on whether the market size is measured by sales in the host country or by the country's GDP. He argues that the output hypothesis is applied to the micro level, postulating a positive relationship between the FDI of a firm in a particular host country and its output or sales in that country. The market size hypothesis, he argues, applies to the macro level. In this case FDI is related positively to market size proxied by GDP. It seems the only difference is that between the total market and the market for the investing firm's products (its market share).

7. Hymer's work first appeared in his Ph.D. dissertation in 1960. In 1976 the dissertation was published as a book.

8. Coase considered four main types of cost: (i) the cost of discovering the correct price; (ii) the cost of arranging the contractual obligations of the parties in an exchange transaction; (iii) the risk of scheduling of goods and inputs; and (iv) the taxes paid on exchange transactions.

9. A report in the 20 November 1995 issue of *Business Week* showed that the hourly wage in Mexico was US$2.57, compared with US$15.73 in Canada. Germany came top of the list with US$27.37.

10. In this sense, it is sometimes argued that short-term changes in exchange rates can influence the timing of FDI decisions. Love and Lage-Hidalgo (2000) find evidence in support of this hypothesis.

11. When, in the late 1970s, Ford wanted to build a new engine plant in Europe, it played one country against another (Spain, Belgium and the UK). Eventually, the UK agreed to pay nearly half the capital cost of the project.

3 The Effects of Foreign Direct Investment

1. It is often the case that an investing MNC has sales or total assets that are bigger than the host country's GDP or government budget. Since 'money talks', concerns about national sovereignty are legitimate and justifiable. Winters (1991, p. 230) argues that MNCs frequently pursue covert political objectives in their host countries. For example, ITT resisted President Allende's regime in Chile in the early 1970s. There is also the question of bribery that has prompted the OECD to issue guidelines urging MNCs not to 'offer, promise, give, or demand a bribe or other undue advantage to obtain or retain business or other improper advantage'.
2. Who thought that the Russians and Chinese would develop a taste for Big Macs?
3. However, social and cultural effects may arise even if the investing and source countries are socially and culturally similar. For example, a US MNC investing in the UK may promote baseball, whereas a British MNC investing in the USA may promote cricket. But at the other extreme, consider the cultural effect of having female executives running an MNC investing in Saudi Arabia, a country where men dominate, and where there are restrictions on the activities of women, including driving.
4. The simple macroeconomic identity is $Y = C + I + X - M$, where Y is GDP, C is consumption, I is investment, X represents exports, and M represents imports. Since $S = Y - C$, where S is saving, it follows that $M - X = I - S$. The saving gap is represented by the right-hand side of the identity, $I - S$, whereas the foreign exchange gap is represented by the left-hand side, $M - X$.
5. This sounds like pump priming with a twist. In pump priming proper, initial government expenditure triggers private expenditure.
6. Unlike other financial resources, FDI funds did not dry up during the Asian and Mexican crises of the 1990s.
7. It is true that capital, just like labour, may at a certain stage experience diminishing returns, in which case further capital accumulation will be unable to contribute to growth, and technology becomes the only factor that can propel economic growth. This must be the case in developed countries, but in developing countries, the capital–labour ratio is so low that additional capital units will have increasing returns. This is indeed the basis of the catch-up hypothesis as an explanation for economic convergence.
8. MNCs frequently circumvent economic policy in developing host countries – for example, by frustrating credit squeezes or avoiding exchange restrictions. What is more disturbing is that this could happen even in developed countries. When Ford (UK) broke the British government's pay policy in 1978, the government proved to be quite powerless.

9. The contradiction between this result and the observation that capital has become increasingly mobile is known as the Feldstein–Horioka puzzle. Many attempts have been made to resolve this puzzle (see, for example, Moosa, 1997).

10. There are two extreme views on patents, as explained in a special report on patents in *The Economist* of 23 June 2001, pp. 25–9. One extreme view is that 'patents kill' as claimed by AIDS activists in South Africa, and farmers in north-west Mexico suffering from a patent issued to an American company giving it the exclusive right to market yellow enola beans in the USA. According to this negative view, 'patents are obviously bad for the poor . . . They are largely the preserve of Western multi-national companies, allowing them to establish monopolies, drive out local competition, divert research and development away from the needs of poor countries and force up the price of everything from seeds to software.' The other extreme view is that 'intellectual property protection is good for poor countries,' because 'it encourages domestic industry, boosts foreign investment and improves access to new technologies'. Where does the truth lie?

11. Simultaneous equation models solve the 'black box' problem associated with single-equation, reduced-form models in the sense that they (simultaneous equation models) explain how the variables in the system interact with each other.

4   International Capital Budgeting

1. By discounting, we obtain the present value of a future cash flow. The present value of a cash flow is the amount which, if invested at the discount rate, will produce the future value of the cash flow. Discounting is therefore carried out to take explicit account of the time value of money arising from the fact that funds available today can be invested to grow in value over time.

2. Normally, it is argued that, for the purpose of calculating NPV, the cash flows should be represented by $O_t(1 - \tau)$ rather than X_t; that is, by the after-tax operating cash flows. We shall elaborate on this point in a subsequent chapter.

3. See Makridakis *et al.* (1983) for ARIMA modelling, smoothing, time series decomposition and forecasting with multivariate models. For structural time series modelling, see Harvey (1989).

4. If $\tau < \tau^*$, then the MNC will be allowed to offset taxes that would be paid on other foreign income.

5. Notice that all of these cash flows are expressed in foreign currency terms, because we are only considering the effect of taxes.

5   Country Risk and Political Risk

1. For more details on the theory and empirics of uncovered interest parity, purchasing power parity and the Fisher equation, see Moosa and Bhatti (1997).

2. Sometimes, a third set of indicators is added: the debt or credit indicators that measure the ability of the country to service its debt and to obtain credit. These indicators are, however, more relevant to international lending than to FDI. But this does not mean that these indicators do not provide useful information for evaluating the risk that is relevant to FDI.
3. Indicative of the importance of political risk relative to economic risk for FDI is the fact that the literature (books and articles on FDI) rarely refers to country risk or economic risk. Invariably, the term 'political risk' is used to indicate country risk.
4. This problem can be circumvented by estimating the relationship in a time-varying parametric framework, which allows the estimated parameters to evolve over time.
5. This representation and the scale used to measure risk are not standard. In fact, it is normally the case that a high score implies low risk, and vice versa, as we shall see later.
6. The *Euromoney* figures are taken from *Euromoney*, September 1999, pp. 251–3.
7. Petras and Morley (1975) describe OPIC as falling within the 'US triple alliance' consisting of the US government, MNCs and the military.

6 International Taxation

1. In a survey of taxation in *The Economist* (29 January 2000) the following statement is made to indicate how ancient taxation is: 'prostitution may be the oldest profession, but tax collection was surely not far behind'. It is also stated that the Bible records that Jesus offered his views on a tax matter and converted a prominent taxman. According to the survey, the origin of modern taxation can be traced to wealthy subjects paying money to their king in lieu of military service.
2. Residency is in this case the basis for incurring a tax liability from the perspective of a particular country. But residency is an elusive concept that could mean anything. Consider, for example, the case of Luciano Pavarotti, the famous Italian opera singer versus the Italian government. The Italian government took Pavarotti to court for tax evasion, claiming that he had incurred a tax liability of US$2 million. Pavarotti claimed that in that particular period he did not spend 183 days a year in Italy, which is the period of time required to confirm residency. He also disputed the other criterion that defines residency by denying that his companies that operated in Italy represented his 'vital economic interests'. His lawyer in fact made the interesting remark that it is true that Pavarotti owns houses in Italy, but so does the Queen of the Netherlands, who obviously does not reside in Italy.
3. William Woods, the chief executive of the Bermuda Stock Exchange, has been quoted as saying that Bill Gates would have been wealthier if he had started Microsoft in Bermuda, and that he [Gates] may have known a lot about computer programming when he started the company [Microsoft], but his ignorance about tax cost him a fortune. It seems, however, that Gates has learned the trick, as he co-founded Teledesic in Bermuda. This is a company that offers broad-band Internet access by satellite (see *The Economist*, 'Survey', 29 January 2000, p. 11).

4. A cartoon once appeared in *The New Yorker* magazine showing two dogs sitting in front of a computer screen, with one telling the other: 'On the Internet nobody knows you are a dog.'
5. For example, an American company, Oakington, is developing a digital cash system called e-Bits, which is not wholly anonymous.
6. One can glean a conclusion to that effect just by reading the title of a report published by Ernst & Young. The title reads 'The sky is not falling: why state and local revenues were not significantly impacted by the Internet in 1998' (see Cline and Neubig, 1999).
7. One reason is that digital goods are a tiny fraction of online purchases and will continue to be small for many years.

7 The International Cost of Capital and the Capital Structure

1. Just to mention a few, other means of obtaining external funds include note issuance facilities, Euro-commercial papers, Eurocredit, parallel loans, credit swaps, government lending, and lending by international development institutions.
2. Parallel loans (also called back-to-back loans) involve two parties lending each other funds of equal amounts, maturing on the same date and denominated in different currencies. The exchange of the principals is based on the spot exchange rate, whereas the interest payments and principal repayments are based on the forward rate. Currency swaps have evolved out of parallel loans. They differ in that the settlement of all payments is carried out on the basis of the exchange rate agreed upon when the contract is initiated (the contract rate).
3. Remember that $Cov(\dot{X}_t^*, \dot{S}_t) = \sigma(\dot{X}_t)\sigma(\dot{S}_t)\rho(\dot{X}_t\dot{S}_t)$.
4. New issues of shares (and bonds) may be sold to investors either by a public offering or a private placement. In the case of a public offering, the issue is advertised and sold to investors via the banks and other financial institutions underwriting the issues. When there is a private placement, the whole issue is sold to one or a few investors, typically institutional investors such as pension funds and insurance companies.
5. The available evidence suggests that markets are neither fully integrated nor completely segmented. Cooper and Kaplanis (2000) explain how to calculate the cost of capital in partially integrated markets.
6. Notice that if $\dot{S}^e(x/y) > 0$, then currency y is expected to appreciate, and vice versa.
7. One of the explanations for the empirical failure of uncovered interest parity is the presence of a risk premium, which implies that agents are not risk neutral.
8. The Fisher equation, named after Irving Fisher, relates the nominal interest rate to expected inflation. It states that the level of the nominal interest rate is determined by two components: the real interest rate, and expected inflation. Since the real interest rate, which is the rate of return on real capital, is assumed to be stable over time, the nominal interest rate changes directly and proportionately with the expected inflation rate.

8 Transfer Pricing

1. Tax avoidance is carried out within the confines of the law, but tax evasion is carried out by illegal means.
2. According to the OECD, around 60 per cent of international trade involves transactions between related parts of MNCs.
3. Market penetration refers to a supplier entering the market with particularly low prices, with the intention of obtaining a large market share as quickly as possible. This is the kind of policy whereby Japanese electronics manufacturers were able to conquer European and American markets. Market skimming, on the other hand, aims at creaming off the early users' willingness to pay, followed by a lowering of prices to open up the market.
4. Notice that the line representing the exchange rate in Figure 8.2 has a slope that is equal to $(1 + \lambda)/S$.
5. Foreign exchange risk is due to fluctuations in exchange rates. Purchasing power risk results from changes in the purchasing power of funds due to inflation. And political risk, as we saw in Chapter 5, results from political factors pertaining to the host country.
6. In Figure 8.4(a) the slope of the $C = XSP^*$ line is XS, in which case the rise in the exchange rate makes the line steeper. In Figure 8.4(b) the slope of the line is XP^*, in which case the reduction in P^* makes the line less steep. This is why the $C = XSP^*$ shifts to the left in Figure 8.4(a) and to the right in Figure 8.4(b).

9 Control and Performance Evaluation in MNCs

1. For a general treatment of fundamental models of exchange rate determination, see Moosa (2000a). For an evaluation of the view that exchange rates are not affected by fundamental macroeconomic factors, see Moosa (2000b). See also Moosa and Shamsuddin (2001) for an explanation of exchange rate volatility in terms of the heterogeneity of traders.
2. Unexpected changes in exchange rates are sometimes taken to be deviations from uncovered interest parity.
3. See Moosa (2000a) for a comprehensive analysis of the role of exchange rate forecasting in financial decision-making.
4. Under inflationary conditions, different results will be obtained by using the FIFO than the LIFO method of inventory accounting. In FIFO accounting inventory acquired first is used first, while in LIFO accounting, inventory that is acquired last is used first. Under inflation, inventory that is acquired last is more expensive, which would affect net income.

References

Abdallah, W. and Keller, D. E. (1985) 'Measuring the Multinational Performance', *Management Accounting*, vol. 67: 26–31.

Agarwal, J. P. (1980) 'Determinants of Foreign Direct Investment: A Survey',
Weltwirtschaftliches Archiv, vol. 116: 739–73.

Agarwal, S. and Ramaswami, S. N. (1992) 'Choice of Foreign Market Entry
Mode: Impact of Ownership, Location and Internalisation Factors', *Journal
of International Business Studies*, vol. 23: 1–27.

Agmon, T. (1985) *Political Economy and Risk in World Financial Markets*
(Lexington, Mass.: Lexington Books).

Agmon, T. and Lessard, D. R. (1977) 'Investor Recognition of Corporate
International Diversification', *Journal of Finance*, vol. 32: 1049–55.

Aharoni, Y. (1966) *The Foreign Investment Decision Process* (Cambridge,
Mass.: Harvard Graduate School of Business).

Aitken, B. J. and Harrison, A. E. (1999) 'Do Domestic Firms Benefit from
Direct Foreign Investment? Evidence from Venezuela', *American Economic Review*, vol. 89: 605–18.

Aizenman, J. (1992) 'Foreign Direct Investment as a Commitment Mechanism in the Presence of Managed Trade', NBER Working Paper
No. 4102.

Al-Eryani, M. F., Alam, P. and Akhter, S. H. (1990) 'Transfer Pricing Determinants of US Multinationals', *Journal of International Business Studies*,
vol. 21: 409–25.

Aliber, R. Z. (1970) 'A Theory of Direct Foreign Investment', in C. P.
Kindleberger (ed.), *The International Corporation: A Symposium* (Cambridge, Mass.: MIT Press).

Aliber, R. Z. (1971) 'The Multinational Enterprise in a Multiple Currency
World', in J. H. Dunning (ed.), *The Multinational Enterprise* (London: Allen
& Unwin).

Altshuler, R., Grubert, H. and Newlon, T. S. (1998) 'Has US Investment Abroad
Become More Sensitive to Tax Rates?', NBER Working Paper No. 6383.

Amin, S. (1974) *Accumulation on a World Scale* (New York: Monthly Review
Press).

Amiti, M., Greenaway, D. and Wakelin, K. (2000) 'Foreign Direct Investment
and Trade: Substitutes or Compliments?', Unpublished paper, University of
Melbourne.

Appleyard, A. R., Strong, N. C. and Walston, P. J. (1990) 'Budgetary Control
of Foreign Subsidiaries', *Management Accounting*, vol. 68: 44–5.

Arpan, J. S. (1972) *Intracorporate Pricing: Non-American Systems and Views*
(New York: Praeger).

Asafu-Adjaye, J. (2000) 'The Effects of Foreign Direct Investment on Indonesian Economic Growth, 1960–1996', *Economic Analysis and Policy*,
vol. 30: 49–62.

Asquith, P. and Mullins, D. W. (1986) 'Equity Issues and Offering Dilution', *Journal of Financial Economics*, vol. 15: 31–60.

Avi-Yonah, R. (1999) 'Globalisation, Tax Competition and the Fiscal Crisis of the Welfare State', Harvard Law School Working Paper, July.

Bailes, J. C. and Assada, T. (1991) 'Empirical Differences between Japanese and American Budget and Performance Evaluation Systems', *International Journal of Accounting*, vol. 26: 131–42.

Bajo-Rubio, O. and Sosvilla-Rivero, S. (1994) 'An Econometric Analysis of Foreign Direct Investment in Spain, 1964–89', *Southern Economic Journal*, vol. 61: 104–20.

Balassa, B. (1966) 'American Direct Investment in the Common Market', *Banco Nazionale del Lavoro Quarterly Review*: 121–46.

Baldwin, R. E. (1995) 'The Effect of Trade and Foreign Direct Investment on Employment and Relative Wages', NBER Working Paper No. 5037.

Bandera, V. N. and White, J. T. (1968) 'U.S. Direct Investments and Domestic Markets in Europe', *Economia Internazionale*, vol. 21: 117–33.

Baranson, J. (1966) 'Transfers of Technical Knowledge by International Corporations to Developing Economies', *American Economic Review*, vol. 56: 256–67.

Baranson, J. (1970) 'Technology Transfer Through the International Firm' *American Economic Review*, vol. 60: 435–40.

Barlow, E. R. and Wender, I. T. (1955) *Foreign Investment and Taxation* (Englewood Cliffs, NJ: Prentice-Hall).

Barratt-Brown, M. (1974) *The Economics of Imperialism* (Harmondsworth: Penguin).

Barrell, R. and Holland, D. (2000) 'Foreign Direct Investment and Enterprise Restructuring in Central Europe', *Economics of Transition*, vol. 8: 477–504.

Barrell, R. and Pain, N. (1996) 'An Econometric Analysis of U.S. Foreign Direct Investment', *Review of Economics and Statistics*, vol. 78: 200–7.

Barrell, R. and Pain, N. (1999) 'Trade Restraints and Japanese Direct Investment Flows', *European Economic Review*, vol. 43: 29–45.

Bartik, T. J. (1985) 'Business Location Decisions in the United States: Estimates of the Effects of Unionization, Taxes and Other Characteristics of States', *Journal of Business and Economic Statistics*, vol. 3: 14–22.

Bartlett, C. A. and Goshal, S. (1989) *Managing Across Borders* (Boston Mass.: Harvard Business School Press).

Basi, R. S. (1963) *Determinants of United States Private Investment in Foreign Countries*. (Kent: Kent University Press).

Baskin, J. and Miranti, P. A. (1997) *History of Corporate Finance* (Cambridge University Press).

Baumann, H. G. (1975) 'Merger Theory, Property Rights and the Pattern of US Investment in Canada', *Weltwirtschaftliches Archiv*, vol. 111: 676–98.

Baumgarten, S. A. and Hausman, A. (2000) 'An Analysis of the Correlates of US Foreign Direct Investment in Latin America', *Journal of Transnational Management Development*, vol. 5: 57–82.

Belderbos, R. and Sleuwaegen, L. (1998) 'Tariff Jumping DFI and Export Substitution: Japanese Electronic Firms in Europe', *International Journal of Industrial Organization*, vol. 16: 601–38.

Benacek, V. (2000) 'Prime Zahranicni Investice v Ceske Ekonomice', *Politicka Ekonomie*, vol. 48: 7–24.

284 *References*

Bergsten, C. F., Horst, T. and Moran, T. H. (1978) *American Multinationals and American Interests* (Washington, DC: The Brookings Institution).

Berman, E., Bound, J. and Griliches, Z. (1994) 'Changes in the Demand for Skilled Labour within U.S. Manufacturing: Evidence from the Annual Survey of Manufacturers', *Quarterly Journal of Economics*, vol. 109: 367–98.

Berthelemy, J. C. and Demurger, S. (2000) 'Foreign Direct Investment and Economic Growth: Theory and Application to China', *Review of Development Economics*, vol. 4: 140–55.

Bhagwati, J. N. (1967) 'Fiscal Policies, the Faking of Foreign Trade Declarations, and the Balance of Payments', *Bulletin of the Oxford University Institute of Economics and Statistics*, vol. 29: 61–7.

Blomstrom, M. and Kokko, A. (1994) 'Home Country Effects of Foreign Direct Investment: Sweden', in S. Globerman (ed.), *Canadian Based Multinationals*, The Industry Canada Research Series, Vol. 4 (Calgary, Atlanta: University of Calgary Press).

Blomstrom, M. and Persson, H. (1983) 'Foreign Investment and Spillover Efficiency in an Underdeveloped Economy: Evidence from the Mexican Manufacturing Industry', *World Development*, vol. 11: 493–501.

Blomstrom, M., Fors, G. and Lipsey, R. (1997) 'Foreign Direct Investment and Employment: Home Country Experience in the United States and Sweden', NBER Working Paper No. 6205.

Blomstrom, M., Lipsey, R. E. and Kulchycky, K. (1988) 'U.S. and Swedish Direct Investments and Exports', in R. E. Baldwin (ed.), *Trade Policy Issues and Empirical Analysis* (Chicago: University of Chicago Press).

Blonigen, B. A. (1999) 'In Search of Substitution Between Foreign Production and Exports', NBER Working Paper No. 7154.

Blonigen, B. A. and Feenstra, R. C. (1996) 'Protectionist Threats and Foreign Direct Investment', NBER Working Paper No. 5475.

Bodinat, H. (1974) 'Multinational Decentralisation', *European Business*, Summer: 64–70.

Bond, E. and Guisinger, S. (1985) 'Investment Incentives as Tariff Substitutes: A Comprehensive Measure of Protection', *Review of Economics and Statistics*, vol. 67: 91–7.

Bonelli, R. (1999) 'A Note on Foreign Direct Investment and Industrial Competitiveness in Brazil', *Oxford Development Studies*, vol. 27: 305–27.

Booth, L. D. (1982) 'Capital Budgeting Frameworks for the Multinational Corporation', *Journal of International Business Studies*, vol. 13: 113–23.

Borensztein, E., De Gregorio, J. and Lee, J. W. (1995) 'How Does Foreign Direct Investment Affect Economic Growth?', NBER Working Paper No. 5057.

Borjas, G. H. and Ramey, V. A. (1993) 'Foreign Competition, Market Power, and Wage Inequality: Theory and Evidence', NBER Working Paper No. 4556.

Borkowski, S. C. (1993) 'International Versus Domestic Managerial Performance Evaluation: Some Evidence', *International Journal of Accounting*, vol. 28: 129–39.

Borkowski, S. C. (1999) 'International Managerial Performance Evaluation: A Five Country Comparison', *Journal of International Business Studies*, vol. 30: 533–55.

Boskin, M. and Gale, W. G. (1987) 'New Results on the Effects of Tax Policy on the International Location of Investment', in M. Feldstein (ed.), *The Effects of Taxation on Capital Accumulation* (Chicago: University of Chicago Press): 201–19.

Bosworth, B. P. and Collins, S. M. (1999) 'Capital Flows to Developing Economies: Implications for Saving and Investment', *Brookings Papers on Economic Activity*, vol. 1: 143–69.

Brainard, S. L. and Riker, D. A. (1997) 'Are U.S. Multinationals Exporting U.S. Jobs?', NBER Working Paper No. 5958.

Brash, D. T. (1966) *American Investment in Australian Industry* (Canberra: Australian National University Press).

Braunerhjelm, P. and Oxelheim, L. (2000) 'Does Foreign Direct Investment Replace Home Country Investment? The Effect of European Integration on the Location of Swedish Investment', *Journal of Common Market Studies*, vol. 38: 199–221.

Brealey, R. A. and Myers, S. C. (1996) *Principles of Corporate Finance*, 5th edn (New York: McGraw Hill).

Brewer, T. L. (1983) 'The Instability of Governments and the Instability of Controls on Funds Transfers by Multinational Corporations', *Journal of International Business Studies*, vol. 14: 147–57.

Brewer, T. L. (1993) 'Foreign Direct Investment in Emerging Market Countries', in L. Oxelheim (ed.), *Global Race for Foreign Direct Investment: Prospects for the Future* (London and Tokyo: Springer).

Brickley, J. A., Smith, C. W. and Zimmerman, J. L. (1997) 'Transfer Pricing and the Control of Internal Corporate Transactions', *Journal of Applied Corporate Finance*, vol. 8: 60–7.

Buckley, A. (1996) *Multinational Finance*, 3rd edn (London: Phillip Allan).

Buckley, P. J. (1988) 'The Limits of Explanation: Testing the Internalization Theory of the Multinational Enterprise', *Journal of International Business Studies*, vol. 19: 181–93.

Buckley, P. J. (1990) 'Macroeconomic Versus International Business Approach to Direct Foreign Investment: A Comment on Professor Kojima's Interpretation', in P. J. Buckley (ed.), *International Investment* (Aldershot: Edward Elgar).

Buckley, P. J. and Casson, M. (1976) *The Future of the Multinational Enterprise* (London: Macmillan).

Buckley, P. J. and Casson, M. (1981) 'The Optimal Timing of a Foreign Direct Investment', *Economic Journal*, vol. 91: 75–87.

Buckley, P. J. and Casson, M. (1988) 'A Theory of Cooperation in International Business', in F. J. Contractor and P. Lorange (eds), *Cooperative Strategies in International Business* (Lexington, Mass.: Lexington Books).

Buckley, P. J. and Casson, M. (1996) 'An Economic Model of International Joint Ventures', *Journal of International Business Studies*, vol. 27: 849–76.

Buckley, P. J. and Casson, M. (2000a) 'Foreign Market Entry: A Formal Extension of Internalization Theory', in M. Casson (ed.), *Economics of International Business* (Cheltenham: Edward Elgar).

Buckley, P. J. and Casson, M. (2000b) 'International Joint Ventures', in M. Casson (ed.), *Economics of International Business* (Cheltenham: Edward Elgar).

Burgmann, T. (1996) 'An Empirical Examination of the Multinational Capital Structure', *Journal of International Business Studies*, vol. 27: 553–70.

Burns, J. O. (1980) 'Transfer Pricing Decisions in US Multinational Corporations', *Journal of International Business Studies*, vol. 11: 23–39.

Burns, J. O. and Ross, R. (1981) 'Establishing International Transfer Pricing Standards for Tax Audits of Multinational Enterprises', *International Journal of Accounting Education and Research*, vol. 17: 161–79.

Bursk, E. C. (1971) *Financial Control of Multinational Operations* (New York: Financial Executives Research Foundation).

Bushman, R., Indjejikian, R. and Smith, A. (1995) 'Aggregate Performance Measures in Business Unit Manager Compensation: The Role of Intrafirm Interdependencies', *Journal of Accounting Research*, vol. 33 (Supplement): 101–28.

Business International Money Report (1979) *Evaluating Overseas Performance I: What are the Problems and How do MNCs Deal with Them?*, 16 November: 385–7.

Cantwell, J. and Bellak, C. (1998) 'How Important is Foreign Direct Investment?', *Oxford Bulletin of Economics and Statistics*, vol. 60: 99–106.

Carlton, D. W. (1983) 'The Location and Employment Choices of New Firms: An Econometric Model with Discrete and Continuous Endogenous Variables', *Review of Economics and Statistics*, vol. 65: 440–9.

Casson, M. (1990) 'The Theory of Foreign Direct Investment', in P. J. Buckley (ed.), *International Investment* (Aldershot: Edward Elgar).

Castilho, M. and Zignago, S. (2000) 'Commerce et IDE dans un Cadre de Regionalisation: Le Cas du Mercosur', *Revue Economique*, vol. 51: 761–74.

Caves, R. E. (1971) 'International Corporations: The Industrial Economics of Foreign Investment', *Economica*, vol. 38: 1–27.

Caves, R. E. (1974a) 'Causes of Direct Investment: Foreign Firms' Shares in Canadian and United States Manufacturing Industries', *Review of Economics and Statistics*, vol. 56: 279–93.

Caves, R. E. (1974b) 'Multinational Firms, Competition and Productivity in Host Country Markets', *Economica*, vol. 41: 176–93.

Caves, R. E. (1982) *Multinational Enterprise and Economic Analysis* (Cambridge University Press).

Caves, R. E. (1988) 'Exchange Rate Movements and Foreign Direct Investment in the United States', Harvard Institute of Economic Research, Discussion Paper Series, No. 1383, May.

Chen, J. R. and Yang, C. H. (1999) 'Determinants of Foreign Direct Investment: Comparison between Expansionary FDI and Defensive FDI', *Taiwan Economic Review*, vol. 27: 215–40.

Chen, T. J. and Ku, Y. H. (2000) 'The Effect of Foreign Direct Investment on Firm Growth: The Case of Taiwan's Manufacturers', *Japan and the World Economy*, vol. 12: 153–72.

Chen, T. Y. (2000) 'Foreign Direct Investment and Intra-Industry Trade: The Case of the United States', *Pacific Economic Papers*, no. 303, May.

Chenery, H. B. (1952) 'Overcapacity and the Acceleration Principle', *Econometrica*, vol. 20: 1–28.

Cheng, L. K. and Kwan, Y. K. (2000) 'What Are the Determinants of the Location of Foreign Direct Investment? The Chinese Experience', *Journal of International Economics*, vol. 51: 379–400.

Choi, F. D. S. and Czechowicz, I. J. (1983) 'Assessing Foreign Performance: A Multinational Comparison', *Management International Review*, vol. 4: 14–25.

Chuang, Y. C. and Lin, C. M. (1999) 'Foreign Direct Investment, R&D and Spillover Efficiency: Evidence from Taiwan's Manufacturing Firms', *Journal of Development Studies*, vol. 35: 117–37.

Clark, E. (1997) 'Valuing Political Risk', *Journal of International Money and Finance*, vol. 16: 477–90.

Cleeve, E. (2000) 'Why Do Japanese Firms Locate in Particular British Regions?', *Asia Pacific Journal of Economics and Business*, vol. 4: 112–24.

Clegg, J. and Scott-Green, S. (1999) 'The Determinants of New FDI Capital Flows into the EC: A Statistical Comparison of the USA and Japan', *Journal of Common Market Studies*, vol. 37: 597–616.

Cline, W. and Neubig, T. (1999) 'The Sky is Not Falling: Why State and Local Revenues Were Not Significantly Impacted by the Internet in 1998', Ernst and Young Economics Consulting and Quantitative Analysis, June.

Co, C. Y. (2000) 'R&D, Foreign Direct Investment and Technology Sourcing?', *Review of International Organization*, vol. 16: 385–97.

Coase, R. H. (1937) 'The Nature of the Firm', *Economica*, vol. 4: 386–405.

Cooper, I. A. and Kaplanis, E. (2000) 'Partially Segmented International Capital Markets and International Capital Budgeting', *Journal of International Money and Finance*, vol. 19: 309–29.

Culem, C. G. (1988) 'The Locational Determinants of Direct Investments Among Industrialised Countries', *European Economic Review*, vol. 32: 885–904.

Cummins, J. G. and Hubbard, R. G. (1995) 'The Tax Sensitivity of Foreign Direct Investment: Evidence from Firm-Level Panel Data', in M. Feldstein, J. Hines and R. G. Hubbard (eds), *The Effect of Taxation on Multinational Corporations* (Chicago: University of Chicago Press).

Cushman, D. (1987) 'The Effects of Real Wages and Labour Productivity on Foreign Direct Investment', *Southern Economic Journal*, vol. 54: 174–85.

Cyert, R. M. and March, J. G. (1963) *A Behavioral Theory of the Firm* (Englewood Cliffs, NJ: Prentice-Hall).

Czechowicz, I. J., Choi, F. D. S and Bavishi, V. (1982) *Assessing Foreign Subsidiary Performance Systems and Practices of Leading Multinational Companies* (New York: Business International Corporation).

Daniels, J. D., Ogram, E. W. and Radebaugh, L. H. (1979) *International Business: Environment and Operations*, 2nd edn (Reading, Mass.: Addison-Wesley).

Das, S. P. (1999) 'Direct Foreign Investment Versus Licensing', *Review of Development Economics*, vol. 3: 86–97.

Davis, S. J. and Haltiwanger, J. (1991) 'Wage Dispersion between and within U.S. Manufacturing Plants, 1963–86', *Brookings Papers on Economic Activity, Microeconomics*: 115–80.

De Andrade-Castro, E. and Teixeira, J. R. (1999) 'Investimento Direto Estrangeiro, Transferencia Tecnologica e Extensoses do Modelo Norte-Sul de Wang', *Revista Brasileira de Economia*, vol. 53: 167–81.

De Mello, L. R. (1999) 'Foreign Direct Investment-led Growth: Evidence from Time Series and Panel Data', *Oxford Economic Papers*, vol. 51: 133–51.

Demirag, I. S. (1987) 'How U.K. Companies Measure Overseas Performance', *Accountancy*, vol. 99: 101–3.

Demirag, I. S. (1988) 'Assessing Foreign Subsidiary Performance: The Currency Choice of UK MNCs', *Journal of International Business Studies*, vol. 19: 257–75.

Demirag, I. S. (1992) 'The State of the Art in Assessing Foreign Currency Operations', *Managerial Finance*, vol. 18: 24–40.

Dickescheid, T. (1999) 'Tax Competition with Multinational Firms', *Finanz-Archiv*, vol. 56: 500–17.

Djankov, S. and Hoekman, B. M. (2000) 'Foreign Investment and Productivity Growth in Czech Enterprises', *World Bank Economic Review*, vol. 14: 49–64.

Donaldson, G. (1961) 'Corporate Debt Capacity: A Study of Corporate Debt Policy and the Determination of Corporate Debt Capacity', Harvard Business School, Division of Research, Harvard University.

Donnenfeld, S. and Weber, S. (2000) 'Exporting Versus Foreign Direct Investment', *Journal of Economic Integration*, vol. 15: 100–26.

Dorrenbacher, C. (2000) 'Measuring Corporate Internationalisation: A Review of Measurement Concepts and Their Use', *Intereconomics*, May/June: 119–26.

Doukas, J. and Travlos, N. G. (1988) 'The Effect of Corporate Multinationalism on Shareholders' Wealth: Evidence from International Acquisitions', *Journal of Finance*, vol. 43: 1161–75.

Driffield, N. (1999) 'Indirect Employment Effects of Foreign Direct Investment into the UK', *Bulletin of Economic Research*, vol. 51: 207–21.

Driffield, N. and Taylor, K. (2000) 'FDI and the Labour Market: A Review of the Evidence and Policy Implications', *Oxford Review of Economic Policy*, vol. 16: 90–103.

Dumas, B. (1993) 'Partial vs. General Equilibrium Models of the International Capital Markets', NBER Working Paper No. 4446.

Dunning, J. H. (1961) 'The Present Role of US Investment in British Industry', *Moorgate and Wall Street*, Spring.

Dunning, J. H. (1969) 'The Role of American Investment in the British Economy', *PEP Broadsheet*: 507.

Dunning, J. H. (1973) 'The Determinants of International Production', *Oxford Economic Papers*, vol. 25: 289–336.

Dunning, J. H. (1977) 'Trade, Location of Economic Activity and the MNE: A Search for an Eclectic Approach', in B. Ohlin, P. O. Hesselborn, and P. M. Wijkman (eds), *The International Allocation of Economic Activity* (London: Macmillan).

Dunning, J. H. (1979) 'Explaining Changing Patterns of International Production: In Defence of the Eclectic Theory', *Oxford Bulletin of Economics and Statistics*, vol. 41: 269–95.

Dunning, J. H. (1988) 'The Eclectic Paradigm of International Production: A Restatement and Some Possible Extensions', *Journal of International Business Studies*, vol. 19: 1–31.

Dunning, J. H. and Dilyard, J. R. (1999) 'Towards a General Paradigm of Foreign Direct and Foreign Portfolio Investment', *Transnational Corporations*, vol. 8: 1–52.

Eaton, J. and Tamura, A. (1996) 'Japanese and U.S. Exports and Investment as Conduits of Growth', NBER Working Paper No. 5457.

Egelhoff, W. G. (1988) *Organizing the Multinational Enterprise: An Information Processing Perspective* (Cambridge, Mass.: Ballinger).

Eichengreen, B. (2000) 'Taming Capital Flows', *World Development*, vol. 28: 1105–16.

Eiteman, D. K. and Stonehill, A. I. (1989) *Multinational Business Finance,* 5th edn (Reading, Mass.: Addison-Wesley).

Elahee, M. N. and Pagan, J. A. (1999) 'Foreign Direct Investment and Economic Growth in East Asia and Latin America', *Journal of Emerging Markets*, vol. 4: 59–67.

Ellingsen, T. and Warneryd, K. (1999) 'Foreign Direct Investment and the Political Economy of Protection', *International Economic Review*, vol. 40: 357–79.

Eng, M. V., Lee, F. A. and Mauer, L. J. (1995) *Global Finance* (New York: HarperCollins).

Erickson, E. (1996) 'Software Royalty Income from Licensing Software: Is it Rental or Sales Income?', *Hightech*, August.

Errunza, V. R. and Senbet, L. W. (1981) 'The Effects of International Operations on the Market Value of the Firm: Theory and Evidence', *Journal of Finance*, vol. 36: 401–17.

Eun, C. S. and Resnick, B. G. (1998) *International Financial Management* (New York: McGraw Hill).

Fan, X. and Dickie, P. M. (2000) 'The Contribution of Foreign Direct Investment to Growth and Stability: A Post-Crisis ASEAN-65 Review', *ASEAN Economic Bulletin*, vol. 17: 312–23.

Feenstra, R. C. and Hanson, G. H. (1995) 'Foreign Direct Investment and Relative Wages: Evidence from Mexico's Maquiladoras', NBER Working Paper No. 5122.

Feldstein, M. (1994) 'Taxes, Leverage and the National Return on Outbound Foreign Direct Investment', NBER Working Paper No. 4689.

Feldstein, M. and Horioka, C. (1980) 'Domestic Saving and International Capital Flows', *Economic Journal*, vol. 90: 314–29.

Figlio, D. N. and Blonigen, B. A. (2000) 'The Effects of Foreign Direct Investment on Local Communities', *Journal of Urban Economics*, vol. 48: 338–63.

Findlay, R. (1978) 'Relative Backwardness, Direct Foreign Investment, and the Transfer of Technology: A Simple Dynamic Model', *Quarterly Journal of Economics*, vol. 92: 1–16.

Fischer, E. O., Heinkel, R. and Zechner, J. (1989) 'Dynamic Capital Structure Choice: Theory and Test', *Journal of Finance*, vol. 44: 19–40.

Flowers, E. B. (1975) 'Oligopolsitic Reaction in European Direct Investment in the United States', Ph.D. dissertation, Georgia State University.

Forsyth, D. J. C. (1972) *Investment in Scotland*, Praeger Special Studies in International Economics and Development (New York: Praeger).

Fosfuri, A. and Motta, M. (1999) 'Multinationals without Advantages', *Scandinavian Journal of Economics*, vol. 101: 617–30.

Frank, I. (1980) *Foreign Enterprise in Developing Countries* (Baltimore, Md: Johns Hopkins University Press.

Froot, K. and Stein, J. C. (1991) 'Exchange Rates and Foreign Direct Investment: An Imperfect Capital Markets Approach', *Quarterly Journal of Economics*, vol. 106: 1191–217.

Froot, K. A. and Krugman, P. R. (1989) *Foreign Direct Investment in the United States* (Washington DC: Institute for International Economics).

Fung, M. K., Zeng, J. and Zhu, L. (1999) 'Foreign Capital, Urban Unemployment and Economic Growth', *Review of International Economics*, vol. 7: 651–64.

Glass, A. J. and Saggi, K. (1999a) 'FDI Policies under Shared Factor Markets', *Journal of International Economics*, vol. 49: 309–32.

Glass, A. J. and Saggi, K. (1999b) 'Foreign Direct Investment and the Nature of R&D', *Canadian Journal of Economics*, vol. 32: 92–117.

Glickman, N. and Woodward, D. P. (1989) *The New Competitor: How Foreign Investors are Changing the U.S. Economy* (New York: Basic Books).

Globerman, S. (1979) 'Foreign Direct Investment and Spillover Efficiency Benefits in Canadian Manufacturing Industries', *Canadian Journal of Economics*, vol. 12: 42–56.

Globerman, S. and Shapiro, D. M. (1999) 'The Impact of Government Policies on Foreign Direct Investment: The Canadian Experience', *Journal of International Business Studies*, vol. 30: 513–32.

Godley, A. C. (1999) 'Pioneering Foreign Direct Investment in British Manufacturing', *Business History Review*, vol. 73: 394–429.

Goldberg, L. S. and Klein, M. W. (1997) 'Foreign Direct Investment, Trade and Real Exchange Rate Linkages in Southeast Asia and Latin America', NBER Working Paper No. 6344.

Goldberg, M. A. (1972) 'The Determinants of US Direct Investment in the EEC: Comment', *American Economic Review*, vol. 62: 692–9.

Goold, M. (1991) 'Strategic Control in the Decentralised Firm', *Sloan Management Review*, vol. 32: 71–81.

Goold, N. C. and Campbell, A. (1987) *Strategies and Styles: The Role of the Centre in Managing Diversified Corporations* (Oxford: Basil Blackwell).

Goolsbee, A. (2000) 'The Value of Broadband and the Deadweight Loss of Taxing New Technologies', Mimeo, University of Chicago, Graduate School of Business.

Goolsbee, A. (2001) 'The Implications of Electronic Commerce for Fiscal Policy (and Vice Versa)', *Journal of Economic Perspectives*, vol. 15: 13–24.

Gopinath, M., Pick, D. and Vasavada, U. (1999) 'The Economics of Foreign Direct Investment and Trade with an Application to the U.S. Food Processing Industry', *American Journal of Agricultural Economics*, vol. 81: 442–52.

Graham, E. M. and Krugman, P. R. (1991) *Foreign Direct Investment in the United States* (Washington DC: Institute for International Economics).

Graham, R. (1999) 'Should the Internet be Taxed? Communities Hurt if the Web Isn't Taxed', *Roll Call*, 22 February.

Gray, H. P. (2000) 'Globalization and Economic Development', *Global Economy Quarterly*, vol. 1: 71–96.

Green, R. (1972) *Political Instability as a Determinant of US Foreign Investment* (Austin, Tx: University of Texas).

Grubaugh, S. G. (1987) 'Determinants of Direct Foreign Investment', *Review of Economics and Statistics*: 149–52.

Gruber, W., Mehta, D. and Vernon, R. (1967) 'The R&D Factor in International Trade and International Investment of United States Industries', *Journal of Political Economy*, vol. 75: 20–37.

Guimaraes, P., Figueiredo, O. and Woodward, D. (2000) 'Agglomeration and the Location of Foreign Direct Investment in Portugal', *Journal of Urban Economics*, vol. 47: 115–35.

Gul, F. A. and Chia, Y. M. (1994) 'The Effect of Management Accounting Systems, Perceived Environmental Uncertainty and Decentralization of Managerial Performance: A Test of Three-Way Interaction', *Accounting, Organizations and Society*, vol. 19: 413–26.

Gupta, A. K. and Govindarajan, V. (1991) 'Knowledge Flows and the Structure of Control within the Multinational Corporations', *Academy of Management Review*, vol. 16: 768–93.

Gyapong, A. O. and Karikari, J. A. (1999) 'Direct Foreign Investment and Economic Performance in Ghana and Ivory Coast', *Journal of Economic Development*, vol. 24: 133–46.

Haaparanta, P. (1996) 'Competition for Foreign Direct Investment', *Journal of Public Economics*, vol. 63: 141–53.

Haddad, M. and Harrison, A. (1993) 'Are There Positive Spillovers from Direct Foreign Investment?', *Journal of Development Economics*, vol. 42: 51–74.

Haendel, D. (1979) 'Foreign Investment and the Management of Political Risk', Westview Special Studies in International Economics and Business (Boulder, Colorado: Westview Press).

Halpern, R. and Srinidhi, B. (1991) 'US Income Tax Transfer Pricing Rules and Resource Allocation: The Case of Decentralised Multinational Enterprises', *Accounting Review*, vol. 66: 141–57.

Harris, R. and Ravenscraft, D. (1991) 'The Role of Acquisitions in Foreign Direct Investment: Evidence from the U.S. Stock Market', *Journal of Finance*, vol. 46: 825–44.

Hartman, D. G. (1981) 'Domestic Tax Policy and Foreign Investment: Some Evidence', NBER Working Paper No. 784.

Hartman, D. G. (1984) 'Tax Policy and Foreign Direct Investment in the United States', *National Tax Journal*, vol. 37: 475–88.

Hartman, D. G. (1985) 'Tax Policy and Foreign Direct Investment', *Journal of Public Economics*, vol. 26: 107–21.

Harvey, A. C. (1989) *Forecasting, Structural Time Series Models and the Kalman Filter* (Cambridge University Press).

Hassel, L. G. (1991) 'Headquarter Reliance on Accounting Performance Measures in a Multinational Context', *Journal of International Financial Management and Accounting*, vol. 13: 17–38.

Hassel, L. G. and Cunningham, G. M. (1993) 'Budget Effectiveness in Multinational Companies: An Empirical Examination of Environmental Interaction on Cognitive and Affective Effects of Two Dimensions of Budgetary Participation', *Scandinavian Journal of Management*, vol. 9: 297–316.

Hassel, L. G. and Cunningham, G. M. (1996) 'Budget Effectiveness in Multinational Corporations: An Empirical Test of the Use of Budget Controls Moderated by Two Dimensions of Budgetary Participation under High and Low Environmental Dynamism', *Management International Review*, vol. 36: 245–66.

Hatzius, J. (2000) 'Foreign Direct Investment and Factor Demand Elasticities', *European Economic Review*, vol. 44: 117–43.

Haufler, A. and Wooton, I. (1999) 'Country Size and Tax Competition for Foreign Direct Investment', *Journal of Public Economics*, vol. 71: 121–39.

Heinrich, J. and Konan, D. E. (2000) 'Foreign Direct Investment and Host-country Trading Blocs', *Journal of Economic Integration*, vol. 15: 565–84.

Helms, L. J. (1985) 'The Effect of State and Local Taxes on Economic Growth: A Time Series Cross Section Approach', *Review of Economics and Statistics*, vol. 67: 574–82.

Helpman, E. (1984) 'A Simple Theory of International Trade with Multi-national Corporations', *Journal of Political Economy*, vol. 92: 451–72.

Henderson, B. D. and Dearden, J. (1966) 'New System for Divisional Control', *Harvard Business Review*, September–October: 144–60.

Henneberger, F. and Ziegler, A. (2000) 'Auslandsinvestitionen Schweizer-ischer Unternehmen: Hat die Unternehmensgrosse einen Einfluss auf die Heimischen Beschaftigungseffekte?', *Ifo-Studien*, vol. 46: 1239–60.

Hines, J. R. (1996) 'Altered States: Taxes and the Location of Foreign Direct Investment in America', *American Economic Review*, vol. 86: 1076–94.

Hines, J. R. (1999) 'Lessons from Behavioral Responses to International Taxation', *National Tax Journal*, June.

Hines, J. R. and Rice, E. M. (1994) 'Fiscal Paradise: Foreign Tax Havens and American Business', *Quarterly Journal of Economics*, vol. 109: 149–82.

Hirsch, S. (1976) 'An International Trade and Investment Theory of the Firm', *Oxford Economic Papers*, vol. 28: 258–70.

Hoelscher, D. H. S. (1975) 'Investment and Capital Structure in the Inter-national Firm: Theoretical and Empirical Analysis', Ph.D. dissertation, University of Pittsburgh.

Hopkins, H. D. (1999) 'Cross-border Mergers and Acquisitions: Global and Regional Perspectives', *Journal of International Management*, vol. 5: 207–39.

Hopwood, A. G. (1972) 'Empirical Study of the Role of Accounting Data in Performance Evaluation', *Journal of Accounting Research*, Empirical Research in Accounting, Selected Studies: 156–93.

Horngren, C. (1977) *Cost Accounting: A Managerial Emphasis* (Englewood Cliffs, NJ: Prentice-Hall).

Horst, T. (1972a) 'Firm and Industry Determinants of the Decision to Invest Abroad: An Empirical Study', *Review of Economics and Statistics*, vol. 54: 258–66.

Horst, T. (1972b) 'The Industrial Composition of U.S. Exports and Subsidiary Sales to the Canadian Market', *American Economic Review*, vol. 62: 37–45.

Hoshower, L. B. and Mandel, L. A. (1986) 'Transfer Pricing Policies of Diversified US Based Multinationals', *International Journal of Accounting Education and Research*, vol. 22, Fall: 51–9.

Hovakimian, A., Opler, T. and Titman, S. (2001) 'The Debt–Equity Choice', *Journal of Financial and Quantitative Analysis*, vol. 36: 1–24.

Hsu, M. and Chen, B. L. (2000) 'Labor Productivity of Small and Large Manufacturing Firms: The Case of Taiwan', *Contemporary Economic Policy*, vol. 18: 270–83.

Hufbauer, G., Lakdawalla, D. and Malani, A. (1994) 'Determinants of Direct Foreign Investment and its Connection to Trade', *UNCTAD Review*: 39–51.

Hufbauer, G. C. (1975) 'The Multinational Corporation and Direct Investment', in P. B. Kenen (ed.), *International Trade and Finance: Frontiers for Research* (Cambridge University Press).

Hymer, S. H. (1976 [1960 as a thesis]) *The International Operations of National Firms: A Study of Direct Foreign Investment* (Cambridge, Mass.: MIT Press).

Ietto-Gillies, G. (1998) 'Different Conceptual Frameworks for the Assessment of the Degree of Internationalization: An Empirical Analysis of Various Indices for the Top 100 Transnational Corporations', *Transnational Corporations*, vol. 7: 17–39.

Ihrig, J. (2000) 'Multinationals' Response to Repatriation Restrictions', *Journal of Economic Dynamics and Control*, vol. 24: 1345–79.

Ijiri, Y. (1983) 'Foreign Currency Accounting and its Transition in Management of Foreign Exchange Risk', in Herring, R. J. (ed.), *Managing Foreign Exchange Risk* (Cambridge University Press).

Jarolim, M. (2000) 'Zahranicni Investice a Produktivita Firem', *Finance-a-Uver*, vol. 50: 478–87.

Jeon, Y. D. (1992) 'The Determinants of Korean Foreign Direct Investment in Manufacturing Industries', *Weltwirtschaftliches Archiv*, vol. 128: 527–41.

Johnson, H. G. (1970) 'The Efficiency and Welfare Implications of the International Corporation', in C. P. Kindleberger (ed.), *The International Corporation* (Boston, Mass.: MIT Press).

Jorgenson, D. W. (1963) 'Capital Theory and Investment Behavior', *American Economic Review*, vol. 53: 247–59.

Jovanovic, B. and Rob, R. (1989) 'The Growth and Diffusion of Knowledge', *Review of Economic Studies*, vol. 56: 569–82.

Jun, J. (1989) 'Tax Policy and International Direct Investment', NBER Working Paper No. 3048.

Karsel, B., Mines, C. and Kopikis, K. (1999) 'From Dial-up to Broad-band', *Forrester Report*, April.

Kearns, A. and Ruane, F. (2001) 'The Tangible Contribution of R&D-spending Foreign-owned Plants to a Host Region: A Plant Level Study of the Irish Manufacturing Sector (1980–1996), *Research Policy*, vol. 30: 227–44.

Keating, A. S. (1997) 'Determinants of Divisional Performance Evaluation Practices', Working paper, University of Rochester, Rochester, NY.

Kelly, M. (1974) 'Evaluating the Risk of Expropriation', *Risk Management*, January: 24.

Keynes, J. M. (1936) *The General Theory of Employment, Interest and Money* (London: Macmillan).

Kindleberger, C. P. (1939) 'Speculation and Forward Exchange', *Journal of Political Economy*, vol. 47: 163–81.

Kindleberger, C. P. (1969) *American Business Abroad: Six Lectures on Direct Investment* (New Haven, Conn.: Yale University Press).

Kirsch, R. J. and Johnson, W. (1991) 'The Impact of Fluctuating Exchange Rates on Multinational Corporate Budgeting for, and Performance Evaluation of, Foreign Subsidiaries', *International Journal of Accounting*, vol. 26: 149–73.

Kiymaz, K. and Taylor, L. (2000) 'Competition for Foreign Direct Investment when Countries are not Sure of Site Values', *International Review of Economics and Finance*, vol. 9: 53–68.

Klein, M. and Rosengren, E. (1994) 'The Real Exchange Rate and Foreign Direct Investment in the United States: Relative Wealth vs Relative Wage Effects', *Journal of International Economics*, vol. 36: 373–89.

Knickerbocker, F. T. (1973) *Oligopolistic Reaction and Multinational Enterprise* (Boston, Mass.: Division of Research, Harvard University Graduate School of Business Administration).

Kobrin, S. J. (1976) 'The Environmental Determinants of Foreign Direct Manufacturing Investment: An Ex Post Empirical Analysis', *Journal of International Business Studies*, vol. 7: 29–42.

Kobrin, S. J. (1979) 'Political Risk: A Review and Reconsideration', *Journal of International Business Studies*, vol. 10: 67–80.

Kobrin, S. J. (1984) 'The Expropriation as an Attempt to Control Foreign Firms in LDCs', *International Studies Quarterly*, vol. 28: 348–57.

Kojima, K. (1973) 'A Macroeconomic Approach to Foreign Direct Investment', *Hitotsubashi Journal of Economics*, vol. 14: 1–21.

Kojima, K. (1975) 'International Trade and Foreign Investment: Substitutes or Complements?', *Hitotsubashi Journal of Economics*, vol. 16: 1–12.

Kojima, K. (1985) 'Japanese and American Direct Investment in Asia: A Comparative Analysis', *Hitotsubashi Journal of Economics*, vol. 26: 1–35.

Kollaritsch, F. P. (1984) 'Managerial Accounting Problems of Multinational Corporations', in Holzer, H. P. (ed.), *International Accounting* (New York: Harper & Row).

Konishi, H., Saggi, K. and Weber, S. (1999) 'Endogeous Trade Policy under Foreign Direct Investment', *Journal of International Economics*, vol. 49: 289–408.

Kopp, R. (1994) 'International Human Resource Policies and Practice in Japanese, European and U.S. Multinationals', *Human Resource Management*, vol. 33: 581–99.

Kosteletou, N. and Liargovas, P. (2000) 'Foreign Direct Investment and Real Exchange Rate Interlinkages', *Open Economies Review*, vol. 11: 135–48.

Koyck, L. M. (1954) *Distributed Lags and Investment Analysis* (Amsterdam: North-Holland).

Kravis, I. B. and Lipsey, R. G. (1982) 'The Location of Overseas Production and Production for Exports by US Multinational Firms', *Journal of International Economics*, vol. 12: 201–23.

Kravis, I. B. and Lipsey, R. E. (1988) 'The Effect of Multinational Firms' Foreign Operations on their Domestic Employment', NBER Working Paper No. 2760.

Kreinin, M. E., Abe, S. and Plummer, M. G. (1999) 'Motives for Japanese FDI: Survey, Analysis and Implications in Light of the Asian Crisis', *Journal of Asian Economics*, vol. 10: 385–94.

Kwack, S. Y. (1972) 'A Model of U.S. Direct Investment Abroad: A Neoclassical Approach', *Western Economic Journal*, vol. 10: 373–83.

Lall, S. (1980) 'Monopolistic Advantages and Foreign Investment by U.S. Manufacturing Industry', *Oxford Economic Papers*, vol. 32: 102–22.

Lall, S. and Streeten, P. (1977) *Foreign Investment, Transnationals and Developing Countries* (London: Macmillan).

Lawrence, R. Z. and Slaughter, M. J. (1993) 'Trade and U.S. Wages: Great Sucking Sound or Small Hiccup?', Paper presented at MICRO-BEPA Meeting, June.

Leahy, D. and Montagna, C. (2000a) 'Temporary Social Dumping, Union Legislation and FDI: A Note on the Strategic Use of Standards', *Journal of International Trade and Economic Development*, vol. 9: 243–59.

Leahy, D. and Montagna, C. (2000b) 'Unionisation and Foreign Direct Investment: Challenging Conventional Wisdom?' *Economic Journal*, vol. 110: C80–C92.

Leamer, E. (1993) 'Wage Effects of a U.S.–Mexico Free Trade Agreement', in P. M. Garber (ed.), *The Mexico–U.S. Free Trade Agreement* (Cambridge, Mass.: MIT Press).

Lehmann, A. (1999) 'Country Risk and the Investment Activity of U.S. Multinationals in Developing Countries', International Monetary Fund Working Paper No. WP/99/133, October.

Leland, H. E. (1994) 'Corporate Debt Value, Bond Covenants and Optimal Capital Structure', *Journal of Finance*, vol. 49: 1213–52.

Leland, H. E. (1998) 'Agency Cost, Risk Management and Capital Structure', *Journal of Finance*, vol. 53: 1213–43.

Lessard, D. R. (1985) 'Evaluating International Projects: An Adjusted Present Value Approach', in Lessard, D. R. (ed.), *International Financial Management: Theory and Applications*, 2nd edn (New York: Wiley): 570–84.

Lessard, D. R. and Lorange, P. (1977) 'Currency Changes and Management Control: Resolving the Centralisation/Decentralisation Dilemma', *Accounting Review*, vol. 3: 628–37.

Lessard, D. R. and Sharp, D. (1983) 'Measuring the Performance of Operations Subject to Fluctuating Exchange Rates', *Midland Corporate Finance Journal*, Summer: 56–71.

Levi, M. D. (1990) *International Finance: The Markets and Financial Management of Multinational Business*, 2nd edn (New York: McGraw-Hill).

Levis, M. (1979) 'Does Political Instability in Developing Countries Affect Foreign Investment Flows? An Empirical Examination', *Management International Review*, vol. 19: 59–68.

Lipsey, R. E. (1999) 'The Role of FDI in International Capital Flows', in M. Feldstein (ed.), *International Capital Flows* (Chicago: University of Chicago Press).

Lipsey, R. E. (2000) 'Interpreting Developed Countries' Foreign Direct Investment', NBER Working Paper No. 7810.

Lipsey, R. E. and Weiss, M. Y. (1981) 'Foreign Production and Exports in Manufacturing Industries', *Review of Economics and Statistics*, vol. 63(LXIII): 488–94.

Lipsey, R. E. and Weiss, M. Y. (1984) 'Foreign Production and Exports of Individual Firms', *Review of Economics and Statistics*, vol. 66(LXVI): 304–8.

List, J. A. and Co, C. Y. (2000) 'The Effects of Environmental Regulations on Foreign Direct Investment', *Journal of Environmental Economics and Management*, vol. 40: 1–20.

Lizondo, J. S. (1991) 'Foreign Direct Investment', in 'International Monetary Fund, Determinants and Systematic Consequences of International Capita Flows', IMF Occasional Papers No. 77 (Washington DC): 68–82.

Love, J. H. and Lage-Hidalgo, F. (2000) 'Analysing the Determinants of US Direct Investment in Mexico', *Applied Economics*, vol. 32: 1259–67.

Lucas, R. B. (1993) 'On the Determinants of Foreign Direct Investment: Evidence from East and Southeast Asia', *World Development*, vol. 21: 391–406.

MacDougal, G. D. A. (1960) 'The Benefits and Costs of Private Investment from Abroad: A Theoretical Approach', *Economic Record*, vol. 36: 13–35.

Magdoff, H. (1972) 'Imperialism without Colonies', in R. Owen and B. Sutcliffe (eds), *Studies in the Theory of Imperialism* (London: Longman).

Mahajan, A. (1990) 'Pricing Expropriation Risk', *Financial Management*, vol. 19: 77–85.

Makridakis, S., Wheelright, S. C. and McGee, V. E. (1983) *Forecasting: Methods and Applications* (New York: John Wiley).

Marinov, M. A. and Marinova, S. T. (1999) 'Foreign Direct Investment Motives and Marketing Strategies in Central and Eastern Europe', *Journal of East–West Business*, vol. 5: 25–55.

Mariti, P. and Smiley, R. H. (1983) 'Co-operative Agreements and the Organization of Industry', *Journal of Industrial Economics*, vol. 31: 437–51.

Markowitz, H. M. (1959) *Portfolio Selection: Efficient Diversification of Investments* (New York: John Wiley).

Markusen, J. R. (1984) 'Multinationals, Multi-plant Economies and the Gains from Trade', *Journal of International Economics*, vol. 16: 205–26.

Markusen, J. R. (2000) 'Foreign Direct Investment and Trade', University of Adelaide, Centre for International Economic Studies, Policy Discussion Paper No. 0019.

Markusen, J. R. and Venables, A. J. (1997) 'Foreign Direct Investment as a Catalyst for Industrial Development', NBER Working Paper No. 6241.

Markusen, J. R., Venables, A. J., Konan, D. E. and Zhang, K. H. (1996) 'A Unified Treatment of Horizontal Direct Investment, Vertical Direct Investment, and the Pattern of Trade in Goods and Services', NBER Working Paper No. 5696.

Martin, P. and Ottaviano, G. I. P. (1999) 'Growth Locations: Industry Location in a Model of Endogenous Growth', *European Economic Review*, vol. 43: 281–302.

Martin, S. (1991) 'Direct Foreign Investment in the United States', *Journal of Economic Behavior and Organization*, vol. 16: 283–93.

Martinez, J. I. and Jarillo, C. (1989) 'The Evolution of Research on Co-ordination Mechanisms in Multinational Corporations', *Journal of International Business Studies*, vol. 20: 489–515.

Masulis, R. and Korwar, A. (1986) 'Seasoned Equity Offerings: An Empirical Investigation', *Journal of Financial Economics*, vol. 15: 91–118.

McCann, M. (2001) 'Cross-Border Acquisitions: The UK Experience', *Applied Economics*, vol. 33: 457–61.

McCauley, R. N. and Zimmer, S. A. (1989) 'Explaining International Differences in the Cost of Capital', *FRBNY Quarterly Review*, Summer: 7–28.

McInnes, J. M. (1971) 'Financial Control Systems for Multinational Operations: An Empirical Investigation', *Journal of International Business Studies*, Fall: 11–28.

McKinnon, R. (1963) 'Foreign Exchange Constraints in Economic Development and Efficient Aid Allocation', *Economic Journal*, vol. 73: 388–409.

McManus, J. C. (1972) 'The Theory of the International Firm', in G. Pacquet (ed.), *The Multinational Firm and the Nation State* (Galt, Ontario: Collier-Macmillan).

Meister, I. W. (1970) *Managing the International Finance Function* (New York: The Conference Board).

Meyer, K. (1997) 'Determinants of Direct Foreign Investment in Transition Economies in Central and Eastern Europe', Ph.D. thesis, University of London.

Meyer, K. and Estrin, S. (1998) 'Entry Mode Choice in Emerging Markets: Greenfield, Acquisition and Brownfield', Center for East European Studies, Copenhagen Business School, Working Paper No. 18, February.

Miller, E. L. (1979) *Accounting Problems of Multinational Enterprises* (Lexington, Mass.: Lexington Books).

Miller, M. (1977) 'Debt and Taxes', *Journal of Finance*, vol. 32: 261–75.

Modigliani, F. and Miller, M. (1963) 'Corporate Income Taxes and the Cost of Capital: A Correction', *American Economic Review*, vol. 53: 433–43.

Mody, A., Dasgupta, S. and Sinha, S. (1999) 'Japanese Multinationals in Asia: Drivers and Attractors', *Oxford Development Studies*, vol. 27: 149–64.

Montiel, P. and Reinhart, C. M. (1999) 'Do Capital Controls and Macroeconomic Policies Influence the Volume and Composition of Capital Flows? Evidence from the 1990s', *Journal of International Money and Finance*, vol. 18: 619–35.

Moore, M. O. (1993) 'Determinants of German Manufacturing Direct Investment in Manufacturing Industries', *Weltwirtschaftliches Archiv*, vol. 129: 120–37.

Moosa, I. A. (1997) 'Resolving the Feldstein–Horioka Puzzle', *Economia Internazionale*, vol. 50: 437–58.

Moosa, I. A. (1998) *International Finance: An Analytical Approach* (Sydney: McGraw Hill).

Moosa, I. A. (2000a) *Exchange Rate Forecasting: Techniques and Applications* (London: Macmillan).

Moosa, I. A. (2000b) 'Exchange Rates and Fundamentals: A Microeconomic Approach', Unpublished paper, La Trobe University, Australia.

Moosa, I. A. and Bhatti, R. H. (1997) *International Parity Conditions: Theory, Econometric Testing and Empirical Evidence* (London: Macmillan).

Moosa, I. A. and Bollen, B. E. (2002) 'A Benchmark for Measuring Bias in Estimated Daily Value at Risk', *International Review of Financial Analysis* (forthcoming).

Moosa, I. A. and Shamsuddin, A. (2001) 'Heterogeneity of Traders as a Source of Exchange Rate Volatility', Unpublished paper, La Trobe University, Australia.

Morsicato, H. G. (1978) *An Investigation of the Interaction of Financial Statement Translation and Multinational Enterprise Performance*, Ph.D. dissertation, Pennsylvania State University.

Moshirian, F. (2001) 'International Investment in Financial Services', *Journal of Banking and Finance*, vol. 25: 317–37.

Mucchielli, J. L., Chedor, S. and Soubaya, I. (2000) 'Investissements Directs a l'Etranger des Multinationales Françaises et Relations Commerciales avec Leurs Filiales: Une Analyses sur Donnees Individuelles d'Entreprises', *Revue Economique*, vol. 51: 747–60.

Myers, S. C. (1984) 'The Capital Structure Puzzle', *Journal of Finance*, vol. 39: 575–92.

Nachum, L. (1999) 'FDI, the Location Advantages of Countries and the Competitiveness of TNCs: US FDI in Professional Service Industries', University of Cambridge, ESRC Centre for Business Research Working Paper No. WP128, June.

Nagy, P. J. (1979) *Country Risk: How to Assess, Quantify and Monitor It* (London: Euromoney Publications).

Nankani, G. T. (1979) *The Intercountry Distribution of Direct Foreign Investment* (New York: Garland).

Narula, R. and Dunning, J. H. (1999) 'Developing Countries Versus Multinational Enterprises in a Globalising World: The Dangers of Falling Behind', *Forum for Development Studies*, vol. 0(2): 261–87.

National Association of Accountants (1960) *Management Accounting Problems in Foreign Operations*, NAA Research Report 36, New York.

Naylor, R. and Santoni, M. (1998) 'Wage Bargaining and Foreign Direct Investment', Mimeo, University of Warwick.

Nelson, R. R. and Phelps, E. (1966) 'Investment in Humans, Technological Diffusion, and Economic Growth', *American Economic Review* (Papers and Proceedings), vol. 56: 69–75.

Newfarmer, R. S. and Mueller, W. F. (1975) *Multinational Corporations in Brazil and Mexico: Structural Sources of Economic and Non-economic Market Power*, Report to the Subcommittee on Multinational Corporations of the Committee on Foreign Relations, US Senate (Washington, DC: US Government).

Newman, N. (1995) 'Prop 13 Meets the Internet: How State and Local Government Finances are Becoming Road Kill on the Information Superhighway', Mimeo, Center for Community Economic Research, University of California, Berkeley.

Newman, R. J. (1983) 'Industry Migration and Growth in the South', *Review of Economics and Statistics*, vol. 65: 76–86.

Newman, R. J. and Sullivan, D. H. (1988) 'Econometric Analysis of Business Tax Impacts on Industrial Location: What Do We Know, and How Do We Know It?', *Journal of Urban Economics*, vol. 23: 215–34.

Nitsch, D., Beamish, P. and Makino, S. (1996) 'Entry Mode and Performance of Japanese FDI in Western Europe', *Management International Review*, vol. 36: 27–43.

OECD (1999) *Foreign Direct Investment and the Environment* (Paris: OECD Centre for Co-operation with Non-Members).

Okamoto, Y. (1999) 'Multinationals, Production Efficiency, and Spillover Effects: The Case of the U.S. Auto Parts Industry', *Weltwirtschaftliches Archiv*, vol. 135: 241–60.

Okposin, S. B. (1999) *The Extent of Singapore's Investments Abroad* (Sydney: Ashgate).

Otley, D. T. (1980) 'The Contingency Theory of Management Accounting: Achievement and Prognosis', *Accounting, Organizations and Society*, vol. 5: 413–20.

Owen, R. and Sutcliffe, R. B. (eds) (1972) *Studies in the Theory of Imperialism* (London: Longman).

Pain, N. (1993) 'An Econometric Analysis of Foreign Direct Investment in the United Kingdom', *Scottish Journal of Political Economy*, vol. 40: 1–23.

Pain, N. and Wakelin, K. (1998) Export Performance and the Role of Foreign Direct Investment, *The Manchester School*, vol. 66: 62–88.

Panic, M. and Joyce, P. L. (1980) 'UK Manufacturing Industry: International Integration and Trade Performance', *Bank of England Quarterly Review*, vol. 1: 42–55.

Papke, L. E. (1987) 'Subnational Taxation and Capital Mobility: Estimates of Tax–Price Elasticities', *National Tax Journal*, vol. 40: 191–204.

Papke, L. E. (1991) 'Interstate Business Tax Differentials and New Firm Location', *Journal of Public Economics*, vol. 45: 47–68.

Parker, J. E. S. (1974) *The Economics of Innovation: The National and Multinational Enterprise in Technological Change* (London: Longman).

Parker, L. (1977) 'A Reassessment of the Role of Control in Corporate Budgeting', *Accounting and Business Research*, Spring: 135–43.

Persen, W. and Lessig, V. (1979) *Evaluating the Financial Performance of Overseas Operations* (New York: Financial Executives Research Foundation).

Petit, M. L. and Sanna-Randaccio, F. (2000) 'Endogenous R&D and Foreign Direct Investment in International Oligopolies', *International Journal of Industrial Organisation*, vol. 18: 339–67.

Petras, J. and Morley, M. (1975) *The United States and Chile: Imperialism and the Overthrow of the Allende Government* (New York: Monthly Review Press).

Petrochilos, G. (1989) *Foreign Direct Investment and the Development Process: The Case of Greece* (Aldershot: Avebury).

Petry, G. H. and Sprow, J. (1993) 'International Trends and Events in Corporate Finance and Management: A Survey', *Financial Practice and Education*: 21–8.

Pistoresi, B. (2000) 'Investimenti Diretti Esteri e Fattori di Localizzazione: L' America Latina e il Sud Est Asiatico', *Rivista di Politica Economica*, vol. 90: 27–44.

Pitelis, C. (2000) 'A Theory of the (Growth of the) Transnational Firm: A Penrosean Perspective', *Contributions to Political Economy*, vol. 19: 71–89.

Prachowny, M. F. J. (1972) 'Direct Investment and the Balance of Payments of the United States: A Portfolio Approach', in F. Machlup, W. S. Salant and L. Tarshis (eds), *International Mobility and Movements of Capital* (New York: NBER).

Pugel, T. A. (1985) 'The United States', in J. H. Dunning (ed.), *Multinational Enterprises, Economic Structure and Industrial Competitiveness* (New York: John Wiley).

Raddock, D. (1986) *Assessing Corporate Political Risk* (Totowa, NJ: Rowman and Littlefield).

Ragazzi, G. (1973) 'Theories of the Determinants of Foreign Direct Investment', *IMF Staff Papers*, vol. 20: 471–98.

Ramcharran, H. (1999) 'Foreign Direct Investment and Country Risk: Further Empirical Evidence', *Global Economic Review*, vol. 28: 49–59.

Razin, A., Sadka, E. and Yuen, C. W. (1996) 'Tax Principles and Capital Inflows: Is it Efficient to Tax Nonresident Income?', NBER Working Paper No. 5513.

Razin, A., Sadka, E. and Yuen, C. W. (1999a) 'An Information-based Model of Foreign Direct Investment: The Gains from Trade Revisited', NBER Working Paper No. 6884.

Razin, A., Sadka, E. and Yuen, C. W. (1999b) 'Excessive FDI Flows Under Asymmetric Information', NBER Working Paper No. 7400.

Reece, J. and Cool, W. (1978) 'Measuring Investment Center Performance', *Harvard Business Review*, vol. 56: 29–30.

Resmini, L. (2000) 'The Determinants of Foreign Direct Investment in the CEECs: New Evidence from Sectoral Patterns', *Economics of Transition*, vol. 8: 665–89.

Reuber, G., Crokell, H., Emersen, M. and Gallais-Hamonno, G. (1973) *Private Foreign Investment in Development* (Oxford: Clarendon Press and OECD).

Riedel, J. (1975) 'The Nature and Determinants of Export-oriented Foreign Direct Investment in a Developing Country: A Case Study of Taiwan', *Weltwirtschaftliches Archiv*, vol. 3: 505–28.

Robbins, S. and Stobaugh, R. (1973a) 'Growth of the Financial Function', *Financial Executive*, July.

Robbins, S. M. and Stobaugh, R. (1973b) 'The Bent Measuring Stick for Foreign Subsidiaries', *Harvard Business Review*, September–October.

Robinson, W. I. and Harris, J. (2000) 'Towards a Global Ruling Class? Globalization and the Transnational Capitalist Class', *Science and Society*, vol. 64: 11–54.

Robock, S. H. (1971) 'Political Risk, Identification and Assessment', *Columbia Journal of World Management Science*, vol. 4: 141–83.

Robock, S. H. and Simmonds, K. (1973) *International Business and Multinational Enterprises* (Homewood, Ill.: Irwin).

Rock, M. T. (1973) 'Cross-country Analysis of the Determinants of U.S. Foreign Direct Investment in Manufacturing in Less Developed Countries', Ph.D. dissertation, University of Pittsburgh.

Roling, J. (1999) 'Bedeuten Deutsche Direktinvestitionen im Ausland Einen Export Duetscher Arbeitsplatze?', *Zeitschrift für Wirtschatfspolitik*, vol. 48: 147–67.

Romer, J. E. (1975) 'U.S.–Japanese Competition in International Markets: A Study of the Trade–Investment Cycle in Modern Capitalism', University of California, Institute of International Studies, Research Series No. 22.

Root, F. R. (1968) 'Attitudes of American Executives Towards Foreign Government and Investment Opportunities', *Economic and Business Bulletin*, vol. 2: 1–9.

Ross, S. A., Westerfield, R. W. and Jaffe, J. (1996) *Corporate Finance*, 4th edn (Burr Ridge, Ill.: Irwin).

Rugman, A. M. (1980) 'Internalization as a General Theory of Foreign Direct Investment: A Re-appraisal of the Literature', *Weltwirtschaftliches Archiv*, vol. 116: 365–79.

Rugman, A. M. (1981) *Inside the Multinationals: The Economics of Internal Markets*, (New York: Columbia University Press).

Rummel, R. and Heenan, D. A. (1978) 'How Multinationals Analyse Political Risk', *Harvard Business Review*, January–February: 67–76.

Safarian, A. E. (1969) *The Performance of Foreign-owned Firms in Canada*, (Washington DC: Canadian–American Committee Sponsored by National Planning Association/Montreal: Private Planning Association of Canada).

Safarian, A. E. (1999) 'Host Country Policies Towards Inward Foreign Direct Investment in the 1950s and 1990s', *Transnational Corporations*, vol. 8: 93–112.

Saggi, K. (1999) 'Foreign Direct Investment, Licensing and Incentives for Innovation', *Review of International Economics*, vol. 7: 699–714.

Sanford, D. M. and Dong, H. (2000) 'Investment in Familiar Territory: Tourism and New Foreign Direct Investment', *Tourism Economics*, vol. 6: 205–19.

Saunders, R. (1983) 'The Determinants of Interindustry Variation of Foreign Ownership in Canadian Manufacturing', *Canadian Journal of Economics*, vol. 15: 77–84.

Schneider, F. and Frey, B. S. (1985) 'Economic and Political Determinants of Foreign Direct Investment', *World Development*, vol. 13: 161–75.

Schnitzer, M. (1999) 'Expropriation and Control Rights: A Dynamic Model of Foreign Direct Investment', *International Journal of Industrial Organization*, vol. 17: 1113–37.

Schoeman, N. J., Robinson, Z. C. and de-Wet, T. J. (2000) 'Foreign Direct Investment Flows and Fiscal Discipline in South Africa', *South African Journal of Economic and Management Sciences*, vol. 3: 235–44.

Scholes, M. S. and Wolfson, M. A. (1990) 'The Effects of Changes in Tax Laws on Corporate Reorganization Activity', *Journal of Business*, vol. 63: S141–S164.

Schweitzer, N. (1976) 'Bayesian Analysis for Intelligence, Some Focus on the Middle East', Paper presented at the International Studies Meeting, Toronto, Canada, February.

Scott, G. M. (1972) 'Financial Control in Multinational Enterprises: The New Challenge to Accountants', *International Journal of Accounting, Education and Research*, vol. 7: 55–68.

Segerstrom, P. S. (1991) 'Innovation, Imitation, and Economic Growth', *Journal of Political Economy*, vol. 99: 807–27.

Sethi, P. S. and Luther, K. N. (1986) 'Political Risk Analysis and Direct Foreign Investment: Some Problems of Definition and Measurement', *California Management Review*, vol. 28: 57–68.

Severn, A. K. (1972) 'Investment and Financial Behaviour of American Direct Investors in Manufacturing', in F. Machlup, W. S. Salant and L. Tarshis (eds), *International Mobility and Movement of Capital* (New York: NBER).

Shapiro, A. (1992) *Multinational Financial Management*, 4th edn (Newton, Mass.: Allyn and Bacon).

Shyam-Sunder, L. and Myers, S. C. (1999) 'Testing Static Tradeoff against Pecking Order Models of Capital Structure', *Journal of Financial Economics*, vol. 51: 219–44.

Sin, C. Y. and Leung, W. F. (2001) 'Impacts of FDI Liberalisation on Investment Inflows', *Applied Economics Letters*, vol. 8: 253–6.

Sjoholm, F. (1999) 'Technology Gap, Competition and Spillovers from Direct Foreign Investment: Evidence from Establishment Data', *Journal of Development Studies*, vol. 36: 53–73.

Slemrod, J. (1989) *Tax Effects on Foreign Direct Investment in the U.S.: Evidence from a Cross-country Comparison*, NBER Working Paper No. 3042.

Slemrod, J. (1990a) 'Tax Effects on Foreign Direct Investment in the United States: Evidence from a Cross-country Comparison', in A. Razin and J. Slemrod (eds), *Taxation in the Global Economy* (Chicago: University of Chicago Press).

Slemrod, J. (1990b) 'The Impact of the Tax Reform Act of 1986 on Foreign Direct Investment to and from the United States', in J. Slemrod (ed.), *Do Taxes Matter? The Impact of the Tax Reform Act of 1986* (Cambridge, Mass.: MIT Press).

Solomon, L. D. (1978) *Multinational Corporations and the Emerging World Order* (Port Washington, NY: Kennikat Press).

Solomon, R. F. and Ingham, K. P. D. (1977) 'Discriminating between MNC Subsidiaries and Indigenous Companies: A Comparative Analysis of British Mechanical Engineering', *Oxford Bulletin of Economics and Statistics*, vol. 39: 127–38.

Solomons, D. (1965) *Divisional Performance: Management and Control* (New York: Financial Executive Research Foundation).

Stanley, M. and Block, S. (1983) 'An Empirical Study of Management and Financial Variables Influencing Capital Budgeting Decisions for Multinational Corporations in the 1980s', *Management International Review*, vol. 23: 61–73.

Stevens, G. (1969) 'Fixed Investment Expenditure of Foreign Manufacturing Affiliates of U.S. Firms: Theoretical Models and Empirical Evidence', *Yale Economic Essays*, vol. 9: 137–200.

Stevens, G. (2000) 'Politics, Economics and Investment: Explaining Plant and Equipment Spending by US Direct Investors in Argentina, Brazil and Mexico', *Journal of International Money and Finance*, vol. 19: 153–83.

Stevens, G. and Lipsey, R. E. (1992) 'Interactions between Domestic and Foreign Investment', *Journal of International Money and Finance*, vol. 11: 40–62.

Stobaugh, R. B. (1970) 'Financing Foreign Subsidiaries of U.S.-controlled Multinational Enterprises', *Journal of International Business Studies*, vol. 1: 43–64.

Stoever, W. A. (1999) 'The Levels of Developing Country Policy Formulation Towards Foreign Direct Investment', *Journal of Emerging Markets*, vol. 4: 45–58.

Stone, S. F. and Jeon, B. N. (2000) 'Foreign Direct Investment and Trade in the Asian-Pacific Region: Complementarity, Distance and Regional Economic Integration', *Journal of Economic Integration*, vol. 15: 460–85.

Sullivan, D. (1994) 'Measuring the Degree of Internationalization of a Firm', *Journal of International Business Studies*, vol. 25: 331.

Sung, H. and Lapan, H. E. (2000) 'Strategic Foreign Direct Investment and Exchange Rate Uncertainty', *International Economic Review*, vol. 41: 411–23.

Svensson, R. (1966) 'Effects of Overseas Production on Home County Exports: Evidence Based on Swedish Multinationals', *Weltwirtschaftliches Archiv*, vol. 132: 304–29.

Svensson, R. (1996) 'Foreign Activities of Swedish Multinational Corporations', Uppsala University, Department of Economics, Economic Studies 25.

Swedenbourg, B. (1979) *The Multinational Operations of Swedish Firms: Analysis of the Determinants and Effects* (Stockholm: Industrial Institute of Economics and Social Research).

Swenson, D. L. (1994) 'The Impact of U.S. Tax Reform on Direct Investment in the United States', *Journal of Public Economics*, vol. 54: 243–66.

Tambunlertchai, S. (1976) 'Foreign Direct Investment in Thailand's Manufacturing Industries', Ph.D. dissertation, Duke University, North Carolina.

Tcha, M. (1998) 'Labour Disputes, Factor Intensity and Direct Foreign Investment: The Experience of Korea in Transmission', *Economic Development and Cultural Change*, vol. 46: 305–28.

Thompson, E. R. and Poon, J. P. H. (2000) 'ASEAN after the Financial Crisis: Links between Foreign Direct Investment and Regulatory Change', *ASEAN Economic Bulletin*, vol. 17: 1–14.

Thunnel, H. L. (1977) *Political Risk in International Business, Investment Behaviour of Multinational Corporations*, Praeger Special Studies in International Business, Trade and Finance (New York: Praeger).

Titman, S. and Wessels, R. (1988) 'The Determinants of Capital Structure Choice', *Journal of Finance*, vol. 43: 1–18.

Tobin, J. (1958) 'Liquidity Preference as Behavior Towards Risk', *Review of Economic Studies*, vol. 25: 65–86.

Traxler, F. and Woitech, B. (2000) 'Transnational Investment and National Labour Market Regimes: A Case of "Regime Shopping"?', *European Journal of Industrial Relations*, vol. 6: 141–59.

Tuman, J. P. and Emmert, C. F. (1999) 'Explaining Japanese Foreign Direct Investment in Latin America, 1979–1992', *Social Science Quarterly*, vol. 80: 539–55.

UNCTAD (1999) *World Investment Report: Foreign Direct Investment and the Challenge of Development* (New York: United Nations).

UNCTAD (2000) *World Investment Report: Cross-border Mergers and Acquisitions and Development* (New York: United Nations).

United Nations (1973) *Multinational Corporations in World Development* (New York: United Nations).

US Congress Committee on Foreign Relations (1973) *Multinational Corporations and United States Foreign Policy* (Washington DC: US Government Printing Office).

US General Accounting Office (2000) 'Sales Taxes: Electronic Commerce Growth Presents Challenges; Revenue Losses are Uncertain', Report to Congressional Requesters, June, GAO/GGD/OEC-00-165.

Vaitsos, C. V. (1976) 'Employment Problems and Transnational Enterprises in Developing Countries: Distortions and Inequality', International Labour Office, World Employment Programme Research, Working Paper II.

Varian, H. (1999) 'Estimating the Demand for Bandwidth', Mimeo, University of California, August.

Varian, H. (2000) 'Taxation of Electronic Commerce', Mimeo, University of California, March.

Vaupel, J. W. (1971) 'Characteristics and Motivations of the U.S. Corporations which Manufacture Abroad', Paper presented at the Meeting of Participating Members of the Atlantic Institute, Paris, June.

Vernon, R. (1966) 'International Investment and International Trade in the Product Cycle', *Quarterly Journal of Economics*, vol. 80: 190–207.

Vernon, R. (1968) 'Conflict and Resolution between Foreign Direct Investment and Less Developed Countries', *Public Policy*, vol. 18: 333–51.

Vernon, R. (1971) *Sovereignty at Bay: The Multinational Spread of U.S. Enterprises*, (London: Pelican).

Vernon, R. (1974) 'The Location of Economic Activity', in J. Dunning (ed.), *Economic Analysis and the Multinational Enterprise* (London: George Allen & Unwin).

Vernon, R. (1977) *Storm Over Multinationals: The Real Issues* (London: Macmillan).

Vernon, R. (1979) 'The Product Cycle Hypothesis in a New International Environment', *Oxford Bulletin of Economics and Statistics*, vol. 41: 255–67.

Wafo, G. L. K. (1998) 'Political Risk and Foreign Direct Investment', Faculty of Economics and Statistics, University of Konstanz, Germany.

Walkenhorst, P. (2000) 'Foreign Direct Investment, Technological Spillovers and Agricultural Transition in Central Europe', *Post Communist Economies*, vol. 12: 61–75.

Wallace, C. D. (1990) *Foreign Direct Investment in the 1990s: A New Climate in the Third World* (Rordrecht: Martinus Nijhoff).

Wang, J. Y. (1990) 'Growth, Technology Transfer, and the Long-run Theory of International Capital Movements', *Journal of International Economics*, vol. 29: 255–71.

Wang, J. Y. and Blomstrom, M. (1992) 'Foreign Investment and Technology Transfer: A Simple Model', *European Economic Review*, vol. 36: 137–55.

Wang, Z. Q. and Swain, N. J. (1995) 'The Determinants of Foreign Direct Investment in Transforming Economies: Empirical Evidence from Hungary and China', *Weltwirtschaftliches Archiv*, vol. 131: 359–82.

Wasylenko, M. (1981) 'The Location of Firms: The Role of Taxes and Fiscal Incentives', in R. Bahl (ed.), *Urban Government Finance: Emerging Trends* (Beverly Hills, Calif.: Sage).

Wasylenko, M. (1991) 'Empirical Evidence on Interregional Business Location Decisions and the Role of Fiscal Incentives in Economic Development', in H. W. Herzog and A. M. Achlottmann (eds), *Industry Location and Public Policy* (Knoxville, Tenn.: University of Tennessee Press).

Wei, S. J. (2000a) 'How Taxing is Corruption on International Investors?', *Review of Economics and Statistics*, vol. 82: 1–11.

Wei, S. J. (2000b) 'Local Corruption and Global Capital Flows', *Brookings Papers on Economic Activity*, 2: 303–46.

Weintraub, R. (1967) 'Studio Emprico Sulle Relazioni di Lungo Andare tra Movimenti di Capitali Rendimenti Differenziali', *Rivista Internazionale di Scienze Economiche e Commerciale*, vol. 14: 401–5.

Wheeler, D. and Mody, A. (1990) *Risk and Rewards in International Location Tournaments: The Case of US Firms* (Washington DC: The World Bank).

Wilamoski, P. and Tinkler, S. (1999) 'The Trade Balance Effects of U.S. Foreign Direct Investment in Mexico', *Atlantic Economic Journal*, vol. 21: 24–37.

Wilkins, M. (1999) 'Two Literatures, Two Storylines: Is a General Paradigm of Foreign Portfolio and Foreign Direct Investment Feasible?', *Transnational Corporations*, vol. 8: 53–116.

Williams, S., Cooperstein, D., Weisman, D. and Oum, T. (1999) 'Post-Web Retail', *The Forrester Report*, September.

Wilson, B. (1980) 'The Propensity of Multinational Companies to Expand Through Aquisitions', *Journal of International Business Studies*, vol. 12: 59–65.

Winters, L. A. (1991) *International Economics*, 4th edn (London: Harper-Collins).

Wood, A. (1994) *North–South Trade, Employment, and Inequality* (Oxford: Clarendon Press).

Wu, F. (1999) 'Intrametropolitan FDI Firm Location in Guangzhou, China: A Poisson and Negative Binomial Analysis', *Annals of Regional Science*, vol. 33: 535–55.

Xu, B. and Wang, J. (2000) 'Trade, FDI and International Technology Diffusion', *Journal of Economic Integration*, vol. 15: 585–601.

Yabuuchi, S. (1999) 'Foreign Direct Investment, Urban Unemployment and Welfare', *Journal of International Trade and Economic Development*, vol. 8: 359–71.

Yang, J. Y. Y., Groenewold, N. and Tcha, M. (2000) 'The Determinants of Foreign Direct Investment in Australia', *Economic Record*, vol. 76: 45–54.

Yang, Q. (1999) 'Repartition Geographique de l'Investissement Direct Etranger en Chine: l'Impact du Capital Humain', *Revue d'Economie du Developpement*, vol. 3: 35–59.

Yu, C. M. and Ito, K. (1988) 'Oligopolistic Reaction and Foreign Direct Investment: The Case of the U.S. Tire and Textiles Industries', *Journal of International Business Studies*, vol. 19: 449–60.

Zeile, W. J. (1999) 'Foreign Direct Investment in the United States: Preliminary Results from the 1997 Benchmark Survey', *Survey of Current Business*, vol. 79: 21–54.

Zejan, M. C. (1990) 'New Ventures or Acquisitions: The Choice of Swedish Multinational Enterprises', *Journal of Industrial Economics*, vol. 38: 349–55.

Zhang, K. H. (1999a) 'Foreign Direct Investment and Economic Growth: Evidence from Ten East Asian Economies', *Economia Internazionale*, vol. 52: 517–35.

Zhang, K. H. (1999b) 'How Does FDI Interact with Economic Growth in a Large Developing Country? The Case of China', *Economic Systems*, vol. 23: 291–303.

Zhang, K. H. (2000) 'Why Is U.S. Direct Investment in China So Small?', *Contemporary Economic Policy*, vol. 18: 82–94.

Zhao, L. (1995) 'Cross-hauling Direct Foreign Investment and Unionised Oligopoly', *European Economic Review*, vol. 39: 1237–53.

Zhao, L. (1998) 'The Impact of Foreign Direct Investment on Wages and Employment', *Oxford Economic Papers*, vol. 50: 284–301.

Zukowska-Gagelmann, K. (2000) 'Productivity Spillovers from Foreign Direct Investment in Poland', *Economic Systems*, vol. 24: 223–56.

Index

Index